T0279918

JOURNEY WITHOUT END

Journey without End

Migration from the Global South through the Americas

**ROB CURRAN AND
ANDREW NELSON**

VANDERBILT UNIVERSITY PRESS

Nashville, Tennessee

Copyright 2022 Vanderbilt University Press
All rights reserved
First printing 2022

Library of Congress Cataloging-in-Publication Data

Names: Curran, Rob, 1975– author. | Nelson, Andrew (Lecturer of
  anthropology), author.
Title: Journey without end : migration from the Global South through the
  Americas / Rob Curran and Andrew Nelson.
Description: Nashville, Tennessee : Vanderbilt University Press, [2022] |
  Includes bibliographical references.
Identifiers: LCCN 2022010477 (print) | LCCN 2022010478 (ebook) | ISBN
  9780826504869 (hardcover) | ISBN 9780826504852 (paperback) | ISBN
  9780826504876 (epub) | ISBN 9780826504883 (pdf)
Subjects: LCSH: Immigrants—United States. | Immigrants—Latin America. |
  Immigrants—Developing countries. | United States—Emigration and
  immigration. | Latin America—Emigration and immigration. | Developing
  countries—Emigration and immigration.
Classification: LCC E184.A1 C875 2022 (print) | LCC E184.A1 (ebook) | DDC
  305.9/069120973—dc23/eng/20220826
LC record available at https://lccn.loc.gov/2022010477
LC ebook record available at https://lccn.loc.gov/2022010478

Cover photo: The open road in Peru's southern desert.
Courtesy of Rob Curran.

For Catherine "Creina" Curran and Don Nelson

CONTENTS

ACKNOWLEDGMENTS

This book would never have materialized if it weren't for the support and encouragement of many.

One of the greatest joys of working on a multi-year and multi-country project is the opportunity to meet so many people along the way. Todd and Lorena Johnson not only gave us a place to stay in Quito, but also served as our guides to the city. It was a serendipitous encounter to meet the American hotel owner in Capurganá, who offered us a perfect base for our research and formative advice. It was a similarly fortuitous twist of fate that led us to Mama Africa's restaurant during our first hour in Tapachula, where we received the global hospitality of Etelvina Hernández López.

To the many migrants we met in Quito, Capurganá, and Tapachula, words cannot sufficiently express our appreciation for their willingness to share their experiences with us. We can only hope that this book expresses some shred of truth to their amazing stories, and contributes to the growing call for the United States, among other countries, to examine the brutality caused by their immigration policies. To Kidane Okubay, in particular, we are heavily indebted for his fearless and selfless willingness to tell his story.

We would like to thank all the photo subjects who appear in the book for their permission to photograph them.

We could not have sustained this project were it not for the patronage of Elizabeth Souder, the long-time Points opinion-page editor of the *Dallas Morning News*. By publishing a series of articles over a number of years that would come to form the core of this book, she took great risks at a time when pro-immigrant perspectives were not popular. Ms. Souder's faith in the project kept us going at times when our own foundered. Thanks also to Katie Zanecchia, who first gave us the idea that our project might make a good book.

Between trips to sites along the *camino duro*, we continued to learn about the journey thanks to the groundbreaking reporting and informative research of many journalists and scholars. In particular, we are indebted to the scholarship of Soledad Velasco Álvarez, Caitlin Fourratt, Elizabeth Nimmons, Juan Thomas Ordóñez, Nanneke Winters, Caitlyn Yates, and Jonathan Echeverri Zuluaga. While we had hoped to meet in-person for a workshop initially planned for April 2020, the virtual conference of August 2020 provided a welcomed exchange of ideas.

Andy would like to thank his colleagues at UNT. He is particularly grateful for the generous support of the Department of Anthropology, the College of Liberal Arts and Social Sciences, and the Office of Faculty Success. Special thanks are due to family—to Carol Nelson-Rea, Sara Nelson, and Scott Nelson for inspiring a desire to travel; to Abraham and Blanca Arellano for providing a loving second home in Miami; and finally, to Melissa and Mateo, the loves of his life.

Rob would like to thank his wife, Sara Fanning, and all the Currans, Moores, and Fannings for their love and support throughout the research and writing process.

INTRODUCTION

Exile is when you live in one place and dream in another. Exile is a dream of going back home. In exile, one is possessed by longing, no matter where the exile takes place. The whole world becomes a prison. Neither Calypso's beauty and passionate love nor a pleasant life on her island could relieve Odysseus's longing for Ithaca. A life in exile is like being condemned in purgatory, a state between life and death, a limbo between here and there.

—SHAHRAM KHOSRAVI, *"Illegal" Traveller*, 2010

It costs about $30 to ride the tourist boat from the Colombian port of Turbo to Capurganá, on the border with Panama. For migrants like Kidane Okubay, who do not have the documents to take the tourist boat, it costs about $550 to take the same ride in the middle of the night, as part of a trans-rainforest smugglers' package. With this boat ride across the heaving Caribbean begins the most treacherous leg of a death-defying journey.

The Gulf of Urabá is shaped like a fishing hook with Turbo on the up-swoop near the tip and Capurganá on the opposite side, near the tie-off. The boats cut through the diagonal, beginning in the brown silty headwaters of the Atrato River and the rolling sapphire Caribbean. For migrants, it's a rough crossing in an open-topped skiff with an outboard motor, a boat more suitable to carry a couple of fishermen than a dozen passengers, huddled with their luggage. The smuggler's boat offers no refunds when the trip is not completed, although there is an understanding that migrants are entitled to a second attempt if the first fails, as Kidane discovered.

On the night of Monday, July 9, 2018, a local smuggler made his second attempt at the crossing with Kidane and about ten other Eritreans—in Colombia, smugglers often divide the migrants by nationality to make communication easier. Kidane and his compatriots were wearing life jackets of the bright orange variety that slip over the head. As the small motorboat entered the open Caribbean, the waves picked up. Near Capurganá, several hours northwest of Turbo, wave crests are often ten feet high. The boats take the waves at speed; for the passenger, it feels like an extreme fairground ride, with a rush to the stomach as the boat climbs the face of the wave, then the sensation of floating in air as it reaches the peak, followed by a plunge down to a hard landing. Even the ferry-sized high-horsepower boat that carries the tourists arrives drenched in spray. On smaller boats—*lanchas* as they are called in Latin America—the engine's roar often kicks up an octave from the strain of climbing the rolling hills. On the way back down, the engine often stutters as it tries to find purchase, and the passenger's heart does the same.

When Kidane's boat stopped, it was still some way short of the beach near the Capurganá harbor. The smuggler ordered his passengers to jump into the sea with their life jackets. Those who did not jump were pushed. They had to swim to shore, carrying backpacks with them.

Kidane, who can swim, remembers the boat stopping about ten yards short of the beach. Some of the non-swimmers on the boat described it, with horror, as being more like fifty yards.

By the time we met Kidane and his group the next day, he and his compatriots, only a handful of whom he had known before Turbo, were drying their clothes on the downstairs railings of a safe house in Capurganá. They were sitting together in an exterior covered porch near the railings, talking over the near disaster of the previous night. The hotel was not that different to the lodges where European and American twentysomethings were vacationing nearby: a brightly painted clapboard building overlooking a sheltered fishing dock. It was a Caribbean idyll. But the dripping clothes provided a glimpse of an experience as far removed from the tourists' Capurganá as possible. Kidane and his friends were on a months-long journey but only carried enough clothes between the eleven of them to cover twenty feet of railings.

We had been staying at a neighboring hotel, when the hotelier, who knew we had come to Capurganá to interview migrants, told us about a group of Eritreans recently arrived next door. We addressed the group across the hotel railing, introducing ourselves as a journalist and an anthropologist. We told them we were writing about the journey migrants from all over the world were

FIGURE 1.1. Kidane and his friends' clothes drying at their hostel.

taking to the US. This prompted a somewhat tetchy debate among the group as to whether they should even talk to us. In the end, about half the group withdrew to talk among themselves around the picnic tables in the common area. A handful, including Kidane and others, came forward to talk. We listened and tried to transcribe, leaning against the top of the railings at times as we scribbled furiously. One pen had to be tossed back into the waterproof zip bag after the ink went faint. We didn't want to miss anything. We divided micro-interview duties. Kidane waited patiently while we interrupted our conversation with him to speak with his friends. Soon, Kidane's friends went back to checking on their clothes and chatting to one another.

Kidane, thirty-one years old at the time, had a short chin-strap beard, which he'd managed to keep sculpted even on the road; a face that was handsome despite being winnowed and washed out by his journey; and warm, if weary, eyes. He projected a calm intelligence. It quickly became clear that Kidane understood what we were trying to do and saw some value in it. He recognized the power of his story to inform Americans about migrants, and to inform the migrants about the path to the US. While others in the group warned him against sharing information, he trusted us as honest brokers. On that first meeting with Kidane, we talked for about twenty minutes.

In the coming days, we would follow up on that interview with Kidane informally several times. We exchanged information, and he expressed relief that he would arrive in the US with a contact. When we returned from the trip to Colombia and Panama, we found Kidane on Facebook. We kept in touch via Facebook Messenger. (Messenger, alongside WhatsApp, another Facebook app, is the preferred method of communication for the migrants we interviewed, likely because these apps can move with phone numbers and data plans. All they require is a WiFi signal and a cheap phone.) Later, we would get to spend one more day with Kidane, a day during which we documented much of his journey, gleaning many of the visceral details that have allowed us to complete this work.

Kidane told us that he kept a diary during the trip, but that very private version of his story he has chosen to keep to himself. Kidane is something of a modern protagonist, a character conscious of his role. Even in that moment of crisis in Capurganá, Kidane had the ability to step back and consider his experience. Among the first things he told us was that he graduated with a degree in library science focused on archives. Perhaps it was his background in books that gave him the perspective to recognize himself as a protagonist in a complex narrative, and to drive some of the narration himself. Recounting the boat incident, he seemed more curious about the motive for the boatman's callous act than expressing the anger of a victim.

"Maybe he was scared," Kidane said. "Maybe he thought the police were coming."

The *Camino Duro*

In numbers that have increased sharply during the last decade, migrants like Kidane from all over the Global South fly to the only nations in the Americas whose borders remain open to them—Ecuador, Brazil, Guyana or, in the case of Eritreans, Bolivia. From there, they travel north by bus, boat, train, plane, and foot to the US border. When we met him, Kidane had already passed through about a dozen countries since he'd left Eritrea three years earlier.

There's an old name in Latin America for the overland—and sea—migrant route to the US: the *camino duro*, the "hard way." It's a journey that's always been hard, but in the past half-decade it's become near impossible.

What was always a daunting proposition now tests the limits of human endurance. The chances of people like Kidane being detained, mugged, deported, tossed off a speedboat, or killed along the way are growing all the time. Sexual assault, long rampant in the Mexican section of the route, is now just as prevalent in the Darién Gap.

"And what, when we get there?" asked one of Kidane's Eritrean friends, a man who didn't wish to be named and who advised Kidane not to trust us.[1] "Prison? This detention center . . . it's prison, no?" The same man described being fired upon by Peruvian police earlier in the journey. While this man told his story, the pitch of his voice rose, as if he were almost giddy at the thought that these things were happening to him.

Kidane and his friends knew when they left Eritrea that they were attempting to pass through the eye of the needle. US border policy and diplomatic pressure on transit countries mean the eye of the needle is narrowing all the time. These policies do not deter migrants as intended but force them onto an obstacle course full of near-impossible challenges, fitful progress, returns and detentions, life-threatening dangers, and unknown risks. If and when they reach the US, as Kidane's compatriot rightly suspected, they do not arrive at a destination. Rather, they enter a kind of gulag, an asylum system that criminalizes applicants.

It's a journey that recalls the most epic quests and pilgrimages of history and myth, from the wanderings of Ulysses to the California Gold Rush. This is the way of the vertiginous Andean pass; the way of the roiling Caribbean Sea; the way of the viper-riddled Panamanian jungle; the way of the forded Guatemalan torrent; the way of the parched Sonoran desert. This is the way of the over-crowded smuggler's boat; the way of the speeding pickup truck; the way of the American ice-box cell. For the vast majority of people in the Global South, this is the only way to the US—the hard way.

These migrants are contributing to the changing face of immigration to the US via the southern border. In 2014, for the first time since records were released in 1970, non-Mexicans outnumbered Mexicans apprehended at the US-Mexico border. Although this shift points to the changing economics of Mexico and increase of Central American immigration to the States, it also hints at the growth of people from Africa, Asia, and the Caribbean migrating to the States through Latin America. The proportion of Asian, African, and Caribbean migrants apprehended at the US-Mexico border has gradually increased from an average of 0.2 percent in the late 2000s to 1.1 percent in 2011, surpassing 2 percent in 2017 and 3 percent in 2018, peaking at 6.9 percent in 2019.[2] Border statistics further to the south confirm this trend. The same group of migrants accounted for 1.56 percent of detentions at Mexico's southern border during the 2000s, but 7.28 percent in the 2010s (even reaching 16 percent in 2016).[3] Finally, the "irregular transit" of foreigners (99.1 percent of whom are from Cuba, Haiti, or Asian or African countries) crossing from Colombia to Panama grew exponentially from less than a thousand in 2010 and 2011, to an average of 19,000 per year from 2015 to 2020.[4]

The questions of why Latin America and why now are answered by shifts in South American and European politics. In Latin America's so-called pink tide politics of the 2000s, several states liberalized their immigration policy creating cracks in global mobility regimes rarely open to the world's poorest countries. In particular, Ecuador's 2008 "Citizen's Revolution" opened the country, if only temporarily, to any nationality on earth, a radical step described by President Rafael Correa as seeking to "unmake the twentieth-century invention of the passport." Ecuador's seemingly revolutionary move was matched by similar gestures of immigration liberalization and regularization in Argentina, Brazil, and Bolivia. At the same time as these American openings, Europe has become increasingly hostile to immigrants. Almost every African and Asian migrant with whom we spoke mentioned weighing travel to the Americas against European options. For many starting in sub-Saharan Africa, it was the horror stories of crossing the Mediterranean or transiting through Libya that pushed them toward the much longer American route.

While the opening of South America and increased closure of Europe has drawn attention to the Latin American route, it should not be considered new. Scholars have identified an Ecuador transit route serving Asian and African migrants since the 1980s.[5] One might even look further back to link contemporary migration with the colonial roots of Asian and African forced migration to the Iberian colonies.[6] Although the current increase to Latin America seems to follow the logic of choice, it is equally configured by global inequalities.

Setting off from a variety of regions facing a range of unstable conditions, tens of thousands of people like Kidane are taking one of the longest migration routes in history, a journey often measuring fifteen thousand miles in length. The *camino duro* starts in a hundred different places, but the starting points share certain forces of displacement: economic despair, some degree of political instability, and robust migrant-smuggling networks.

Joining Kidane's group of Eritreans fleeing the authoritarian rule of liberator-turned-dictator Isaias Afwerki are other migrants from the Horn of Africa—Ethiopians, Somalis, Sudanese, Yemeni, as well as Congolese and Ugandans escaping from economic downturns and conflict.

We met an equal number of West Africans, particularly people from Nigeria, Cameroon, and Ghana, but also heard of migrants coming from Angola and Equatorial Guinea. Government statistics suggest that nationals of

Guinea, Senegal, Mali, Gambia, Togo, Burkina Faso, Mauritania, and Ivory Coast have also made the trip. Since 2015, English-speaking Cameroonians are the most common West Africans on the route, fleeing persecution and civil war of their Francophone-ruled homeland.

From South Asia, the official story tends to be escape from some form of persecution: Bangladeshis from the Awami League's repression, Indians (mostly from Gujarat and Punjab) from Hindu nationalism, Nepalis from the threats of Maoist militants, Sri Lankan Tamils from Sinhala rule, and Pakistanis and Afghanis from general violence. In spite of their religious and ethnic diversity, in Latin America, South Asians tend to be collectively known as "Hindu" (regardless of their religious identification) to avoid confusion with the Spanish "Indio" term for indigenous people. But their reasons and circumstances for entering the journey vary widely, and as we explore, their journeys tend to be costlier, often tapping into smuggling networks spanning continents.

Finally, starting from places that are, at least on a map, closer to the US, Haitians and Cubans line the *camino duro*. But their journey is anything but direct. Most Haitians come to the route via Brazil or Chile, where economic downturns and anti-immigrant policies have propelled them northward. Cuban presence on the route greatly increased in 2015 amid rumors that then-US president Obama would end the "wet foot, dry foot" policy granting pathways to citizenship for all Cubans reaching US territory. Under this policy, the US distinguished between Cubans intercepted at sea, who were returned to their homeland, and those that made it to the US shore, who were allowed to apply for asylum. The Cuban migrants anticipated—correctly, as it turned out—that the exception to migration laws would end as relations between the Obama administration and the Castro regime were "normalized." Trump, in spite of rolling back Obama's other normalization policies with Cuba, did not restart the immigration exemption. As the US Coast Guard made boat arrivals on US soil nearly impossible, land routes via Ecuador became the preferred route. In 2015 alone, there was an 83 percent increase of Cuban asylees in the US over 2014.[7]

Migrants from these four global regions mix with other mobile people. In the asylum offices of South, Central, and North American countries, South Asian, African, and Caribbean migrants rub shoulders with Venezuelans, the largest displaced nationality in the Americas over the past five years; Colombians uncertain about their peace accord; Chinese nationals rumored to use the same routes but through other networks; and, from Mexico northward, Hondurans, Salvadorans, and Guatemalans. For the sake of consistency, our focus remains on those who enter South America and cross the ten-plus borders in hopes of reaching the US.

As shall become clear, migrants leaving Africa and Asia have a similar experience—and often a very similar route—to those who come from Haiti and Cuba. The length and trials of a migrant's journey are not decided by the physical location of their home, but rather by the location of that home in the global hierarchy of nations. That's because, as we shall show, many of the obstacles on this route were—and are—deliberately placed in the migrants' way. We will show how President Trump and his administration circumscribed this treacherous itinerary for people from what he, in the statement that defined his callous and facile immigration policy, called "shithole" countries.

Extracontinentales, a Problematic Label

Along their route in Latin America, the migrants are easily identifiable, picked out by their appearance or by the "mochilas"—small backpacks—they travel with, or simply by the size of their traveling parties. Latin American citizens, reporters, and governments often dub these migrants *extracontinentales,* a label that, much like the US term *alien,* is politically loaded with an intrinsic emphasis on exclusion. It's a reductive and hopelessly inadequate term that we use sparingly.[8]

The word *extra-continental* has a troubled etymology, with origins in ecology—to discuss invasive species, and in foreign policy—often in reference to "extra-continental military incursions" of the Cold War era. These uses invoke the xenophobic trope of migrant invasion fitting a Trumpian worldview. Another politically fraught term is *refugee* or asylum-seeker. Most of the people we interviewed sounded like they had legitimate claims to permanent asylum or temporary protection because of jeopardy, war, or deprivation at home. But the term *refugee* has been stretched by governments in the global north into some kind of litmus test to distinguish between the worthy and the unworthy ("economic migrants") on often arbitrary and politically biased grounds.[9]

As we struggled with these inadequate definitions, we came to see this book as an effort to put a more nuanced treatment of the *extracontinentales* and "asylum-seekers on the border" on the public record by documenting their incredible journey. The phrase "Global South," as a relatively new one, initially smacked of academic faddishness. As work progressed, it seemed the best general description of the places our protagonists were leaving. Global South is certainly preferable to the "Third World" or "developing world," phrases that long ago transferred from any geographic meaning to the realm of insult. Nothing else seemed broad enough to encompass the range of departure points in a respectful fashion.

While Global South is often used, like third world, to refer to the formerly colonized parts of the globe, it has come to mean much more. Beyond a geographic designation, Global South invokes the shared struggles of those exploited by the racialized and uneven economic development of global capitalism.[10] It is this more conceptual meaning that aligns with our impressions of agency and solidarities emerging from global south-south migration.

We take inspiration from recent turns in urban studies that refuse to cast Asian, African, and Latin American cities as failures of planning, instead recognizing their adaptive responses to the destructive conditions of imposed neoliberalism.[11] What some label "southern" or "peripheral" urbanism are the creative acts of urban residents to build their cities, working from the bottom-up rather than using the top-down approach of the state or private developers so common in the northern hemisphere.[12] This kind of city-making consists of improvised small acts of self-built infrastructure and the creation of shadow economies. Importantly, it emerges out of struggle and unexpected solidarities.

Migration from Asia, Africa, and the Caribbean through Latin America requires the same kind of creative adaptations. The US and other powers have committed formidable resources to slowing mobility on the *camino duro* and are constantly shifting tactics in the name of so-called deterrence. For the migrant, this journey requires months or years of adaptive struggle. As we shall show, each migrant depends on a network of others taking the journey—a digital and physical network—to survive.

How the US Policy of Deterrence Shapes the Journey

The leading anti-mobility power in the western hemisphere is the United States. Looming large over each border and national set of policies is the externalization of US immigration control. More than any other country in the western hemisphere, the US government has an end-to-end overview of this obstacle course and direct knowledge of the lives it claims every day.

Instead of trying to lower the obstacles, the best minds in the US immigration service have long been applied to raising the bar on existing obstacles and adding brand new ones.

US efforts to stop or slow regional migration are certainly not new, but reached new levels under Trump. Our research time frame, 2015 to 2020, overlapped with Trump's presidency, giving us a front-row seat to the lesser-noticed effects of his anti-immigration policies on the other side of the "wall" extending far south of the Rio Grande. The Trump administration has deliberately made the *camino duro* even *mas duro*. In the name of "deterrence," the US has employed all the bureaucratic and diplomatic resources at its disposal to stop or slow northward migration. They employ obstacles to wear down people's will to exert their human rights.

The Trump administration pushed "deterrence," we will demonstrate, to an extreme that entered the realm of what the anthropologist Jason de León interprets as "necropolitics"—a concept made popular by Achille Mbembe's studies of how colonial states governed through death. De León's research shows how US policy purposefully redirects migrants through the Sonoran desert, the most treacherous part of the US-Mexico border.[13] This diversion, he argues, outsources border deterrence to nature through the threat of death imposed by the desert. But the Sonoran desert is far from the only natural barrier exploited by the US. Using their influence with countries along the *camino duro*, the Trump administration worked hard to ensure the Americas became an ever-more deadly obstacle course.

In this most brutal form of deterrence, the US has harnessed the destructive power of natural obstacles and human-made barriers along the route to control the flow of migrants. The migrants face live fire from border guards, robbery and extortion from Colombian and Mexican drug cartels, Nicaraguan curfews, and American manacles. At great altitude, in high seas, and in forbidding jungle and desert terrain, the migrants are constantly diverted to the most treacherous path. But this natural deterrence is anything but "natural."

At the center of the journey is the near impassability of the Darién jungle at the Colombia-Panama borderlands. This part of the migration route has long been in use, but, unlike almost any other part of the Americas of comparable size (the Darién National Park in Panama is about 2,300 square miles), it remains unserved by road, air, sea, or even river. The Darién's reputation for deadliness is, arguably, the only effective part of the US and Central American allies' "deterrence" policy. As such, the Darién is wielded in a way reminiscent of ancient practices of banishment. The Roman and Greek empires chose the most inhospitable parts of their dominions for individuals sentenced to banishment. With the globe to work with, the US and allies appear to have chosen the Darién, an area where terrain, weather, dangerous animals, and armed groups are particularly abundant, as the destination for banishment as a deterrence. Due to US pressure on Panama since 2017, crossing the Darién has become even more treacherous forcing migrants into midnight boat rides and multi-day jungle hikes without consistent guides.

When a Cuban migrant, whom we call Armando, stumbled upon the dehydrated corpses of four people, including a child, in the Panamanian jungle, he knew the Panamanian authorities were not coming to bury them. In fact, the corpses that often litter the Darién Gap are part and parcel of policies euphemized as "deterrence" and "controlled flow." US pressure and funding built walls of military sharpshooters, walls of exhausted migrants in lines outside immigration offices, biometric data collection, and, most insidiously, walls of bureaucratic attrition. The brutal family separation at the US border was not the only infringement of human rights conventions. Our reporting suggests that migrants are subjected to deliberate delays and slow-pedaling of paperwork at every possible turn.

One particularly horrific example: asylum applicants are required to fill out the US Customs and Immigration Service's I-589 form. One exasperated immigration advocate lamented to us how, under the Trump administration, if a migrant neglected to fill out any of the dozens of fields on the form, even a "not applicable" field, the application was automatically rejected. Deterrence becomes a spectrum from the visceral brutality of the jungle on one end to the slow-downs and surveillance of migrant control at the other end.

The migrants we interviewed on the route told us they knew who their principal antagonist was. They knew that the Trump administration bestrode the whole route, prepared to assail them like the giant Maul in Bunyan's *Pilgrim's Progress*. They knew that migrants who took the *camino duro* before the age of Trump did not find it quite as *duro*.

But the strategy of the US anti-mobility regime long predates the most recent administration, emanating from both Republican and Democrat presidents. Since the advent of visas, powerful nation-states have used immigration policy as a form of foreign policy by "remote border control."[14] In the case of the Americas, the externalization of US policy has followed the logic of its anti-communist Cold War, and subsequent wars on drugs and terror. Through the promise of aid, free trade agreements, and military support, the US has outsourced anti-migration control through Mexico and, increasingly, Central American and South American states.

As we show, in spite of Correa's desire for Ecuador's open border experiment to counter US restrictions, the policy was partially undermined by US maneuvering, which included lobbying to restrict entry to certain nationalities, and support for detention centers and other anti-migration enforcements. Beyond Ecuador, the route is littered with reminders of US' overbearing influence. From Panama's *flujo controlado* (controlled flow) to Nicaragua's *muro de contención* (containment wall) and Mexico's Plan Sur and Mérida Initiative, each transit country has implemented anti-migration measures. While the policies' stated aims are to reduce trafficking and criminal activity, in practice, they serve the US agenda of tracking migrants, detaining or slowing them, all in the name of deterrence.

Deterrence policy does not deter, as a simple review of border-apprehension statistics confirms. The number of apprehensions at the US-Mexico border hit a twelve-year high in fiscal year 2019.[15] We have found that, while the threats of detentions, deportations, asylum rejection, violence, and natural dangers are well known and worrisome to migrants, they seldom outweigh calculations of what could be. Moreover, this sort of journey often lasts a year, extending the feedback loop on deterrence policies beyond the impatience of election cycles. Finally, transit countries are not mere puppets of northern hegemons, but often express refusals or face internal pressures to resist imposed restrictions from above, culminating in occasional and momentary cracks and openings.[16] Migrant trails are like rivers. The economic and political forces that set them in motion are too powerful for even the most committed—or cruel—national policy to stop. Policies of deterrence and *flujo controlado* do not fully control what happens on the *camino duro* any more than dams and levees control the course of the Mississippi. What deterrence policies do achieve, however, is a stalled and seemingly endless journey that is made increasingly dangerous—and, for smugglers, profitable—by each new policy barrier. Deterrence does not stop migration; it simply redirects it.

The Role of the Shadow Travel Industry

For every deterrent action, we will show, a shadow travel industry quickly produces a reaction. And this reaction often comes at the expense of the migrant. As soon as another section of the wall is built, the ladders—and the price for scaling the ladders—go up. It is an industry grounded in the paradox of the contemporary state's political wish to "control" its borders while also working to supply an exploitable labor pool. As a result, ballooned budgets devoted to border security are created, which filter, ironically, down as more profit, and demand, for smugglers and agents.[17]

Instead of understanding smuggling as a response to government policies, popular discourse often blames the smuggler for the miserable conditions of irregular migrants. In this simple binary, the smuggler is imagined as the "unscrupulous criminal" preying on migrant victims. But the multi-billion-dollar migration industry is far from being so simple. It encompasses an ethical spectrum that stretches from organized human traffickers to licensed travel agents and visa procurers. As numerous scholars of migration have illustrated, the diverse global industry of migration profiteers blurs the lines of legal and illegal, licit and illicit.[18] In nations such as Nepal and Eritrea, where few other economic opportunities exist, the rich incentives in the shadow travel industry create a push factor all of their own.

The distinction between human trafficking and what we call the shadow travel industry is hardly a bright line. We are not here to deny the existence of heinous exploitation by organized crime along the route we have traced. The broad implications of trafficking are that the smuggler deliberately misrepresents the services sold to the migrant, and effectively makes the migrant themselves the product. They might, for example, promise the migrant a job upon arrival only for the migrant to end up as something akin to an underpaid indentured servant. More specifically, abducting vulnerable women for sexual exploitation—domestically and internationally—has become a major crime. We did not meet anyone who alleged they were trafficked in either of these fashions. One Nepali man in Quito had arrived there for what appeared to be a prearranged and underpaid job. He complained about his job, but he did not have the experience of being "trafficked." We did not meet anyone who became involved in the sex trade. It's possible that the smugglers who arranged travel for the migrants we interviewed were also involved in sex trafficking or other sales of migrant laborpower. The vast majority of migrants we interviewed paid smugglers for passage along specific sections of the route. The terms were agreed in advance, and the migrants were not under any illusion that the smugglers would help them in any other way. The shadow travel industry certainly has very dark fringes. We frequently heard about betrayal, extortion, and abuse committed by coyotes, as the smuggler-guides are known in Latin America. Prices are inflated, and many migrants will never repay the loans they must take out to afford these travel services.

Since the 1990s, migration scholars have been discussing the notion of a "migration industry" to draw attention to the business of intermediaries who negotiate between the global labor market, national immigration policies, and the migrants.[19] While it was often assumed that migration agents, the center of the industry, are "entrepreneurial criminals" who use informal business practices to exploit migrants, more recent work has complicated any easy judgments.[20] This scholarship shows a spectrum of actors and actions, ranging from exploitation by transnational criminal networks to the less illicit work of guides, drivers, brokers, cooks, recruiters, lookouts, and handlers.[21] On one hand, this industry is sales-driven, helping to generate the vast numbers of people on the move, and how closely entwined it is with Global South economies and people—the unregulated moneylending industry. But the industry also includes the less profiteering work of restaurateurs, hoteliers, and humanitarians, who combine work with compassion to offer a grass-roots form of cosmopolitan solidarity with migrants.

It's a lucrative business whose owners do not file paperwork with securities regulators—much less visa offices. In other ways, it functions much like the conventional travel industry, with independent agents in dozens of countries coordinating complex and often extremely expensive itineraries. For this reason, we use the term "shadow" to reflect its parallel character to the more conventional travel industry. Sometimes migrants use the latter—in the form of regulated commercial travel on ticketed planes and buses. At other times, it follows its own logics. For instance, the alternative "ticketing" of a forwarded cellphone message picture of the migrants eating a meal to prove they have been serviced.

Smuggler-migrant relations are equally complex, often based on gendered expectations, kinship, friendship, or other ties of social proximity based on trust and reciprocity.[22] Smugglers can be migrants themselves, sharing social connections to the community from which migrants are coming.[23] In some cases, smugglers conceive of their activity as a moral duty, even philanthropy or a form of resistance.[24] But, any such "chains of trust" diminish with increased anti-migrant surveillance and regulation, allowing more exploitative relations to take root.[25]

From Kathmandu labor recruitment offices to Quito restaurants, tourist hostels in Capurganá's beachside resorts, and restaurants surrounding Tapachula's central plaza, the agents of the route span an expansive economic network that can be hardly considered one unified conglomerate. Industry actors, motives, and social characteristics shift based on place, ranging from a side-business for narco-paramilitaries to a cooperative form of co-ethnic support, from a dangerous and organized form of smuggling to an independent and open "mobile commons."

The diverse spectrum of industry actors is reflected in the range of migrant travel options: the full-board "escorted" migrants guided—and watched—along the way; the half-board travelers who occasionally work with smugglers for border crossings, but often remained on their own; finally, the independent "self-catering" migrants who sort it out as they go. This spectrum of services mirrors global hierarchies of class, race, and nationality. As we explore further, the migrant's ability to pay—upward of US$50,000—for the full-board escorted journey requires considerable financial planning. Loans provided by the shadow travel industry and backed by their families' landholdings fund many of the South Asian journeys on the *camino*. Like luxury travelers in the conventional travel industry, these escorted migrants are subject to special protocols. They are often trained to act as tourists and are closely monitored by handlers, giving their experience a chaperoned sort of feel. While all migrants must rely on the information and support of fellow migrants, the goodwill of humanitarian helpers, or find opportunities to work along the way, it was the independent travelers who were most exploited. Such exploitation goes hand-in-hand with the racialization of Haitian and African migrants along the *camino*, evidenced in references to "*los morenos*" as the problem-makers.[26] Cubans, due to knowing Spanish and having diasporas along the route, travel on the other side of the spectrum. They have tended to create nationalized forms of support with marked safe-houses and guides, one-time migrants who return to the *camino*—to guide and profit from co-nationals.

Whether escorted or independent, there are no guarantees in the shadow travel industry. As we show, reaching the US border might mark the finish line from the smuggler's perspective, but the start of a whole new set of travails. Even release from a detention center offers little solace witnessed in our main protagonist's decision to leave the US for Canada. For this reason, we use the term travel, instead of migration, industry to emphasize the indeterminacy of such mobility. Migration implies a fixed destination and trajectory. Thanks to the extended encounter of deterrence barriers, the journey has no clear ending. From the view of migrants, the goal is to keep moving.

When a Journey Becomes an Existence

The entrepreneurial and cooperative nature of migrant community points to our third and final main observation: the way that migrants create a life in transit. While the industry relations often commodify migrants with dehumanizing language of being called chicken, pigs, snakes or sheep, the immense amount of negotiation required to survive on the journey reveals the agency of migrants.[27] They are not passively "smuggled." Rather, they are active decision makers who calculate choices based on many social factors.[28]

It's our hope that we allow our sources to gradually define themselves as their stories unfold. We hope to reveal migrants as narrators of their own stories, both in their interviews with us and in their digital communications with one another and the homeland. While Global South migrants have undertaken epic journeys for decades, their epicness has largely failed to register. In the stories told from the US or European perspective, migrants are portrayed as hapless flotsam, washed up in areas significant to western life—usually the US-Mexico border or the northern coasts of the Mediterranean Sea. If there is any agency in the journey, it's attributed to the smuggler, who is thought to accompany the migrant every step of the way. Even when the migrant's circuitous route is taken into account, there's an assumption that the person from the Global South could never appreciate the complex combination of desperate danger and thrilling adventure that's part of more celebrated epic journeys.

The multi-continental geography—and sheer duration—of these journeys requires expanding our conceptual toolkit beyond the limited dualities of push and pull, origins and destination, sending and receiving countries. Building on the "transit turn" in migration studies, the journey itself is the focus of this book.[29] This journey is not only a major event in migrants' lives; for some, including Kidane, it becomes their lives for years on end. Policy debates in the 1980s treated "transit" as a category of person, often conflated with illegal status.[30] This view of transit evokes a "panic" of mobile hordes passing through corrupt and inefficient southern countries, an image serving the imperialistic urges of Global North states to extend their control over intermediate spaces.

We hope this book divorces the concept of transit from its policy origins. We build on the work of scholars who have framed transit as a condition of fragmentation, ambiguity, uncertainty, and precariousness common across migration experiences.[31] In particular, we apply Jonathan Echeverri Zuluaga's use of the concept "errance" to express the uncertain nature of undocumented global travel.[32] Based on research with migrants in Dakar, Senegal and Quito, Ecuador, Echeverri Zuluaga theorizes errance as a state of being in which borders, people, documents, and identities are dislocated, closed one day but open to negotiation the next. Amid the fluctuating dynamics of errance, there are no destinations, just next best options for continuing movement. It's clear, from speaking with Kidane and others, that the uncertainty of the journey is a defining part of their life experience. That's true because of the heightened life-or-death reality of the trip, but also because, more than a half-decade later, Kidane and thousands in similar situations are still, effectively, in transit.

Migration, for the migrants featured in this book, is neither linear nor constant, but rather consists of fitful starts and stops, returns and detentions, not to mention periods of waiting. The journeys we describe do not have clear starting or finish lines, but rather an overarching sensibility of being stuck in limbo—even while physically moving. Transit, thus, is a study in contradictions between exploitation and solidarity, mobility and control, alienation and connection.

What we add to this ontological understanding of transit is the creative sharing of information/knowledge, the thrill of the journey, and the boredom of waiting. One reason these journeys are not more celebrated is that they lack the documented trappings of the traditional Western voyage: the maps, sea charts and compasses. However, Kidane and others used and shared information via texted communications and apps the way sailors once pooled maps—a cooperative phenomenon that recalls the concept of the "digital commons," or what we call a digital grapevine.[33] The messages not only provide physical directions, but also range from advice, such as what to say to immigration officials or how to receive money, to explaining what to expect along the way and encouragement to keep going. One scholar has astutely described this exchange of community knowledge as "refugee protection from below."[34]

Like any story of endurance, this is also one of adventure. From the agents' offices of Kathmandu to shelters for asylees awaiting trial in the US, we heard migrants describe the thrill of a multi-country journey, making it clear that the travails of the route were part of America's allure. The journey also requires an adaptive creativity contingent on a wide possibility of shifting circumstances. Migrants must be able to perform different roles ranging in visibility from being hidden "tourists" in surveilled spaces to papers-seeking advocates at governmental offices. Engaging with police, agents, and service providers requires a similar array of negotiation and performative skills. Additionally, knowing when and how to align with other migrants entails a linguistic and cultural know-how that crosses categories of nationality, religion, gender, and regional affiliation.

A Special Blend of Personalities and Approaches

We do not see ourselves as protagonists in this book. But the storyteller can never stay out of the story entirely. As we set the scene and paint the backgrounds, some of own scenes and our own backgrounds will be revealed, whether we like it or not.

We have our own journeys. There was the journey from small-town journalism in suburban Ireland to riding taxis across South American borders with anxious Haitian migrants; and the journey from ethnographic research on urbanization in Nepal to a global migration network stretching from Kathmandu to Southern Mexico. It was, perhaps, a shared experience and love of circuitous journeys that made the course of researching and writing this book so smooth.

Curran had originally arrived in the US as a migrant in 2000. Due to his own carelessness, he had lost his fiancé visa and become, effectively, an undocumented migrant for the year during which his permanent-resident application was being processed. Later, Curran's urge to journey led him to supplement his work in financial journalism with travel assignments. Curran was still searching for something deeper when he accompanied his wife, Sara Fanning, a scholar of Haitian history, on a research trip to Haiti in 2014.

When Curran arrived, Port au Prince was little more than the shattered remains of the 2010 earthquake. The streets were mostly churned-up clay and concrete, with occasional piles of rubble, a city turned inside out. An extensive tented district was still standing near the center. Most people had moved back into corrugated-iron shacks, constructed on the ruins of their prior houses. Partly due to the lack of shelter, the streets were thronged. Everyone seemed to be selling something, and nobody seemed to be buying. The lucky ones sold coconuts from beneath multicolored umbrellas, while most had nothing to cover their heads from the beating sun other than the trays of shellfish or water bottles.

When Curran returned from Haiti, he had an experience common to many northern visitors to the Global South. It was difficult to leave Haiti behind, difficult to find anything to write about in the US as urgent or meaningful as the struggles of the Haitians.

Not long after his return, he got to talking to Nelson, as they watched their kids play together on the grounds of Cornerstone Cooperative preschool in the authors' hometown of Denton, Texas. Nelson told him a fascinating story about a part of the Global South incredibly distant from Haiti, and yet somehow reminiscent of it. Dads enrolled in the school typically cooperate on shed building or grass maintenance. These two started cooperating on a research project.

Nelson's understanding of global migration started with a study abroad trip to Nepal in 1999. While taking courses on Nepali language and society during the day, he would spend his evenings and weekends with a host-brother, Manoj. Like many youth of Kathmandu, Manoj was unemployed and disinterested in working his family's fields on the city's outskirts. The closest he came to a job came in regular visits to a labor recruitment office, or "manpower agency" as they are known in Nepal, to seek work abroad in Malaysia.

Manoj's cousin Krishna had just returned from two years in Kuala Lumpur and would often regale the neighborhood with adventures of his time living and earning abroad. Over late night beers and momos (Nepali dumplings), Krishna would tell Manoj and Nelson a less enviable version of his experience. From the moment he arrived, his agent stripped him of his passport making it impossible to leave his worksite or hostel. He was essentially an indentured servant stuck in back-breaking twelve-hour construction shifts until he paid off his debt.

To Nelson's surprise, Krishna's revelations did little to dim Manoj's desire to travel abroad, or "go outside." As Nelson would learn later, Nepal's liberalization of passports in the early 1990s started a surge of labor migration, most often to southeast Asia or the Gulf. Manoj's generation saw foreign labor—hellish conditions and all—as preferable to the diminished prospects in Nepal during a civil war.

Where Manoj truly desired to travel was the United States. The naïve college student Nelson tried to help. As it turned out being good friends with a US citizen was insufficient grounds for the embassy to grant a visa to a working-class Nepali youth. Twice Manoj was denied a tourist visa to the US. On Nelson's subsequent trips to Nepal, in 2001 and 2002 as an English teacher, and 2007 to 2009 as a researcher, Manoj would explain new strategies for getting out of Nepal, one of which included entering the US from Mexico. However, after ten years of trying to migrate, Manoj decided to get married in 2009 and commit himself to business ventures in Nepal, such as opening a fast-food restaurant and a tomato farm.

Nearly everyone else in the neighborhood would leave. Manoj's best friend became a driver in Saudi Arabia; his brother-in-law a repairman in a Qatari hotel; a cousin taught Buddhism classes in Japan. But, only one person, his sister Ganga, would make it to the US. After working as a nanny in Germany for three years, she successfully secured a tourist visa to the States, where she remains today as a health-care worker in the Bay Area.

Although Nelson's research was focused on the urbanization of Kathmandu Valley, migration would often factor into conversations with research participants. Many viewed laboring abroad as the vehicle to securing land and home ownership in the city. What tied city-making and migration together was the central role of intermediary dealers, known as *dalals*, who negotiate between the booming industries of land and labor migration. When Nelson started seeing news reports about Nepalis being detained in South and Central American countries in the early 2010s, he connected the dots between Manoj's Mexico plan and the *dalal* networks extending from Nepal into the western hemisphere.

When Nelson visited Kathmandu in the summer of 2015 to study the city's response to the earthquake, he stumbled upon Surendra Poudel's reporting of Latin American journeys and met several aspiring migrants. When Nelson returned from Nepal to Texas, he and Curran got talking in the Cornerstone playground.

The book is the product of a collaboration between a journalist and an anthropologist, a melding of two different approaches to knowing the world. We have sought to marry the best of the journalist's rapid networking and seeking official comment with the anthropologist's slower focus on rapport-building.

We did so in a series of reporting trips, as follows:

In June 2016, we went to Quito, Ecuador, not sure what we would find. It did not take long to stumble upon a vibrant "Little India" in the heart of the city's tourist neighborhood, La Mariscal. Settled in next to other bars and restaurants, ten South Asian restaurants lined the streets of Juan León Mera and Reina Victoria just blocks from the central Plaza Foch. Inside these restaurants we spoke with restaurateurs and workers about their "American dream" and observations of their compatriots coming through on their way to El Norte along the *camino*. Under the name of Indian, or "Hindu," the restaurants offer pan-South Asian social spaces that mix nationalities, regions, and languages from the subcontinent. Many, we discovered, were involved in the industry, managing northward movements, at least through to northern Colombia, to the small town of Turbo. As we argue, this industry provides an alternative formation along the spectrum of profiteering smugglers and humanitarian migrant supporters. It was here that we first experienced the blurred lines between exploitative smuggling, co-ethnic solidarity, and opportunistic informal marketeering found in many communities along the route.

Two years later, in July 2018, we traveled to Colombia, first to Turbo on the southern edge of the Gulf of Urabá, where we met plenty of fishermen, but no migrants. "Go to Capurganá," we were told, and so we embarked on the two-and-a-half hour tourist boat ride to the small beachside tourist town where we met Kidane. Coincidentally, we managed to book a hostel directly in front of the other dock, not the tourist's entry point, but the fisher's spot-by-day, migrant departure spot-by-night, filling small dinghy boats on their way to Panama, from where they start treks into the Darién jungle.

We felt conflicted about never braving the Darién jungle shoulder-to-shoulder with the migrants. Maybe one day. But the truth is, we can never fully share their experience. Just by dint of being white and documented, we have a safety net that they are purposely denied. To paraphrase the British band Pulp, if we called our consular support, we could stop it all. The Darién jungle is treacherous for extreme-sports survivalists that take it on. But theirs are not the bones that litter the path. Migrants pass through the Darién with reminders of death on all sides, conscious that the slightest misstep could mean disaster.

From narratives by Kidane and other migrants, we have also learned another side of the Darién—that of solidarity. While much of the journey is organized according to nationality, the challenge of the jungle requires mutual support across social divisions, informal ethical codes of leaving no one behind, and men helping women. The Darién is also where the digital grapevine becomes most critical, with the accuracy of WhatsApp messages a life-or-death issue.

Emerging from the jungle means reconnecting with the ease of road travel through the rest of Central America, but also facing new barriers in the form of shifting border policies and mobility regimes, camps/detention centers, and new fees—those officially demanded by the state and those unofficially demanded by police and thieves. The shifting sands of US relations and proxy policy in these nations means that every migrant must become versed in the latest Central American politics.

When Kidane's group reached Mexico, they waited in the cosmopolitan border town of Tapachula for two weeks to secure a transit pass, the paperwork which granted them twenty days to move through the country. For less fortunate migrants, this provides enough time for a long bus ride to the border. For those able to afford plane travel, it means a one-stop flight from Tapachula to the border towns of Tijuana, Cuidad Juárez, or Reynosa via the capital.

In early January 2020, we retraced Kidane's steps in Tapachula. There, we ate at Mama Africa's—a restaurant run by an older Mexican woman who has learned the favorite dishes and phrases of the route's many migrants. But the city had changed since Kidane came through it in 2018. Due to the pressure of the Trump administration on Mexico to "stop caravans," transit passes had all but stopped being issued in Tapachula, creating a bottleneck along the route like no other. We observed a transformation of the Octava Avenida Norte guesthouses, built for temporary transit, into long-term boarding houses. The Siglo XXI detention center had become a mandatory stay and the lines at the Las Vegas Immigration Office had become crowds of frustrated applicants.

If and when migrants are able to leave Tapachula and reach the US border, they enter a new maze of shifting immigration policies. The Trump administration's effective cancellation of asylum left migrants in a limbo of detention and deportation orders, often waiting for removal. For many, the impossibility of entering or remaining in the US entailed the shame and danger of returning home or a return to Mexico or further south, which, as we show, takes a considerable toll on the mental health and economic condition of migrants. And indeed, part of this is on purpose. Many were treated as "special interest aliens" (SIA), which is often code for nationals of countries listed on the ever-fluctuating terrorism watch list. As SIA, their asylum pleas are treated with additional scrutiny, usually guaranteeing their immediate transfer to detention centers. With the adoption of the Migration Protection Protocol (MPP), better known as the Trump administration's "Stay in Mexico" policy, in 2019, many asylum-seekers, including SIA, have to wait on the other side of the Rio Grande.

In a mixture of English, Spanish, Nepali (Nelson), very rudimentary Hindi (Nelson), and Haitian Creole (Curran), we have interviewed migrants from Nepal, India, Bangladesh, Pakistan, Cameroon, Ghana, Nigeria, Haiti, Cuba, Uganda, Eritrea, and Ethiopia. We have spoken with lawyers in Ecuador, Colombia, and the US, and with human rights workers in Ecuador, Colombia, Panama, and Mexico. Our methods have included not just interviews but also the act of crossing borders. From Tulcan, Ecuador, to Ipiales, Colombia, we drove and took a taxi across the border, spending time in the "no man's land" between the two. From Sapzurro, Colombia, we walked over the hill to La Miel, Panama, to learn how the migrant pathways into the Darién had shifted. From Tecun Uman, Guatemala, we walked the banks of the Suchiate River, and then over the bridge into Cuidad Hidalgo, Mexico.

This book is also a culmination of two different approaches to writing. Much of it has emerged from revised versions of narrative-driven articles published in the *Dallas Morning News*. Other parts come from several of Nelson's academic publications with more attention to social science literature and analysis. In combining these two approaches, we have sought to integrate the immediacy of journalistic character portraits with an anthropological concern for historical and cultural context.

The heart of the book is rooted in the experiences of several migrants who have generously shared their stories with us and maintained contact over the years. As introduced above, the circuitous journey of Kidane serves as the anchor and foundation of the book. His faithful and patient answering of our questions and good friendship has provided not just our data, but also our motivation to share his story with wider audiences. As fathers ourselves, we feel his heartbreak of having left his pregnant wife five years ago, forced to get to know his son via web-calls. Although not yet fixed, we are hopeful that his story ends with reunion when he finally obtains Canadian residency and family reunification.

Others, too, have given much to the making of this book. A Nepali couple stuck in Quito unable to continue north or return home; a Punjabi "tourist" in Ecuador excited to post his trip's adventures on Facebook; a Cameroonian woman's circular travails between Panama and Colombia and horrific detention in the US; a Ugandan man fleeing a family feud now stranded in Tapachula; and many others. We are also indebted to the contributions of key observers, an expatriate hotelier in Capurganá, and several smugglers "retired" in the US and Dominican Republic. We contextualize these personal narratives with historical and policy sources, expert interviews, as well as our fieldwork observations and experiences. To keep the focus on migrant narratives, we provide the direct words of respondents as much as possible in the text.

The narrative structure of the book follows Kidane's route through the Americas, which overlaps with the journeys of other migrants we have interviewed and with our own research trips. Neither the migrants we interviewed nor we ourselves have followed every spur of the trail, but we believe we have documented the main route as it was traveled during the Trump administration.

CHAPTER 1

The Leaving Business

Leaving Sweet Bihat

Kidane Okubay had no greater desire to leave Eritrea than Ulysses had to leave Ithaca.

In 2015, his wife, Hiwet, had just become pregnant with their first child. But the moment when most young people feel the urge to feather their nest at home—the joyful discovery of imminent parenthood—was the moment that made Kidane realize he had to seek a life elsewhere. How can you raise a son in a society where the only future is conscription and poverty?

Kidane is a very personable young man, easy in any company, even after a treacherous all-night boat trip in Colombia. The trip had somewhat depleted his frame when we first met, but years of manual labor have earned him a square chest and broad shoulders. He is quick to smile, and to slough off worries. But he is not blind to the almost fantastical length and difficulties of the journey he has undertaken. He knows he has a story to tell, and he has always been eager to share it with us. We use Kidane's first name because of how well we feel we have come to know him, in hours of interviews and countless messages.

Interviewing Kidane is refreshing because he does not distrust media and scholarship as so many people now do. A writer—and a reader—often wonders about a subject's "angle." Why do they want to tell their story? Years later, after Curran published a piece in the *Dallas Morning News* based on Kidane's tip-offs about atrocities in Tigray, he was explicit about why he chose to share so much with us.

"This is what I want, voice for the voiceless," he said, in a Facebook Message.

Kidane's urge to tell his story is born of his faith in humanity, and his knowledge of humanist thought. He kept a diary of his journey because he knew it was extraordinary, and he made his trials public because he knew their publication was one of the few possible ways those trials could be eased for the countrymen who came after him.

The guiding force of Kidane's moral compass was clear from the moment we met him. The note of outrage in Kidane's voice when he spoke about mistreatment by South American police and US immigration court, and the light of urgency in his eyes when he spoke about the tyranny of the Eritrean regime could be read as naïve. But a naïve Kidane could never have slipped out of Eritrea, much less navigated his way through the Americas.

Migration stories often start with a complex mixture of push and pull factors. For migrants who commit to the duress of the *camino duro*, the pulls are especially wrenching and the pushes often brutal. Kidane described the calculation to us. He knew from accounts that there was no easy way out of Eritrea, and no easy way into the US. Like tens of thousands of migrants, he weighed the long-term misery of a future in his oppressed homeland against the short-term misery of the *camino duro*.

Kidane's push factor had a name: Isaias Afwerki. For most of Kidane's thirty-six years of life, Eritrea has been ruled by the former freedom fighter. When Mr. Isaias became Eritrea's first president in 1993 after leading the long war of independence against Ethiopia, he was hailed by President Bill Clinton and others as a visionary leader. But he never gave up the ways of war, engaging in the Badme conflict with Ethiopia, a border squabble that claimed an estimated 100,000 lives and lasted two decades. He also turned his wrath on his own people.

In Kidane's Eritrea, the web was only as wide and worldly as Isaias allowed it to be. There were, effectively, no telephones—only party lines, with the Eritrean secret police always acting as the third party.

The Eritrean secret police have infiltrated every community institution, even the churches, where they pressure deacons and others to inform on people who speak out against the government or who they suspect of planning to run away, said John Stauffer, the president of The America Team for Displaced Eritreans. Mr. Stauffer had worked in the Peace Corps in Eritrea before independence, and he now runs a nonprofit advocating for and providing services to Eritrean refugees.

One man who Mr. Stauffer's organization assisted in the US was a public opponent of the regime, a dangerous role, before he escaped to Eastern Europe about five years ago. The man soon learned that his mother was imprisoned in retribution.

"He spoke to someone in the Eritrean embassy, and he was told they knew who he was and asked [to] come back," said Mr. Stauffer.

The act of holding the dissident's mother hostage "serves different purposes. For one thing, it's outright punishment. It also serves as an example to other people: 'don't go against the government, don't run away.'"

Many of the refugees whom Mr. Stauffer assists never had any intention of running from Eritrea. The first they heard of emigration was often when they were seized by the secret police and accused of plotting an escape, explained Mr. Stauffer. Humanitarian group Amnesty International has mapped out hundreds of makeshift jails in the country for such alleged offenders, which it calls an "infrastructure of repression." These jails often consist of little more than freight trailers where prisoners are "crammed" in horrifying conditions, said Mr. Stauffer. The refugees often flee during a lapse in security, when they're "let outside to do their business, and there might be a rainstorm, or very few guards, or they're being transferred in a truck and they jump out."

As Kidane told a US judge who asked him if he had used government phones or government computers: in Eritrea, all phones and computers are government phones and computers. He could not repeat that self-evidently effective defense to us without exasperation. Among the biggest insults he bore was the accusation that he had conspired with his persecutor. In 2014, the year before Kidane left, Human Rights Watch described Eritrea as being "among the most closed countries in the world." It was once ranked at the bottom of the global pile for press freedoms.[1]

Isaias's Eritrea richly deserves its reputation as "the North Korea of Africa," said Stauffer.

Isaias's power is so absolute that he even banned home construction in 2006, according to an Al Jazeera report.[2] One of Kidane's friends built a home for himself only to see it bulldozed by government forces enforcing the ban on private property.

Kidane grew up in a village called Bihat, a farming community in the south of the country, less than ten miles from the mountainous Ethiopian border. The nearest big town is Senafe, known for the ancient Matara ruins and stark, bare-rock mountains in the shape of tombstones.

The Bihat community grew "sorghum, maize, barley, wheat, and others which I do not know their name in English," wrote Kidane, in an e-mail in the summer of 2020. "Even we grow vegetables like tomato, potato, onion, lettuce, spinach and others."

"We use oxes to plough the land," wrote Kidane. "That way of ploughing is [passed down] from our forefathers. Still continues."

Kidane describes growing up in Bihat as a pastoral idyll. He has fond memories of riding horses, and, especially, eating hearty feasts with friends and family. He credits his own sunny, philosophical demeanor to the warmth of the community from which he emerged.

But Bihat also has a long tradition of political and food instability. Kidane is from a Tigrinya-speaking community, and Bihat is almost culturally identical to the communities in the Tigray region of Ethiopia, just across the border. It was the Tigray region of Ethiopia (and Eritrea) that felt the initial brunt of the 1983 to 1985 Ethiopian famine. Some historians even cite the Ethiopian communist leader Megistu Haile Mariam's efforts to divert grain from the Tigray rebels as a major aggravating factor in that famine.

During Kidane's journey, Hiwet and Yoel—like Ulysses's Penelope and Telemachus—have faced growing threats from their neighbors. In 2020, the longstanding tensions between the Tigray and other Ethiopian ethnic groups (including the largest, the Amhara) combusted into the latest of a series of wars, with Ethiopia's national army laying siege to large parts of the region. New Ethiopian Prime Minster Abiy Ahmed was determined to crush the Tigray political establishment, which had long held power in Addis Ababa until his election in 2018.

The US State Department is among many observers calling for a full investigation into reported atrocities in the Tigray province, many of them allegedly committed by the Eritrean army. Fortunately, Kidane's wife and son had moved to Addis Ababa when the shooting and bombing started in the Tigray region in late 2020. They might easily have stayed in a refugee camp on the Ethiopian side of the border. The vengeful, Stalin-like malice that Isaias bears on the diaspora is clear from the allegations of troop behavior in these camps. Using an alliance with Ethiopian troops as a pretext to cross the border, the Eritrean soldiers allegedly rampaged through the refugee camps, raping, killing, and abducting civilians, according to accounts from United Nations officials and Mr. Stauffer's local sources. Eritrean troops have also blocked humanitarian aid to Tigray, reducing as many as 400,000 people to famine conditions. The abducted Eritrean refugees face a forced return to the nation they had escaped, a nation where the mere intention to emigrate is treated as a crime.

Kidane is used to the shadow of armed conflict. In 2000, his parents were forced to move the family for a year, staying near the capital Asmara, because of displacement in the Badme border war.

Isaias uses these wars as leverage for more power. He demanded indefinite national service from all citizens throughout the twenty years of the Badme conflict, and has not lifted that requirement since that war ended in 2018. It's a policy of Kafkaesque cruelty. The work is practically voluntary, with payments set at such a pittance that advancement is meaningless. Leaving is not an option. Isaias has forbidden the issuance of passports until such time as this indefinite service was deemed fulfilled.

Like almost all Eritrean men of his generation, Kidane was sent to Sawa, a sprawling military-training camp in the west of Eritrea the year before graduating secondary school. There, in 2005, he went through brutal boot camp–style training and completed his education. At the end of the year, the graduating class at Sawa must sit matriculation exams. Kidane scored highly enough to continue his education. Otherwise, he would have been pressed into the army as a foot soldier, like many of his classmates.

Kidane attended Mai Nefhi University near the capital Asmara, now the Eritrea Institute of Technology. He earned a degree in library science, qualifying as an archivist. He served eighteen months in a support role in the army and was then transferred to national service in the civilian sector.

He married a young woman he had known since childhood. He showed us a picture of her. Hiwet is even more attractive than Kidane.

They marked the wedding in traditional Tigray ceremonies—"not like what you know in [a] hotel"—in both Asmara, where Hiwet's family had moved, and in their hometown of Bihat. When Kidane left in 2015, Hiwet, by then pregnant, stayed with his parents in Bihat.

For Kidane, the main pull factor was the Eritrean-Ethiopian diaspora. Throughout North America and Europe, there are welcoming Tigrinya-speaking communities who recreate the food-centric culture of Bihat. As with the Irish and Jewish in centuries past, the concept of Eritrean identity has dispersed into little Eritreas everywhere.

From Eritreans with knowledge of the smuggling routes, Kidane learned he would need roughly $20,000 to pay for passage to North America. He borrowed $5,000 from a nephew, enough to get out of Eritrea on purchased documents. ("I will give it back to him," Kidane vowed, during an interview.)

For the balance, he relied on smaller loans from other family's savings and whatever work he found along the way.

The decision to leave was the critical one ahead of the trip. Kidane was aiming for the US, but not committed to that destination. On the *camino duro*, destinations are seen as secondary, and necessarily fungible, goals. Kidane also weighed the European option. In 2015, many Eritreans were going north to Europe, part of a surge of migrants crossing the Sahara desert in the wake of the Arab spring. This was gaining a reputation as an even more treacherous journey than the route through the Americas, according to Kidane and other Eritreans.

Kidane's decision not to take the Saharan route to Europe may have saved his life. Daniel Berhane, an Eritrean man we met in Colombia with Kidane, said his brother was stabbed to death while crossing the world's largest desert. Some years after Kidane left Bihat, one of his nieces traveled to Libya, hoping to make a Mediterranean crossing. Recent reports have documented Libyan smugglers selling Eritrean and other African migrants in slave markets, which follows a legacy of Eritreans being abducted in eastern Sudan and sold to gangs along the Egypt-Sudan border.[3] Kidane forwarded footage of a building where he said his niece was taken by smugglers. It looked like a large warehouse converted into a dormitory, with camp beds but little else. At least three men were lying on stretchers. A woman was screaming.

"The army began to shoot us, they killed two guys," said the man taking the camera-phone video. "More than thirty people are injured."

When Kidane forwarded this video, it was with an appeal: "This is what Eritrean refugees got problems in Libya. . . . If possible, please do your best to expose these difficulties."

Kidane said his niece and more than ninety other people were trapped in the building. As of August 2022, Kidane had not heard from his niece in three years.

In February 2015, with the help of the documents from the Eritrean shadow travel industry, Kidane crossed into Ethiopia, Eritrea's former parent state and, until the peace treaty signed in 2018, its nominal enemy. He spent three months in a refugee camp, established to shelter those caught in the crossfire of the conflict. Kidane is at home with Ethiopians. As is often the case in internecine conflict, Ethiopians and Eritreans have much in common. As Irish people are immersed in English culture so are Eritreans more Ethiopian than the Ethiopians themselves.

From there, he made his way to Addis Ababa, the Ethiopian capital, where he spent eight months scratching around for work. He heard that work was better paid in South Sudan, the oil-rich nation that had just broken away from Sudan.

As the crow flies, it's less than a thousand miles from Addis Ababa to Juba. But Kidane's routes seldom overlap with those of the crow. He traveled more than twice that distance, taking a bus to Kenya and traveling through Uganda via bus and motorbike taxi. His route was almost perfectly circular, a reflection of the complex geopolitics of sub-Saharan East Africa.

To paraphrase the Irish rebel and writer Brendan Behan, the first thing on the agenda after a nation's war of independence is often a civil war. When Kidane arrived, South Sudan was already three years into civil strife, with the South Sudan People's Liberation Army fighting government forces. But the fighting had moved away from the capital city of Juba. Initially, Kidane's situation in South Sudan was promising. He worked for two years in a hardware store. He showed us a picture of the soccer team he formed with his colleagues. But neither Kidane nor South Sudan seemed to be able to get away from warfare.

One day, he heard shooting outside his place of work. Most of his colleagues hunkered down in place. One lady was determined to go home. As Kidane watched, she ran into the street where she was caught in the crossfire and killed.

Kidane decided to move on again. Using the papers acquired in Eritrea, Kidane flew from South Sudan to Dubai. There, he worked as a laborer, packaging exports bound for his homeland.

In 2017, Kidane decided to make his way to North America by way of Dubai. He had to pay a smuggler in the UAE city $16,000 up front for an Eritrean passport, visas, plane tickets and the assistance of *coyotes*, smuggler-guides, in Latin America. The man, he said, claimed to have contacts in the Jordanian consulate who would help ensure that the paperwork was legitimate. On his first attempt, Kidane flew from Dubai to Havana, Cuba, via Moscow. He got as far as the immigration control in Cuba, where his visa was rejected. In 2018, he tried again, this time flying to Santa Cruz, Bolivia via Brazil.

Three years after his journey had begun, he had one foot in the Americas. Now for the hard part.

A Nurse Driven Out of Cameroon

Many of the people Kidane met on his journey through the Americas were from Cameroon. After decades of relative stability, Cameroon's colonial divisions re-emerged in the form of sectarian fighting between the franco-phone-dominant state and anglophone separatists.

We were introduced to Jane Mtebe by the same woman who pointed us in the direction of Kidane in Capurganá, Colombia, an American woman we will call Kristina. Kristina was part of what we have come to think of as an underground railroad, a loose association of people, mainly women, who provide the kind of support that the states on the *camino duro* deny migrants. They might be called humanitarians, although their work is so direct and reactive that it almost feels like something more immediate than what we know as humanitarianism. The first contact we had with Ms. Mtebe was after she had returned to the US. Kristina introduced us over one of the preferred channels of communication on the *camino duro*—Facebook Messenger.

At first, Ms. Mtebe stated frankly that she had found her journey too harrowing to relive in a retelling. She allowed that she might be willing to share when time had healed some of her trauma. Her responses to our questions on the messenger app were understandably curt. It was unclear whether Ms. Mtebe wanted anything to do with the project.

Nevertheless, we stayed in touch. As winter 2018 descended, we had a brief conversation by telephone. Ms. Mtebe was still not ready to do an extended interview. She was still settling in the Boston area, and very concerned about the descending winter. As long as her building was halfway insulated and she had a heavy jacket, we reassured her, everything would be fine. She seemed to appreciate the tip. When we asked about scheduling an interview, she sighed. "Not yet," she said. Now, we were sure that Ms. Mtebe was just being polite. Communication almost stopped.

In March 2020, Ms. Mtebe messaged. She was ready to tell her story. She still could not speak about the harrowing experience without tremors in her voice, but she had decided she must speak, tremors and all.

Ms. Mtebe had a vastly different experience to Kidane's on the *camino duro*. When we met him, Kidane was clearly drained. But Kidane is robust and athletic, and he was used to horse-riding and hiking in rough terrain in Eritrea. The same slog of a journey that depleted Kidane physically very nearly killed Ms. Mtebe. As a general rule, it is the young men from Global South families who make the first attempt at the *camino duro*, sometimes hoping, like Kidane, that their immediate family can follow by a less grueling route. The journey takes a far greater toll on women. In addition to the threat of robbery that Kidane faced, Ms. Mtebe had to worry about sexual assaults. While Ms. Mtebe led an active life in Cameroon, she expressed that she had, at times, struggled with her weight. She knew before she set out that she wasn't cut out for the *camino duro*, but she didn't feel as though she had a choice.

Ms. Mtebe was working as a nurse practitioner near her family's ancestral home in the breakaway anglophone Cameroonian region of Ambazonia. Ambazonia is located in the northwest of Cameroon, on the Nigerian border, roughly corresponding with a former British colony known as "Southern Cameroons." In 2016, minority English speakers launched protests against the appointment of francophone judges in the region, effectively starting an Ambazonian separatist movement. The francophone government brutally suppressed the protests, and armed Ambazonian groups formed. The Cameroonian government declared war on the Ambazonia Defense Forces in 2017. Much of the state's fighting has been attributed to the Rapid Intervention Battalion (BIR), which has been funded and trained by the US since 2010.[4] In the ongoing violence, at least six thousand people have been killed, the majority of them civilians, and half a million have been displaced.

When war broke out, Ms. Mtebe was working in the village drug store. Anyone entering a hospital with a gunshot wound had to be interviewed by the police. This was a fate almost as bad as death; anyone suspected of being a rebel could be locked up indefinitely. Many suspected rebels were simply executed, Ms. Mtebe said. Injured rebels were loath to go to hospitals, and subject themselves to police interrogation. So the makeshift pharmacy where Ms. Mtebe worked in her hometown became an alternative to the hospitals.

"[They were] kind of using us as [a] hospital to take care of them, providing medicines, treated their wounds and stuff like that," Ms. Mtebe said.

The authorities, who were watching the store, suspected Ms. Mtebe of black-market pharmaceutical sales. They apparently developed a theory that the steady stream of rebels who came to the drug store asking for Ms. Mtebe indicated she was donating profits from this activity to the anglophone independence movement, a claim she said was ridiculous. She simply did not want to see her contemporaries die or disappear, she said.

At this time, Ms. Mtebe was studying for a master's degree in nursing education in the University of Buea, and she walked the three hours from her home in Tiko. One day, she was intercepted by police on her walk. They accused her of selling pharmaceuticals without a pharmacist's license.

In April, the police had interviewed Ms. Mtebe about an extortion attempt. The wife of Ms. Mtebe's boss at the Tiko store had received a WhatsApp message, demanding a ransom of 20 million Cameroonian francs (about US$35,000) or "something would happen." The police had apprehended the young man who had sent the extortion demand. They had discovered Ms. Mtebe's name on his contact list.

Ms. Mtebe explained that her boss's wife had forwarded her the extortion threat, which had sounded amateurish to her. When the forwarded message arrived on her phone, its sender was identified as someone who was already in Ms. Mtebe's contacts. The man was a longtime neighbor of Ms. Mtebe's. The only reason she contacted the man in April, she said, was to demand an explanation for the threat. The man denied that he had sent the extortion threat. When Ms. Mtebe reported this to her boss's wife, the woman was angry: "'Like, why did you talk to this person?'" (Ms. Mtebe sometimes wondered the same thing.) The man was arrested and briefly imprisoned for the offense.

During the April questioning, "the police tried to turn it around on me," and suggest that she had somehow instigated the extortion, said Ms. Mtebe. All interrogations were conducted in French, which is Ms. Mtebe's third language.

> When this second incident happened they said, "she's already involved. . . . This thing happened in April . . ." because they had the report. No matter what I was trying to say they wouldn't believe me. They were backed by the government to do whatever they had to do to anyone who was linked to Ambazonia. So I just had to leave.

As a Cameroonian national, the furthest north Ms. Mtebe could get without a visa was Benin. She flew there and arranged for onward transportation with smugglers.

The smugglers drove her north to the border with Togo, where they paid a border guard a bribe. They crossed Togo and, at the border of Ghana, transferred to motorbikes. In Ghana, one of the wealthiest countries in West Africa, Ms. Mtebe paused to take stock of the situation.

In Ghana, Ms. Mtebe contacted friends back in Cameroon. She explained her plight, and said she could not decide whether to flee beyond Africa or to bide her time and plan a return to Cameroon. Ms. Mtebe's friend was adamant. Cameroon was not safe for Ms. Mtebe. Ms. Mtebe had heard rumors of others taking a grueling trek through South America. It did not sound like her cup of tea.

> He said, "It's better you run, if you stay to look for a visa, your life is at risk." This friend told this girl I traveled with about me. She called me and said she,

too, wanted to leave. She encouraged me to leave. I said 'I'm scared . . . I don't know how far I could go on this journey . . . do you think we could survive it?' I'd never been outside Cameroon. She said we should go. She was pregnant, and that's what encouraged me. She had brothers that had made the journey.

The woman, whom we will call Gloria, convinced Ms. Mtebe that she could make it. After all, Gloria said, she was willing to undertake this trip and she was several months pregnant.

The two women paid large sums to smugglers in Ghana, and they were soon on a plane to Ecuador.

The Sending Industry, Kathmandu, Nepal—July 2015

Like Eritrea and Cameroon, Nepal has had its fair share of violence and political instability, not to mention natural disaster, over the past three decades: a ten-year civil war from 1996 to 2006, a royal massacre in 2001, a royal coup in 2005, constituent assembly from 2006 to 2015, and earthquakes in 2015. Beyond these push factors there is a vibrant sending industry that greases the chains of Nepali emigration, turning youth discontent into one of the country's most profitable enterprises.

When Nelson visited Kathmandu in July 2015 with a question about migration via Latin America, it didn't take long to find folks in the know. His host brother Manoj, who had first mentioned going to Mexico in 2007, took him to meet with Bhim Tamang, a friend who was planning one such trip. Mr. Tamang ran a cornershop in the Boudha neighborhood of northeastern Kathmandu, an area associated with its namesake Buddhist stupa and communities of Tibeto-Burman language-speaking ethnicities, known as Janajati in Nepal. Due to the lack of zoning of Kathmandu residential neighborhoods, homeowners often convert bottom floors of houses into small shops selling everything from rice to shaving cream.

These shops become one more way to profit from home ownership, but for Mr. Tamang, managing the store was just a way to pass the hours while aspiring to leave the country. He had passed the class 10 School Leaving Certificate (SLC), but didn't continue his education thereafter. He interpreted the recent earthquake, just three months prior, as a sign that it was time to start planning his departure. But, more so than the quake or a lack of future opportunities in Nepal, it was Kathmandu's sending industry that motivated

FIGURE 1.2. Earthquake destruction to guesthouses in the Gongabu neighborhood of Kathmandu.

his leaving plans. He likened this industry to a conveyor belt on an assembly line. At the time of our conversation he was compiling the 30 million rupees (approximately US$30,000) he would need to pay for the trip.

The migration industry is so prominent in Nepal's capital of Kathmandu that it has its own neighborhood, Gongabu, close to the city's main bus station, among many more locations. The bus station is where people leaving the rural districts of Nepal arrive and wait for papers to go abroad. In the April 2015 earthquake, this district was one of the most devastated areas of Kathmandu as additional floors hastily added to dozens of boarding houses to meet the migrant demand simply toppled.

A few months after the quake, the rubble was still piled up. Unlike the quake's wide devastation of surrounding rural districts, Kathmandu Valley's built environment suffered an uneven destruction that disproportionately ravaged working class and older neighborhoods. When Nelson arrived in July, tent cities still existed in public spaces, and reconstruction efforts were just starting to pick up pace. But the nearby migration markets bustled with even more urgency than usual. Around each Embassy and the Nepali passport office, crowds passed storefronts painted with advertisements for visa services. People waited for service at photo booths, travel agencies, medical check clinics, remittance banks, internet cafes, and shops where clerks offered assistance with filling out forms.

Since the 1990s, young Nepalis have been leaving their country in record numbers to find opportunities abroad. The World Bank recently estimated that 57 percent of all Nepalis who reach working age leave the country shortly thereafter. Half of Nepali households have a member living abroad.[5] While the mass exodus of youth creates social instability, it has also kept the country's economy afloat as remittances of labor migrants contribute more than one-third of Nepal's GDP. The cottage industry facilitating migration has grown into one of the most visible and powerful commercial sectors in many parts of Kathmandu and rural Nepal.

Emigration is by no means new to Nepal. Stretching back to the colonial era of Gurkha soldiers recruited into the British Indian military or state policies encouraging relocation from highlands to India-bordering Tarai plains, mobility is written into the national culture, even identified as a rite of passage.[6] However, out-migration reached unprecedented levels after several national and global shifts in the 1980s. As the Middle East oil boom created large demand for workers, Nepal's government liberalized its laws, deregulating the requirements for migrant laborers. A private industry sprouted to negotiate the "middle space of migration" between growing foreign labor demand and a hands-off government unwilling to regulate the migrant economy.[7]

The Dalal Paradox

Migration is now one of the biggest commercial sectors—formal or informal—in Nepal. By one estimate, there are nearly 80,000 migrant agents in the nation.[8] Recruitment agencies, colloquially known as "manpower," operate in cities, sending out local recruiters, or *dalals*, to entice rural youth into migration ventures.[9]

Borrowed from Arabic and Farsi, the Nepali term *dalal* refers to people who facilitate exchange between two parties. The term stems from the Semitic root term *dal-lam*, which carries the meaning of guiding, pointing something out, or even directing someone toward something. In the Sanskritic languages of northern South Asia, it has come to refer to all types of middlemen— brokers, traders, recruiters, intermediaries of business transactions. In Nepali, it seems to have a more specific meaning, referring to people who broker or sell land, "manpower" recruiters and senders, and prostitution pimps.

The general reputation of *dalals* is overwhelmingly negative within Nepali society. In land sales, a *dalal* is considered untrustworthy and cunning. They are rumored to sell land plots that do not exist or are not for sale; charge high commission rates; or do not provide promised services. There is no better depiction of the *dalal* than in the comedic sketch "Lalpurja" by the Mahajodi comedians, where the *dalal* is a rapacious rip-off merchant.

While the legal standing of manpower agents is somewhat firmer than other *dalals*, they are commonly perceived as exploitative and deceitful, recognized as "conmen" for exploiting the growing number of Nepalis seeking legitimate labor opportunities in foreign countries.[10] In a 2014 expose by the Centre for the Study of Labour and Migration (CESLAM), the list of grievances against migration agents is staggering: they take fees, often at inflated rates, before delivering positions, and sometimes do not return fees to clients not given employment; they fake and forge documents; they lend money at exorbitant rates, all the while leaving the worker in the dark about the process.[11] A quotation in a 2018 *Kathmandu Post* article put it more bluntly: "Manpower agencies . . . suck the blood of 30 million Nepalis."

In spite of their universal condemnation, the migration *dalal* often represents a paradox. While the general category of the *dalal* is deplored as corrupt, deceptive, and untrustworthy, none of these complaints are linked to one's specific *dalal* agent, who is often an *aphno* (one's own), or at least, *chinneko manche* (known person) from back home. This personal connection renders the agent more transparent, predictable, and less of a threat than the obscure processes of the state's labor migration schemes.[12] Whatever corruption takes place, then, is a known and familiar exploitation versus the unknown and unpredictable bureaucratic processes of the state. There's a Nepali proverb to this effect: *Tadha ko deuta banda najik ko bhut kaam lagcha*—roughly translated, "better the devil you know."

According to a 2013 Asian Foundation study of migrant-agent relations, one-third of migrants know their intermediary before entering into a deal; half are introduced to the intermediary by a family member, neighbor, or friend.[13] Meanwhile, no one in the study recorded having found foreign employment through government advertisements or other formal means.

For Mr. Tamang, then in his early twenties, his agent was actually his maternal uncle. As a US green card holder, his uncle was skilled in navigating the cross-continental migration process, particularly the US immigration system. Just one year prior, in 2014, he had successfully "sent" Mr. Tamang's older sister to the States, where she was currently working as a nanny in New York.

Mr. Tamang, like several other Nepali migrants we've interviewed, was raised in Kathmandu, attended private schools, and came from a landowning family. Without some land to put up as collateral, it would be impossible to raise the minimum of three million Nepali rupees (30 lakh, in South Asian parlance) required for the journey to the US. Almost all of the global migrants that we met in the Americas had at least a secondary-school education, belying the Trumpian conflation of undocumented immigrants with uneducated immigrants. Several had college degrees, and Ms. Mtebe, the Cameroonian woman, had an advanced degree.

Migration-Finance Nexus

Mr. Tamang compared manpower offices to ordering at a restaurant. But, instead of food, one is offered a menu of country destinations. Prices vary widely, which means preexisting class distinctions shape Nepali migration patterns. The shadow travel industry, it turns out, has just as many classes, plans, and itinerary price points as the conventional industry. So, in Kathmandu, where and how migrants go abroad reflects their position in Nepal's class hierarchy. Affluent and educated youth from urban areas tend to seek educational visas in Europe, Australia, and North America; working class youth in urban and rural areas (who make up the majority of migrants) follow the cheaper opportunities of labor migration to the Gulf countries and Malaysia, while the poorest rural folk tend to go to India. Each of these destinations has a going rate. Top of the menu, at an estimated 3 to 4 million Nepali rupees (or US$30,000–40,000), is undocumented travel to the United States.

The *dalals* arranging unauthorized travel often work closely with village merchants who serve as local moneylenders—an essential source of financing in areas not reached by banks. In one CESLAM study nearly half of all migrant laborers received loans from village merchants who charge up to 33 percent interest.[14] Characterizing the "rent-seeking behavior" of recruitment agents, the study demonstrated how labor recruitment has less to do with supply-demand economics and more to do with commission profitability. For all but the wealthiest Nepalis, that fee must be financed.

Outside of Kathmandu and other cities, it's difficult to get a loan of a few thousand dollars for a house or a small business. A 2014 report from the United Nations Capital Development Fund found that only about one in ten Nepalis have an outstanding loan—of any kind—from a formal bank.

But $20,000 to pay an emigration *dalal*? That can be had at the drop of a hat. Some borrow from their friends and relatives but most from a local moneylender, who typically works closely with the *dalal*. To some extent, the *dalals* and lenders are still in the land business because the collateral for these loans is usually the title to the emigrant's family land. With conditions both on the journey and at the destination tenuous at best, seizure of the collateral is almost an assumption in these deals. According to the 2013 Asia Foundation report, most emigrants returning to Nepal were still paying off loans in monthly installments. More than one fifth of the fifty returned migrants to Nepal interviewed in the study cited "inducement by agent, family or friends" as the primary reason for their decision to migrate in the first place.[15]

Based on conversations across the globe, with Nepali lawyers in New York, Nepalis in Nepal, and South Asians in Ecuador, it is much easier to secure a loan for travel to the United States than, say, for entrepreneurial ventures at home.

Going to America . . . via Malawi?

Intrinsic to the migrant journey via Latin America to the US is the implicit understanding that the agent will only guarantee so much of your travel. It's generally understood that an agent can only guarantee passage to the Americas, after which everything is subject to risk. Even this first step is no easy feat as it's contingent on the constantly shifting policies and practices of numerous states, airline companies, and airports along the way.

On the *camino duro*, whether it starts in Brazil, Ecuador, or Bolivia, migrants from all over the Global South cross more than a dozen borders by planes, trains, and automobiles (plus boats, horses, and on foot). For those beginning in Nepal, however, the route is even more convoluted. Many journeys begin from New Delhi, taking advantage of the Nepal-India open border and the ability to obtain Indian passports, which open more doors than Nepali ones. Between Delhi and South America, migrants sometimes take detours through Russia or Southeast Asia. In one extreme case, migrants traveled via southern Africa, a story that came to light when four Nepali migrants went to the police in Malawi, alleging they were being held hostage in that country.[16] According to a report in the Kathmandu daily *Kantipur*, these four men had paid a large sum of money to a *dalal* in India, who had guaranteed them passage to the US. After a few weeks in Vietnam, the men were flown to a series of locations in the Middle East and Africa before arriving in Malawi to face demands of further money.

In 2015, Nelson met with "Sano Bhai" (little brother) in his north Kathmandu neighborhood, while he was preparing for what he called his third and final attempt to reach the US. Although his first attempt never materialized in actual travel, his second—just one year prior—took him as far as Phnom Penh, Cambodia. Along with three other Nepali men, he paid 150,000 NRs (US$1,500) to a Kathmandu agent to fly to Bangkok. There, the group was instructed to pose as tourists. It was a surreal piece of theater, one that we've seen repeated on other legs of the journey. Sano Bhai dressed up in swim shorts and shades and posed as a tourist on the beach, while awaiting the next leg of their journey.

After the prolonged tourist theatre, he was met by the main agent who drove the group to the Cambodian capital promising to arrange for a US visa at the Embassy. (The premise of the scam was that it would be easier to obtain visas from an Embassy outside of Nepal.) However, after several weeks of waiting and 1.2 million additional NRs (US$12,000) paid, the agent disappeared, leaving Sano Bhai's group to find their own way home. A year later, Sano Bhai was in the process of negotiating an additional loan from his local moneylender [to whom he was already re-paying 17,000 NRs (US$170) per month, a monthly cost for which he expected to be indebted for the rest of his life] for the three million to pay for another try.

With a Nepali passport, a migrant's options for entering the Western hemisphere without a pre-arranged visa are very slim. A Nepali citizen can enter the small Caribbean island, Dominica, for twenty-one days without a visa and stay for up to three months in Haiti. Bolivia is the only other option, with ninety-day visas available. On an Indian passport, options are more diverse, partly thanks to colonial-era ties. There are a number of Caribbean Commonwealth countries: Trinidad and Tobago, St. Vincent and Grenadines, St. Kitts and Nevis, Jamaica, Grenada, and Dominica in which an Indian national can enter without a visa and stay for periods ranging from thirty days to six months. Indian passport holders can also enter El Salvador, Ecuador, and Bolivia and stay for ninety days without a visa. Brazil, one of the nations that has a "reciprocal policy," allows transit visas.

According to the investigative work of Nepali journalist Surendra Poudel (writing in the Nepali-language daily *Kantipur*), the South Asia–Latin America–US route has taken several shifts over the last decade. At first, the smugglers would send migrants to Qatar directly from Kathmandu, from where they would fly to São Paulo and transit to Santa Cruz, Bolivia. From there they would begin the journey to the US border. However, in 2013, Qatari and Brazilian officials began intercepting and deporting Nepalis traveling on this route, which prompted a detour through southeast Asia. In 2014, Poudel documented a new route from Kathmandu to Delhi to Bangkok by plane, then van to Cambodia and Vietnam followed by flights to Dubai and Brazil. It seems that Sano Bhai's group was led down this route before being stranded in Cambodia. The migrants pay nearly half of their fee (US$12,000–15,000) up front to the main agent in Kathmandu before starting. They then pay the rest while en route, often having to cover their own food and hotel expenses as well as meeting the demands of drivers and smugglers along the way.

America as Dreamed by Migrants

Reaching South America marks an arrival of sorts, but just the beginning of new sorts of decisions and agent negotiations. As Echeverri Zuluaga describes, in migrations of errance, destinations are fungible.[17] Although migrants enter the western hemisphere with the United States as a goal, they often get redirected. Nelson's research with Nepalis living in Chile exposed him to the many ways in which migrants conceive of and negotiate mobility through the Americas.

Nelson met Dipendra Poudel in Iquique, Chile, where he had set up a Latin-South Asian fusion restaurant. Why Mr. Poudel ended up in Chile required multiple coincidences to fall into place. In 2012, while living as a college student in Kathmandu, Poudel's roommate was planning a US$8,000 migration to Norway. Just as the roommate paid his migration broker a down payment, however, he broke his leg. Mr. Poudel, wanting to save his friend's money, decided to go in "his place." Within weeks he was on a plane to Singapore where he stayed for one week before flying to Quito. It was there that agents convinced him to exchange Norway for the US. The only problem was that they were asking for US$13,000 to 14,000 more. While he claimed to have the ability to raise enough, he turned it down because of risk, saying, "We only have one life to live, right?" The agent then offered to send him to Iquique, where a free-trade zone full of Indian-owned businesses was looking for laborers. However, his first attempt at a Chilean visa was rejected in Lima. From there he entered Bolivia, where he successfully obtained a tourist visa to Chile.

The supposed first Nepalis in Iquique, whom we'll call Krishna and Arjun, had a similarly circuitous trip. They entered the western hemisphere in 2007 with promises of work in the Dominican Republic and a subsequent visa to the US. While en route, they were detained at the Montevideo airport and forced to stay in Uruguay. As their temporary visa in Uruguay was about to expire, they obtained a tourist visa to Chile after buying a ticket for a cruise ship. In Santiago, they stayed several months at the Majestic Hotel, a place they called an "Indian refugee camp" for its reputation for housing South Asian migrants. After two months, the owner offered them jobs in Iquique's free trade zone where he owned a store.

While Chile might be in the Americas—one step closer to the United States—it is not the US. It is a "stepwise migration" in which labor migrants seek out intermediate countries with less restrictive immigration policies and accessible labor opportunities after being denied their first choice.[18] Among Nepalis in Chile, there exists a joke that Latin America should be called "Let-in America." Chile represents a progressive move from the more socially repressive Gulf labor migration options, but conditions there are still far below the imagined pay and "developed" lifestyles in the US. Travel to Chile remains a migration of "errance," as it is conceived as coincidental and uncertain, a suspension that can be either temporary or long-term.[19] As one community leader, Dilip, explained to Nelson, "90 percent of Nepalis come to Chile with the US on their mind. They see the two- to three-year wait for PR [permanent residency] cards as a waiting period needed to obtain a US visa." As one pair of scholars put it, "South America is not an end point of a carefully planned trip" but, usually, "a stage on a longer journey to North America" contingent on economic conditions.[20]

For many, being in the Americas is close enough. Another member of the small but growing Nepali in Chile community commented that "we tell our families that we are sending them money from America, they don't know the difference between south and north." The social media accounts of Nepalis in Chile often play with the double meaning of "America" by identifying their homes on Facebook in US cities, such as Chicago, San Antonio, and San Francisco.

As in many parts of the world, the mythology of the US remains a major pull for Nepalis. The "myth of America" has survived decades of leftist movements and influence from powerful neighbors. America has been created and imagined as the land of opportunity in Nepali popular culture in spite of the numerous reports to the contrary from Nepalis living in the States.

But there were also more practical reasons the US had become a premium destination. In response to the April 25 earthquake and subsequent aftershocks, on June 24, 2015, President Obama granted Nepali citizens Temporary Protected Status (TPS) for eighteen months, which allowed them to reside and work in the country without threat of deportation until at least December 2016. This announcement sent migration agents to the Nepali countryside to recruit young men and women eager to reach the United States—despite the fact that TPS was contingent on proving one's presence in the US on or before the day of the announcement.

On the ground in Kathmandu, the details of TPS were ignored in favor of an understanding that the US was now open to Nepali migrants. The challenge, many imagined, would be reaching the border, for which each had a strategy. Mr. Tamang was fully aware of the many dangers of the route from the perils of walking through a jungle in Panama to the likelihood of being robbed by the "Mexican mafia." He had heard stories of boatloads of migrants dying at sea. Despite these risks, he talked with excitement about the trip itself.

Mr. Tamang was certain that if he reached Mexico, he would make it to the US. "In Mexico, they are corrupt like Nepal—so they will let you pass for a bribe," he insisted. Once across the border, he claimed that if caught, he would need to pay US$5,000 to be freed and allowed to work, presumably referring to the typical bond amount issued to Nepali asylum applicants.

Another man, Kedar Sherpa, wanted to join his older brother and wife who live in Texas. Mr. Sherpa was under the impression that it is "easy to enter, but hard to find work" in the United States. He believed that it would be easy to enter as a member of a "Buddhist" caste. He had heard that Nepal's traditionally Buddhist and Tibeto-Burman language speaking groups (known as Janajati) were less likely to be detained than Nepal's Hindu castes (traditionally Indo-European language speakers) who he said "look more like people from Spanish-speaking countries." When Nelson responded that Janajati might be less likely to be misidentified as Latino and thus more likely to be detained, Mr. Sherpa clarified that the United States gave visas to Tibetan Buddhists escaping from China, and, thus, Nepali Buddhists would likely be extended the same hospitality.[21]

As we shall see along the route, migrants use misidentification to their advantage while crossing Latin American borders. As their own TPS status expired, many Haitians reportedly sought to pass themselves off as francophone Africans from nations such as the Congo. To avoid quick and easy deportations, smugglers take the passports from migrants when they arrive in South America. Without documentation, immigration officials seek to interview migrants, whom according to Poudel, are trained to say in English, "We are refugees from Nepal, we had to leave for political reasons," but otherwise show no understanding of English. Linguistic barriers can lead to bureaucratic confusion and long detentions, but they also incentivize expedient resolutions.

Ultimately, the only incentive that *dalals* in Kathmandu have to act in good faith is the power of word-of-mouth. Much like the California gold rush and the Oregon trail, the *camino duro* is promoted by communication from those who make it to the other side. From the perspective of the *dalal* in Kathmandu, there is no recourse for an unsatisfied customer, but a satisfied customer is almost sure to send their family and friends the *dalal*'s way.

For the migrant, the only guarantee that *dalals*—or the *coyotes* along the way—offer is assistance in leaving the point of departure. Arrival is something that Kidane and all the migrants on the route must achieve for themselves.

CHAPTER 2

Entering the Americas

Into the Paws of the Coyotes

It was, fittingly, an Ethiopian Airlines flight that took Kidane to the Americas. He flew from Dubai to Addis Ababa, near where he had once stayed in a refugee camp. From there, he flew to Santa Cruz, Bolivia via São Paulo. There he met a *coyote* and five other Eritreans. Kidane bonded quickly with his fellow travelers, which was just as well because they would soon depend on each other for their lives.

The deal in Dubai was that Kidane's US$16,000 covered passage as far as the northern coast of Colombia. The bulk of the travel in South America was by public transportation. Only at national borders did the travel become more clandestine.

Santa Cruz is a balmy city on the fringes of the butterfly-and-hummingbird haunted, mist-wreathed cloud-forest zone. These forests proliferate on the lower slopes of the leeward, east side of the Andes. Shortly after arrival, Kidane and his compatriots were taken on a bus to the Bolivian capital, La Paz, where they waited in a safe house for ten days while their visas were processed. La Paz is five hundred miles and several climate zones away from Santa Cruz. This is the high Andes, the cordillera, the treeless glacier zone where stepping into the fresh air feels like plunging into ice water. Kidane and his friends had braced themselves, but the cold was still a shock.

Kidane's route through South America crisscrossed the cordillera, passing through areas where many of the world's ecosystems collide. For centuries, these mountain passes were all but impassable for any but the most daring mountaineers. By some accounts, it was easier to get to London and New York from the Peruvian Amazon in the early twentieth century—thanks to the river network—than it was to Lima, on the other side of the Andes.[1] A mini-bus took Kidane on the mountainous route from La Paz to the border with Peru, somewhere between Puerto Acasta on Lake Titicaca and the Madre de Dios rain forest to the north. Kidane described arriving on the banks of a river late at night. It was narrow enough, approximately seven meters, he estimated, to cross by rowboat. It was almost certainly the Heath River, which forms the border between Bolivia and Peru for a couple of hundred miles north of Lake Titicaca.

When Curran drove through the Peruvian Andes, the vertiginous heights turned his legs to jelly. He drank liter after liter of water just to keep the pounding altitude headaches at bay. In some of the towns, the main street felt as though it had originated as a horizontal house row in some kind of concertina-type pop-up-book, and that the page was now only half-opened, rendering the street at an improbable 45 degrees. It was both thrilling and disorienting to experience winter weather a day's drive from the equator. The children of the family in the little café where he stopped wore woolen hats, even inside. Between Cuzco and Nazca, the road was blocked more than once by freshly landed avalanches, forcing him to wait while local crews cleared the road, or to swerve around the debris. Nothing speaks to the tenuous position of humans in the mountains as clearly as a pile of boulders and rubble straddling one lane of a road, the dust still rising from the impact.

From there, the road swooped down to the windward, west side of the Andes, via foothills that look like half-baked muffins—round-topped and bare. There you enter Peru's coastal desert, which itself feels like an extension of the Pacific beaches. There's even a gigantic version of the lifeguard tower, constructed to view the ancient desert art of Nazca. Roadside restaurants serve fish dragged in from the rumbling ocean.

In the coastal towns, the modes of transportation also change. Motorbikes are a popular form of transportation throughout South America but, in Peruvian coastal towns such as Pisco, the tuk-tuk rickshaws swarm the streets until it feels as though the driver is trapped inside a chemical reaction, with electrons pinging everywhere. The bristling streets of tuk-tuks make even the most straightforward route a thrill ride of constant swerving and weaving. Collision is to be expected, with minor damage the best hope.

Kidane took a similar route through Peru. His journey was facilitated by *coyotes*, but without the full concierge service the group had experienced in

FIGURE 2.1. The open road in Peru's southern desert.

Bolivia. Like that of tour guides in the conventional travel industry, the role of the *coyote* is often to smooth out the transitions in a traveler's experience rather than to accompany them every step of the way. In Peru, Kidane's group traveled alone on buses, but were confident that *coyotes* would be on hand to deal with any logistical matters. For example, *coyotes* always purchased the bus tickets to avoid awkward questions about identification or encounters with law enforcement at the bus stations.

> There was another guy waiting in Peru. Two guys were coming to us, took us to the bus stop, near the border. They took us to a hotel, all paid for. In Peru, we went by public transportation. It took three days or something. Sometimes, we passed the whole night on the bus. It was a long way by bus to Lima. In Lima, we stayed in a hotel near the bus station one night. It was a big, big city.

If the *dalal* and moneylenders maintain the financial engine, the person that keeps the wheels of the irregular migration industry turning is the one who guides migrants through otherwise impassable borders. In Latin America, these migrant escorts are known as *coyotes* or *coyoteros*, while their charges are known as *pollos*, revealing the long history of predatory behavior in the profession.[2]

One of the biggest risks for any migrant taking on the *camino duro* is that they will be double-crossed, one way or another, by their *coyote*. This sometimes means abandonment at a particularly dangerous moment. One of the Eritrean men who joined Kidane later in his journey told us that Peruvian border police tried to intercept his party as they were about to cross the border to Ecuador. The *coyotes* were leading the group across a bridge when the Peruvian police called out. Their guides fled, ignoring the group's pleas for assistance, taking off in the vehicle that waited on the other side of the bridge. The Eritrean men hesitated for an instant, and took off running across the bridge. The police started to fire at his group, he said.

Recounting the tale, the Eritrean man gesticulated, whipping fingers past his head. "Whew-wheown-wheown," he said, showing how the bullets whizzed past his ears, and practically brushed his hair. He and his group took cover under the bridge on the Ecuadorian side of the border. They called the number they had for the agent, who eventually sent another group of *coyotes* to bring them to the next destination.

Coyotes are notorious for such acts of abandonment. But they can also turn on their groups more directly. Several sources have told us their *coyotes* demanded further payment in violation of previous agreements. *Coyotes* are often accused of gunpoint robbery and rape. Still, decades of guiding migrants along forbidden paths has created a complex identity. In parts of Ecuador, there are even shrines dedicated to *coyotes*, much as there might be in other parts of Latin America for fishermen or shepherds.[3]

The relay-race nature of the smuggling route creates a challenge for both the *coyote*'s contractor and their customers—the *dalal*/smuggler network side and the migrant side. How do the migrants make sure they are still working with the same network? How do the smugglers know they are intercepting the right group of migrants at each handover?

Kidane was curious how the baton would be passed, how his payment in Dubai would be honored by the chain of smugglers along the route. The system turned out to be as rigorous and foolproof as those used by travel agencies. Every time they met a new *coyote*, the man would check their faces against digital photos forwarded to him.

"The smugglers always checked the photos to make sure they had the right group," said Kidane. "They also took photos of us eating meals, to show that they were feeding us."

Kidane showed us one of the meal photos, where he and his group were hunkered down in the bush at the side of the road near the Peruvian-Ecuadorian border. These meal pictures appeared to serve two purposes. The *coyotes* could conceivably send them to agents in home countries so that migrant families would have "proof of life" (and proof of good service). But they were also, Kidane surmised, a form of expense accounting. *Coyotes* likely sent the food snapshots to higher-ups as a request for reimbursement.

On the northern border of Peru, near Ecuador, the smugglers guided the group through mountainous scrubland. Kidane showed us the spot on a map, and it appeared he crossed near the Peruvian border post of Aguas Verdes.

> One guy with a pickup truck was waiting on the other side of the border. One house was there . . . we passed one night there. . . . One guy from the house asked for money. The smugglers gave him money . . . that was their work, not our work.

From there, the group took a bus north to Quito, the capital of Ecuador. Kidane stayed in a hotel in the center of Quito a night or two. Some Africans and Asians on the *camino duro* end up staying in nearby neighborhoods for months, or even years.

CHAPTER 3

Quito's Little India

The Last Nepali in Quito

Quito is situated in the natural fortress of an Andean valley, bounded by peaks including the Cotopaxi—an ice-capped, smoking-crater-topped, inverted-*v* of a volcano such as principally exist only in picture books. Like comparably situated Mexico City and Kathmandu, Quito has its own microclimate and micro-atmosphere, making the visitor feel as if they were admitted entry to some enchanted citadel. Roses and bougainvillea tumble over the arches of garden walls all over the city, and the equatorial sun battles the cool alpine air to a temperate standstill.

The latticed stone of the cathedral spires, natural beauty, and eighteenth-century neighborhoods made Quito the first urban UNESCO World Heritage site. Picturesque landscapes and historic architecture is not all Kathmandu and Quito have in common. From the moment we met Roshan Dhakal—on break from his shift at the Alexandra Café, a shawarma shop in the central La Mariscal neighborhood—he started talking about earthquakes. It was Nepal's quakes in 2015 that convinced his wife, Bhawani, to join him in Ecuador, five years after he had moved there. The natural disaster destroyed her rented apartment in Kathmandu forcing her to move to the village with Roshan's parents before relocating to Quito. One week short of a calendar year later, Ecuador experienced a major earthquake oddly of the same 7.8 Richter scale reading.

Roshan migrated to Quito in 2010. He came from meager means in an agrarian village on the outskirts of Pokhara, Nepal's second largest city. He

FIGURE 3.1. Quito's skyline looking south from city center.

had just married Bhawani the year before and wanted to work abroad to send money home to his family. His brother and many of his friends had left Nepal for the more common labor destinations in the Gulf—namely Qatar, Dubai, and Kuwait where they worked in construction, gas stations, and hotels.

Many other Nepali migrant laborers go to Malaysia or East Asia, but Ecuador? He had never heard of the South American country until a "didi" (older sister, fictive kin) returned from there speaking of its beauty and job opportunities, immediately intriguing Roshan. The cost for Ecuador would be US$5,000, slightly more than his friends paid to go to the Gulf, but much less than the US$30,000 price tag for the United States.

He entered Ecuador under the "universal citizenship" policy, which allowed any nationality to obtain a tourist visa at the airport, a unique possibility for many African and Asian nationalities otherwise denied entry to the Americas. Importantly, this policy, part of Ecuador's shift to the political left, served as a counter to the increasingly hemispheric reach of US deterrence agenda. Although universal citizenship was not intended to create international diasporas in Quito, it facilitated the conditions for clandestine migration networks and ethnic restaurants to emerge in a thriving tourist neighborhood of the capital, La Mariscal Sucre.

When Roshan first arrived, there were "hundreds" of Nepalis in Quito, some working, most waiting for their agents to give them the greenlight to move toward the US. Among a larger South Asian network of mostly Indian and Pakistani restaurateurs and migration agents, there were several Nepali agents and one momo restaurant that served the famous Nepali dumpling among other South Asian dishes. However, by 2016, they had all disappeared—to the US, to Chile, or returned to Nepal. Besides his wife, Roshan could only think of one other Nepali in Ecuador, a restaurant owner who was now in the hospital suffering from a heart condition.

Arun Magar, who Nelson met in Chile, said he never saw Ecuador as anything more than a stopover. In 2010, he paid US$8,000 to travel from Kathmandu to Quito, via Singapore, with the understanding that Spain would be his ultimate destination. However, after the Spanish embassy in Ecuador rejected his visa application (another member of his group was already deported from the Madrid Airport), he was left in Quito living above a restaurant in the central Carolina Parque neighborhood where he would wash dishes and learn Spanish.

After being denied by Spain, staying in Ecuador was not an option—Mr. Magar and other Nepalis in Chile dismissed it and Bolivia as "poor" countries. But, unable to afford, and afraid about the dangers of, travel to the US, agents offered him journeys to the Dominican Republic ($2,000), Brazil ($4,000), or Chile ($3,000). The promise of a job in Iquique's free-trade zone seemed to be his best bet so he boarded a bus for northern Chile.

The disappearance of Nepalis from Quito reflects the letdown of Ecuador's experiment with open borders. What started as a utopian exercise in reimagining the relationship between the state and immigrants was gradually undermined by the xenophobia of local biases and US extra-territorial pressure on the region.

Ecuador's Universal Citizenship: Radical Anti-Imperialism or Shallow Political Tool?

Ecuador's migration history involves an interesting reversal from being a "sending" in the twentieth century to a "receiving" or "transit" country in the twenty-first century. Ecuador's role in the opening of the *camino duro* to the entire Global South also reflects political trends in Latin America. The electoral success of US nemesis Hugo Chavez in Venezuela inspired the "pink tide" swing to the Chavista left across Latin America in the 2000s. Leftist and populist leaders positioned themselves as counterweights to US power in the region. Casting their rivals and predecessors as quislings to an imperialist power, these premiers sought to defy Washington DC at every turn.

The 2006 presidential elections of leftist politicians Rafael Correa in Ecuador and Evo Morales in neighboring Bolivia would generate border policies that would accelerate transit through their countries, vastly increasing traffic along the *camino duro* from other parts of the Global South. Correa recognized that one of the main things the US wanted from its Latin American allies was to outsource border control to their nations. In the spirit of defiance, Correa quickly did the exact opposite. His government rewrote Ecuador's Citizen's Revolution constitution in the spirit of anti-imperialism and post-neoliberalism. Laying the groundwork for a shift in border policy, Correa ejected the US military from its base in Manta, Ecuador, bringing US surveillance of the coastline and migrant-occupied boats to an end in 2009. More fundamentally, Correa established the Ministry of the Migrant in November 2007 followed by the inclusion of "universal citizenship" in the new constitution, which Correa characterized as "a campaign to dismantle the twentieth-century invention of passports and visas."

The Citizen's Revolution constitution "advocates the principle of universal citizenship, the free movement of all inhabitants of the planet, and the progressive extinction of the status of alien or foreigner as an element to transform the unequal relations between countries, especially those between North and South" (Article 416). Moreover, it states "foreign persons in Ecuadorian territory shall have the same rights and duties as those of Ecuadorians" (Article 9); that "no human being will be considered illegal because of their migratory condition" (Article 40); guaranteeing free mobility, asylum-seeking, and refugee status as rights (Article 41). In any other context, this high-minded rhetoric might have been a geopolitical curiosity. But the shadow travel industry is alert to the smallest shift in border law. And this change lived up to the "revolutionary" billing. What the pro-immigrant constitutional discourse translated into for migrants was simple: anyone from anywhere in the world could enter Ecuador and receive a ninety-day tourist visa. It was a foothold in the Americas.

Before the global migrants braved the odyssey, it was Ecuadorians and other South Americans who pioneered the *camino duro*. When Ecuadorian production of the Panama hat declined in the 1950s and 1960s, the industry shifted from sending hats to sending people to the US.[1] Many hat traders became migration merchants, or *tramitadores*, consisting of recruiters, moneylenders, and smugglers with the goal of sending migrants, mostly from the southern provinces of Cañar and Azuay, to the States by plane, boat, or foot.[2] A migration industry called 'coyoterismo' emerged, rooted in indigenous social norms of solidarity and trust.[3]

Many of the Incan pan-pipes buskers in major American cities come from Ecuador. We met a man selling rugs and novelties in the Otavalo market who told us about his trips to the US during the 1980s and '90s as part of an Incan band (he was one of the lucky few who did so through a short-term visa program).

Several shifts in Ecuadorian economics and politics in the 2000s helped the migration industry pivot from sending Ecuadorians to sending the entire world.[4] In 2000, amid economic crisis and massive inflation of the sucre currency, Ecuador decided to switch to the dollar, making it a more convenient business center for international smuggling. Additionally, due to increased displacement caused by the US-sponsored Plan Colombia, Ecuador started receiving record arrivals of Colombians fleeing violence, making it Latin America's top recipient of refugees.

A stated goal of universal citizenship was to entice Ecuadorian emigrants (10 percent of the country's population) to return and repatriate.[5] From the US perspective, the more consequential outcome of the policy was, of course, to invite thousands of migrants from Asia, Africa, and the Caribbean to fly into Quito or Guayaquil from where they would start the journey northward. Within the first year, Chinese migration to Ecuador grew exponentially, with numbers of South Asians, West- and East Africans, and Caribbeans growing as well.

Almost immediately, the visa exemption policy faced resistance from internal sources anxious about the "foreign threat." Immigration police lobbied against it by expressing concern for the perception of growing numbers of Colombians, Chinese, and South Asians.[6] Similarly, intelligence agencies "clearly rejected" visa liberalization, building on media sources expounding "racist concerns" that exaggerated that security and criminal risks of increased migrants.[7] NGO representatives, meanwhile, made a humanitarian defense of the policy, painting an image of "poor, desperate immigrants, fleeing warfare and hunger in Africa and Asia" inconsistent with the higher education levels and financial support that one social scientist found in interviews with migrants.[8] In practice, however, Ecuador's emerging status as a transit country become an "open secret" that officials were unwilling to address because it allowed migration to be a profitable business.[9]

Importantly, Ecuador, and later Bolivia, became transit countries not just to the US, but also to the Southern Cone countries. A leftward turn in the immigration policies of Argentina and Brazil had complemented Ecuador's reforms.[10] Rejecting the securitized and often racist restrictionism of earlier military regimes, policies adopted by the Kirchner governments of Argentina and Lula/Roussef governments of Brazil recognized migration as a human right. In particular, Senegalese immigrants to Argentina, and Angolan immigrants to Brazil have led the increases.[11] Chile, too, has transformed from being a "sending country" during the repressive military regime of the 1970s and 1980s into a "receiving" country.[12] However, unlike its neighbors, it has been Chile's economic promise, rather than immigration policy reform, that has attracted migrants. But, for all three of these southern cone cases, much of new immigration flows are "irregular" in the sense that they tend to transit from Ecuador and Bolivia.[13]

It did not take long for Ecuador's transit country reputation to gain the attention of foreign governments. First it was China that exerted pressure to exempt their own or other nationalities from the visa waivers, trying to avert an exodus. Within just six months of launching the program, Ecuador reinstated pre-arrival visa requirements for Chinese nationals. Thanks to a cable published by WikiLeaks, we also know that the US expressed concerns over Ecuador becoming a "trampoline" to the States, at one point even threatening to cut aid.[14] The US Embassy also initiated regular trainings of Ecuadorian officials on border control tactics, which had an immediate impact.[15] In 2011 three Pakistani smugglers were arrested in Miami for helping to transport members of a US-recognized terrorist group, Tehrik-e Taliban Pakistan, which they tied back to an "operation" in Quito.[16]

Eighteen months after the policy started, Ecuador decided to reinstate visa requirements for ten nationalities: Afghanis, Bangladeshis, Eritreans, Kenyans, Ethiopians, Nepalis, Nigerians, Pakistanis, and Somalians.[17] Officially, the government justified the reintroduction of requirements as a form of protection for migrants victimized by traffickers and smugglers. However, the exclusion of other more regional nationalities with clear smuggling networks, such as Cuba and Haiti, show that regional ties transcended more global forms of solidarity in the president's thinking.[18] Further reducing its pro-migration rhetoric, in 2012 Ecuador converted a central Quito hotel into a detention center.

Correa's embrace of a pro-mobility agenda was never enshrined in laws, giving him the ability to use universal citizenship as a "slogan for the political benefit of his government's agenda."[19] As a result, the new migration initiatives are largely dependent on presidential discretion, which can be used to exclude certain groups. Until 2017, Ecuador's official migration policy dated back to a 1971 law implemented by a dictatorship openly hostile and repressive toward immigrants. Correa offered little more than a "change in rhetoric," but he ultimately perpetuated exclusionary state practices. For migrants, this produced a disconnect between Ecuador's promise and an inhospitable experience defined by labor discrimination, racism and general precariousness.[20] In spite of the unwelcoming conditions, however, some have stayed and helped transform several Quito neighborhoods.

La Mariscal: Quito's Little India

The tension between the open-borders rhetoric and increasingly restrictive "on-the-ground" policies in Ecuador have left migrants in an ambiguous middle ground between licit and illicit, formal and informal. In one unforeseen outcome of the policy, a dual service industry of restaurants and migration agents has taken root in at least two districts of Quito, expanding the global diversity of the city. For example, a neighborhood of evangelical churches, barbershops, restaurants, and bars catering to Africans exists around Quito's Avenida Amazonas. Contrasted with the ethnic or national sociality of other nodes of migrants in Dakar, Senegal, Quito's spaces of congregation create pan-African identities.[21] National identity waxes and wanes along the migration route, with migrants sometimes organizing themselves this way, and sometimes identifying with broader groups.

Several blocks away in the central La Mariscal Sucre neighborhood, a similar South Asian neighborhood has emerged. Everyone in Quito knows the Mariscal. It's the bar district, one of those places with a nocturnal architecture of plain walls and lamplit signs, where the clink of beer bottles and hum of conversation is never far away. With its narrow streets, short blocks, stone arches, and crowded patios, it could be the waterfront quarter of a Spanish port city. When we visited in June 2016, the central square, "the Foch," was thronged with tourists, students, cigar-sellers, and street hustlers, one in a beaconlike white linen suit. The port atmosphere was reinforced by the passers-through from far-off places, and by the illicit secrets that seemed to echo around the narrow streets. We were, perhaps, made paranoid by the sensitive nature of the interviews we conducted in the Mariscal. But there were times when it seemed like we were as much observed as we were observing.

Since 2008, La Mariscal has become known as an enclave of South Asian restaurants. In 2016, we counted ten South Asian-themed joints with *India*, *Bengal*, *Pakistani*, *tandoori*, or *tadkha* in their title lining the streets of Juan León Mera and Reina Victoria, just blocks off the main Plaza Foch. Almost all

FIGURE 3.2. A Pakistani restaurant in La Mariscal.

the South Asians we interviewed in the Mariscal knew about Quito's place as the first stop on the road from their homelands to the US.

The current South Asian presence in Quito goes back at least twenty years according to several men claiming to be the first arrivals. Raja Naeen, originally from Islamabad, said he started the restaurant Chandni Tandoori in 2000. He was recruited by a Jesuit priest who convinced him to introduce Pakistani food to Ecuador. He soon learned Spanish and married an Ecuadorian woman, with whom he has three kids.

One block over from Chandni Tandoori is the more expensive Sher-e-Punjab started by the Boparai family, Punjabis who migrated to Quito in late 1990s. The co-owner came with his father to Ecuador when he was just a teenager. Preferring Spanish to English, he speaks of Quito as his home, India as a place he occasionally visits. The Boparai family founded the Ecuadorian Indian Association, a group of mostly settled Punjabis who host annual Diwali and Holi parties.

Although Chandni Tandoori and Sher-e-Punjab were established long before the policy shift in 2008, they have become entangled in the migration industry. The presence of compatriots in transit has provided both with transitory employees. Mr. Naeen commented that he has seen many South Asians come and mostly go. He admitted that the smuggling industry is the draw to Ecuador and laments that several of his workers have become "filthy rich" through agent, or *dalal*, work. One, in fact, was arrested by the police, which led to his restaurant being closed for several days. Similarly, Mr. Boparai spoke of the effect of migration on his staff. He complained that while Ecuadorians refuse to work in service, South Asians don't stay: "They will be here for a year, and then suddenly, without any warning, they are gone in the night." He has since decided only to hire family from India or Cubans who have married Ecuadorians.

Since 2008, another kind of Indian restaurant has opened up, catering to South Asian migrants and students. They are called "shawarma shops," colloquial references to the Lebanese influence in Ecuador, known for their snacks and fast-food menus. These more recent places attract the student and tourist crowd looking for a quick snack or a beer, or even a place for karaoke. Whereas one might find the TV displaying recent Bollywood films and songs at Sher-e-Punjab, the TV at the fast-food shawarma places is stuck on futból games and telenovelas. In these restaurants, a mix of tourists, Latin migrants, Ecuadorians, and South Asians mingle reflecting the cosmopolitan feeling of La Mariscal.

One such shawarma shop is Taste of India owned by Panchal, an outgoing Gujarati man who came to Ecuador six years ago with his wife, one of the few South Asian women we met in the Mariscal. They gained residency and later citizenship through their daughter's birth in the country. At Taste of India, which offers dishes like chana masala alongside salchipapas (fries and sausage) and Cuban sandwiches, Panchal has a Cuban cook and a part-time Punjabi assistant, Projit, who just arrived one month prior.

Although further migrations to the States appeared to be on the minds of the shawarma workers, they are also creating a life and community in Quito. Panchal said he had seen many Indians and Nepalis pass through Quito: "thousands come, but few stay," he said. Thinking he would immigrate to Uruguay, Projit changed his destination to Ecuador at the last minute and is weighing whether to continue on to the US or not. "All come here with going to the US in their mind," Projit told us. Panchal also desired to go to the US, but "only the legal way." After all, he continued, "I'm making dollars here in Ecuador the legal way, why trade that for an illegal life up there?" He added, "Now I have a daughter, I can't think of going the illegal way."

Others in La Mariscal have rejected the allure of "America." It seems a more critical view of the US developed long before Trump's election. The owners of the Green Bengal, a shawarma restaurant and take-out spot, are three Bangladeshi men who came to Ecuador in 2010 with hopes of reaching the US. They soon fell in love with Ecuador, calling it "tranquilo" and calculating that it offered a much better standard of living than any life they could imagine in the US. Another restaurateur, a Punjabi Hindu, explained that he turned down the "high-stress" work atmosphere of the US for Ecuador where "I can relax and take my time, life is not just about work." His business has received contracts to cater events for the recent arrival of the Indian Tata Company in Quito, which has brought approximately 180 Indian families to Ecuador. In addition to catering to foreign investment in Ecuador's growing economy, the shawarma shops provide a social space to South Asian migrants, many of whom are weighing their options whether to stay or migrate.

We saw further evidence of the growing Asian and Middle Eastern communities in Quito at a newly opened mosque, in a grand architectural style that would not be out of place in Istanbul or Islamabad.

La Mariscal's Other Industry

Several restaurateurs warned us not to ask too many questions about smuggling and migration around the Mariscal. Most we talked to seemed to hint that everyone in the neighborhood had some link to the shadow travel industry, everyone, of course, apart from they themselves. The shrugged shoulders, raised eyebrows, and nods toward the street gave us the impression of an underworld, just below the surface that locals tiptoed around. Vague nods and cryptic references all seemed to point to one bar, a karaoke venue, as a place of interest.

We originally went to the bar as part of our research into South Asian migrants working in Quito. The manager was an Indian man, about thirty years old, who we found serving drinks behind the bar. He agreed to sit down and chat during the afternoon lull. In a venue that could accommodate dozens, there was only one couple going through the catalog. Like several of the businesspeople in the Mariscal, the bar manager appeared to come from a more privileged background than the South Asian migrants who we would later meet. He was proud of his position as a Brahmin in the Hindu caste system, and of his education. He spoke English relatively well and recounted his life story like a business-school case study. Arriving in Quito as an immigrant, he had started his own bar, he said. The tilt toward workers' rights and high taxation during the Correa presidency had caused him great trouble, and he had closed the bar. He came to work in the karaoke bar, which, he said, belonged to his uncle.

As the interview became increasingly congenial, we asked the manager if he had ever harbored US migration plans, a topic that we'd begun exploring with the other migrants we'd interviewed. The question irked him. Why would we ask him that? He wondered. We explained that a lot of the other people we had interviewed mentioned pursuing American ambitions at some stage. After some further nudging, the bar owner said the low cost of living in Quito, and the fact that the dollar was the de facto currency had persuaded him he was better off in Ecuador than in the US. The questions had clearly peeved him, and the interview quickly ended.

"What's this for again?" the bar manager asked, as we packed our notebooks. It was clear that he was having second thoughts about his participation. We explained ourselves as best we could, and he seemed to accept the explanation about our research on migrants.

Before we left, we gave the bar manager Nelson's business card, identifying him as a professor at the University of North Texas. We assumed that we had seen the last of the bar manager.

The shawarma place where we interviewed Roshan an hour or two later was just down the street from the karaoke bar. While finishing our chat with Roshan, the karaoke bar manager entered the shawarma restaurant, and stormed straight over to our table. It felt as though he had been informed of our presence, a disconcerting development in itself. He leaned on the table, with Nelson's business card in his hand. This time, he was interviewing us.

"If you are writing about Ecuador, why do you keep asking about America?" the bar manager asked, eyes still fixed on the card.

"It's just another part of the story," we said. "It's about the immigrants who travel to the US, and those who stay in Ecuador."

"Look, I'm not saying . . ." the man said. "But the questions you ask . . . you sound like the police."

"I'm a professor of anthropology, like I told you," said Nelson, gesturing at the card. "You can check the Web site."

"What's your phone number?"

"It's on the card," said Nelson.

"Your phone number in Ecuador," said the man, still leaning on his knuckles.

"We don't have a phone in Ecuador, we're only here for a few days," said Nelson.

Now, as a journalist and academic who have traveled extensively, we are not completely street dumb. But we are not exactly Crockett and Tubbs either.

The request seemed reasonable. We almost mentioned the Ecuadorian cell phone we had borrowed from a friend. Fortunately, the bar manager was too peremptory to allow us to take this risk.

"You!" said the man, gesturing to Curran's camera case. "You look like you are in the FBI with this thing."

It was a harmless gibe. But the karaoke bar manager had good reason to fear law enforcement, if he was a black-market agent. According to Roshan, much more than the 2010 decision to remove Nepalis from the list of nationalities automatically receiving visas, it was a 2014 raid that ended Nepali migration to Ecuador. Roshan noted that four Nepalis and two Punjabis were supposedly arrested by the FBI and remained in prisons outside of Quito. Since that time, it appeared, Nepali migration networks had shifted from Ecuador to Bolivia.

Although the Nepali population had decreased, Quito remained a vibrant center of smuggling in 2016. Despite the bar manager's concern, it did not take long for us to distinguish agents from restaurateurs and migrants. At almost every one of our stops, a recurring cast of characters would show up to stand near the door, observing us from a distance. Some were even more willing to engage with us. It was clear in Quito, as elsewhere, that the frissons of danger and power associated with the smuggling route were as much of a draw for some people working with migrants as the share of illicit profits.

Another man, Hamza, told us he had migrated from Pakistan to Quito in the late 1990s, and soon thereafter married an Ecuadorian woman with whom he has children. He had owned a "discotek" until several months prior to our meeting, selling it because of an economic downturn in the city. It seemed every restaurant or bar we entered, Hamza was there. He was often with an Indian man known as a Hindi equivalent of "Uncle." Hamza and Uncle speak fluent Spanish and blend in easily with the cosmopolitan crowd of the Mariscal.

One afternoon we met Hamza at the Juan Valdez Café in the Foch. He refused a coffee since he was fasting for Ramadan but was eager to talk of the people who have made it to the United States. When we asked him how he knows about the journeys, he responded, "We hear things on Facebook," but then directly added, "but no one will talk to you about it here." He immediately proceeded to talk about it. While there used to be more Pakistanis and Nepalis, now they have more or less stopped coming, replaced by a constant flow of Indians. Mostly, it is Punjabis and Gujaratis, he explained. Like colonial-era migration schemes based on sardar middlemen recruiting indentured servants from particular regions to serve production in the far-flung corners of the British empire, it seemed the Ecuadorian route depended on the regional-ethnic ties of middlemen.

If we had any doubt that the Mariscal was a way station on the migration route, it was settled on our last night at the Taste of India.

A kebab skewer spun slowly in front of a blue neon grill bar, filling the restaurant with the sumptuous smell of crisp meat as we chatted to the owner. A man from Gujarat who was still toying with the idea of undertaking the US trip, the kebab-store manager was as gregarious as the karaoke-bar manager had been wary. He seemed intrigued that we would find his journey to or from Ecuador intriguing. He was even more amused that we would find migrants and their agents so significant. He hinted, at times, that he knew more than he was telling, but it was hard to imagine such an open and honest man holding much back.

At about 9 p.m., the kebab-restaurant manager gave us an ambiguous nod.

Four men—who Nelson recognized as Punjabi from their speech and who appeared to be in their late teens or early twenties—had entered the restaurant. We had all but despaired of getting clear answers about the *camino duro* in the secretive demi-monde of the Mariscal. Now, we looked at one another. These young men might have a story to tell, and fewer reasons not to tell it.

The young man who spoke the best English introduced himself cheerily as Akashbir Singh. Dressed in llama-printed tourist tops and chatting excitedly, Mr. Singh and his friends had the air of high-school students on the first night of a school tour. They snapped photographs of each other in playful poses and cracked jokes while they waited for their food. The manager of the restaurant teased them as their chicken sizzled and dal bubbled.

Mr. Singh was an avid photographer—he said he worked in the field before he left Punjab, and insisted on our taking his contact information so we could send him the photos we took.

The chaperones on this school tour were the aforementioned Uncle and a larger Venezuelan man who we had not seen before. The tall and beefy Venezuelan, who we will call Mr. Guerrero, had a contrasting wardrobe to the rest of the party, wearing the kind of half-length black leather coat favored by bouncers and police detectives. He had some of the street-hardened aura that goes with these professions, though he deflected our questions in a friendly manner.

While their chaperones watched a Copa America match between Mexico and Venezuela, the boys laughed and ate heartily.

"What are you doing in Ecuador?" We asked the young men.

"Oh, tourism," said Mr. Singh, fiddling with our camera. This sounded very convincing. Life to Mr. Singh and his friends was clearly a lark, and they were certainly dressed for tourism. The migrants we were looking for were about to embark on a trek where perishing was somewhere between very possible and quite likely. They would be in a state of existential crisis, we had assumed. This apparently affluent group and their light-hearted banter did not fit the profile we had envisioned.

"Where will you visit?" we asked. "Just Quito?"

"Tomorrow, we go to Turbo," said Singh.

"Turbo?"

"Turbo."

Turbo is nine hundred miles, more than twenty hours by car, from Quito, on the northern Caribbean coast of Colombia. It is not in any of the tourist guidebooks, but it is often the next major stop in the migrants' pathway to the north. It is the port where the roads north run out and migrants must take to the sea before entering the treacherous Darién Gap.

Mr. Guerrero, a bit more relaxed after Venezuela scored a goal, confirmed to us that he would be driving the young men across the border into Colombia the following day. He would take them to Turbo, en route to the US. It was unclear how long Mr. Guerrero did this job. He told us before he left that he would soon go to Chile, another country to which migrants from Haiti and elsewhere often go with smugglers. In vague terms, he agreed to tell us about his work driving migrants. He was also open to the idea of us traveling with him one day. But he was always difficult to pin down. A month or so later, his Facebook account indicated he had returned to Maracaibo, Venezuela. There, he said, life was very difficult. After that, the account went dark for a couple of months before he resurfaced, in some triumph, in the Dominican Republic.

As with several of the *coyotes* we have encountered, Mr. Guerrero appeared to fall into a contingent position in the industry during a time when he himself was in transit. One man, who was identified to us by two different people as a *coyote* in Colombia, took offense to the suggestion he would work in such a capacity. The temporary and sporadic nature of the work for such people belies the image, promulgated in the US, of *coyotes* as mafiosi- or narco-gangster-style cold-blooded professionals swimming in illicit cash.

Stuck in La Mariscal

For those unable to afford travel northward, Ecuador had become a trap of sorts. Before coming to Quito, Roshan was promised that he could earn $70 a day, enough to be able to afford a trip to the US within several years. However, when he first arrived, he would make just five to six dollars a day after food and rent was subtracted from his pay. He was also expected to work twelve-hour shifts. When we met, he was making $15 to $20 per day, which was better but still required a frugal life stuck in an apartment on the edge of the city with no computer or TV.

As our interview proceeded with Roshan, his Afghani boss grew increasingly displeased. He yelled at the restaurant chef, a Bangladeshi working the stove, who then yelled at Roshan to restock the fridge. Nelson was reminded of many Dallas-Fort Worth area gas stations in which he has witnessed Indian or Pakistani owners taking considerable advantage of Nepali workers, a reproduction of South Asian geopolitics in the diasporic labor market. Roshan lamented how before he could, at least, work alongside other Nepalis—but now there were none left.

Without a job, friends, or even rudimentary Spanish, his wife Bhawani has nothing to do but sit at home waiting for her husband to finish his twelve-hour shift. Roshan had hoped that she would start working alongside him in La Mariscal in a South Asian-owned establishment. But now, unable to find work for her, he turned his sights not to the north or staying in Ecuador, but rather to returning to Nepal: "I have a sixty-nine-year-old father back in the village to take care of" and he adds, "barley and rice fields to cultivate."

Roshan does not have the money to think of moving north; neither does he have the social contacts to rise in the hierarchy of La Mariscal. He is a product of Ecuador's experiment with open borders. While it opened the door to unprecedented global migration, which in turn established opportunities for service-migration businesses to emerge catering to pan-ethnic communities, it has not provided sufficient conditions for those communities to thrive. Presidential politics, internal criticism, and external pressure have undermined the reality of universal citizenship, rendering Quito's Little India a mere transit stop for some, a dead end for others.

CHAPTER 4

Self-Catering on the
Ecuador-Colombia Border

The Three Coyote Price Plans

As in the tourist industry, smugglers sell *camino duro* travel services at many different levels and price points.

The offerings and pricing, like that of the conventional travel industry, are dynamic. One critical input might easily be based on a World Bank chart of incomes across the Global South. People from emerging economy nations, such as India, command the top-dollar services and the poorest of the poor, such as Haitians, are rarely seen in the company of *coyotes* at all.

Mr. Singh was on what might be called the "all-inclusive" plan. Many Punjabis and South Asians, we came to learn, are afforded white-glove treatment by smugglers in Latin America. When we met people from the Punjab, escorts like Mr. Guerrero were never far behind. One person with knowledge of the smuggling business told us that paramilitary organizations in Colombia consider the Punjabi travelers the most lucrative group and, for this reason, made it known to small-time smugglers that this group was off limits. Mr. Singh and his friends still faced a harrowing road to the US from Quito, but they would, at least, have a guide for almost every step of the way.

For the first-class traveler, a long line of smuggling agents wait for migrants in each country along the way. This is where the migration industry overlaps most closely with the organized crime of drug smuggling. The smugglers on the route tend to insist on strict protocols, and we came to recognize groups on this travel plan instantly from their answers to our questions: "we're not supposed to talk to anyone," we were told by a Nepali group in Tapachula. "We are here as tourists. After our vacation, we're going back to India," we were told by two different Punjabi groups, a thousand miles and two years apart, almost verbatim.[1] Much like Sano Bhai in Thailand, the Punjabis we met in Quito were outfitted in ostentatiously touristic garb, with one man donning a woven sweater with llama logos. It's an ingenious way of blending in by sticking out. The presence of a group of young South Asian men could provoke questions in the mind of a customs official or policeman, but the tourist clothes could well provide answers to those questions before the official posed them to the migrant.[2]

Even in first class, a single *coyote* would rarely if ever accompany the *pollos* for the entire distance.

They might be South Asian intermediaries or they might be Latin American paramilitary leaders, but it appears only one or two masterminds have a view of the entire chain. Our reporting and records of criminal smuggling cases suggests that the Clan del Golfo in Colombia have end-to-end oversight for some South Asian migrants, and that independent agents in Quito, Ecuador, oversee large parts of other South Asians' journeys.

Kidane traveled on the second type of plan, which could be called "half board," and is similar to the trip that Mr. Tamang was trying to arrange with his maternal uncle. A variation on the first-class ticket, this trip is almost as expensive, but lacks the "door-to-door" concierge service. The migrants pay for some initial part of the passage (for Kidane, this leg was Dubai-to-Turbo, Colombia), and must organize their own onward passage from the agreed destination, liaising with independent smugglers along the way.

Like people who have spent thousands of dollars in the conventional travel industry, Kidane and his Eritrean friends had an impression of what their considerable outlay covered. Kidane was conscious that some mishaps could arise beyond the *coyotes'* control, but he had an experienced traveler's notion that he should be getting the same kind of treatment as others in his situation. A steady stream of texts from Eritreans further along the route—some even in the US—informed him of what conditions should be expected. If an independent *coyote*'s sales pitch did not line up with what the previous migrants had told them was in store, they would wave off the proposal. It was another example of the digital grapevine at work: the WhatsApp and Facebook Messenger communications functioned for migrants trying to make it on the *camino duro* as the Irish bars in the Woodlawn neighborhood of the Bronx once functioned for migrants trying to make it in New York.

One of the mantras on the WhatsApp texts was that Kidane and his friends should expect to be nickel-and-dimed by their *coyotes*, even on a half-board plan.

"You have to pay more and more and more," one of the Eritreans told us.

The third option is the one that is favored by most Cuban and Venezuelan migrants, and many of the poorest migrants from Africa, Haiti and elsewhere: call it the "self-catering" model.

When we were in Quito, we heard rumors emanating from the Cuban community that there were maps for sale around the major bus stations for migrants passing through independently. You could buy the "one-dollar map," basically a crude roadmap of upper South and Central America. The "two-dollar map" reputedly provided more exact coordinates for border crossings.

A growing network of very small-time, local smugglers has emerged to handle the self-catering crowd, who arrive in the Americas without any *coyote* phone numbers.

Mr. Guerrero, the smuggler escorting Mr. Singh and his friends, had assured us there would be few stops between Quito and Turbo in his van. He was leaving the morning after the "last supper" in the Taste of India and planned to be in Turbo the following night. For self-catering migrants, however, borders present much more of an impediment. The first stop for this group after Quito is the bus station in Tulcan, a small town roughly 150 miles north of Quito, just below the tree-line in the Andes of northern Ecuador.

The African and Haitian Experience—Extra Legs on the *Camino Duro*

When we visited the Tulcan bus station, it provided perhaps the clearest impression of the scale of global south-south migration. This hub, in a town of roughly fifty thousand residents, felt more like an international airport than a provincial highland bus station. Every few minutes, another bus from Quito or Colombia pulled in and disgorged a surprisingly international group of passengers. We had heard at least three different languages spoken within twenty minutes of arrival.

We approached two men who we took for Haitians. We will call them Frederick Mensah and Michael Boateng. At first, Mr. Mensah and Mr. Boateng didn't want to talk to us. Both were clearly shaken, reluctant to stand still, casting nervous glances around the station as if they were being pursued. Mr. Boateng's knapsack hardly looked big enough for a day at the beach. He appeared to be wearing most of his clothes, the elasticated waist of a colorful pair of shorts peeping out of his ragged trousers. When we asked them if we could help them with anything, they asked us for water. By a news stand in the bus station, they told us their story.

"We are from Ghana," said Mr. Mensah.

At this stage, we knew in theory that the *camino duro* had drawn people from all over the Global South. Still, the word "Ghana" hit us with a thump. The West African nation had not even come up so far in our research. Their presence in this bus station, combined with the steady flow of buses from Quito, suggested we were encountering the tip of an iceberg. The Tulcan bus station, clearly, was where the shadow travel industry intersected with the conventional, regional Latin American travel industry.

Mr. Mensah and Mr. Boateng had been traveling with four African friends, they told us. They had taken a bus the previous night from Tulcan to Cali, in the south of Colombia, a route that tourist guidebooks warn can be plagued by bandits. They fell asleep after the Colombian border, and were rudely awoken by the bus driver in the dead of night. They did not speak Spanish so never learned why he kicked all six men off the bus in the middle of nowhere. It seemed likely that the bus driver was a conspirator in the crime that followed. There, on the dark road, they were approached by armed men. Frightened, the two men's friends ran off into the night. Mr. Mensah and Mr. Boateng were frisked by the thieves, and most of their cash was taken from them.

"This is the only money we have left," said Mr. Mensah.

He showed us what looked like a small wad of dollars he had hidden in a money-belt beneath his shirt. Kidane and other migrants had told us how important it was to separate cash between as many hidden receptacles as possible because of the high incidence of such robberies. It was heart wrenching to think of all the expenses, for black-market or conventional travel, that lay ahead of the men now left with so few resources to pay for it. Mr. Mensah and Mr. Boateng were shaken by their encounter with the Colombian police. They were worried about their friends who had ran into the scrub in the dead of night, and they were clearly traumatized by their experience at gunpoint. But they also demonstrated understanding of how to play the game, by producing documents they considered to be a small ladder at the foot of the giant chute they'd just descended.

The police had issued them with *salvoconductos*. These transit visas permitted the men ten days to pass through Colombia. The passes reflected the de facto policy in Ecuador, Colombia, and Panama before the Trump administration applied pressure: "move on and we won't bother you."

Clearly, Mr. Mensah and Mr. Boateng—and all the migrants we saw in the Tulcan bus station—were on the "self-catering" plan, only interacting with smugglers when there was no other way forward. Travelers on the *camino duro* view the shadow travel industry much as tourists view the conventional travel industry: a necessary evil that must be approached with one hand on your pocketbook.

At first, it was a mystery to us how the independent migrants arriving in the bus station intended to cross the Colombian border. Most would not have Michael and Frederick's *salvoconducto*, and none appeared to have any *coyote* assistance. They all went to the taxi rank—again reminiscent of a mid-sized airport or tourist town rather than a provincial backwater—and were quickly whisked away by drivers who, presumably, did not speak their language.

Our first suspicion was that the migrants would go from Tulcan to the much smaller border town of Tufiño near the El Angel natural reserve. This area is desolate even by Andean standards, a singular ecosystem. The páramo is a temperate desert, where vast mountainsides are covered with cacti that resemble dwarf palm trees or rows of tiny windmills. But Ecuadorian authorities had shut this back door to Colombia by the time we arrived. We were stopped at a roadblock by an Ecuadorian soldier. When we did get to the Colombian side of the border, the narrow road wound around mountains strangely reminiscent of England's Lake District, with Friesian cows grazing the shaggy grass on the steep slopes.

We returned to the Tulcan bus station to find out how the independent travelers proceeded from there. We met with a Haitian family group: two men, a woman, and a young child. They had ponderous luggage, large duffel bags and canvas totes more suitable for air travel than backpacking. One of the Haitian men, we'll call him Julius Delmas, introduced himself and shook our hands somewhat warily. We offered to assist the party in their dealings with the taxi drivers, and before we knew it, we had joined them.

We asked the taxi drivers where they were taking migrants, and they said they were going to a bridge on the border. Misunderstanding our inquiry, one driver offered to bring us (Nelson and Curran) for about $2.50. It wasn't far, he said. No problem. When the Haitian party began loading their luggage in his trunk, the taxi-driver jumped to his feet. This wasn't the deal! He didn't take "French," he said. The next two taxi-drivers agreed to take the whole party: for $5 per taxi, twice the going rate.

FIGURE 4.1. The high Andes of southern Colombia.

The Haitian group did not seem to register the risible discrimination, and only expressed frustration at having to move their bags from one taxi trunk to the next.

Now it became clear how the independent migrants were getting to the border. The taxi-drivers were acting as de facto, short-hop *coyotes*. This is a common occurrence; local people who might be part of the conventional travel or service industry who opportunistically participate in the informal market. The Haitians were so nervous about the proximity of the border (where the risk of apprehension is always highest) that they did not question the prices quoted. They just wanted to get on their way.

In the taxi, Julius Delmas told us they had come from São Paulo, Brazil.

"How did you get through Brazil?" we asked, in broken French.

"Walking."

We weren't sure we had understood. *Marcher* did mean walking, right? It seemed beyond belief.

"Only walking? Did you take buses?'

"No buses," the man said. "Only walking."

At the time, only Mr. Delmas' gaunt cheeks could convince us this could be true. Many Haitians like Mr. Delmas have done an extra leg on the *camino duro*, making the incredible journey that much further beyond belief. In 2012, Curran visited a Brazilian border post in Assis Brasil near the Peruvian town of Iñapari in the Madre de Dios part of the Amazonian rain forest. A Brazilian border guard, with an AK-47 resting at his side, sat in the shade outside the main building, staring into space as cars zipped under the awnings unmolested. It was clear that the vast majority of cars were driven by people who divided their daily lives between Brazil and Peru.

But this sleepy border post would soon awaken, as Haitians like Mr. Delmas began using it, first as an entry and, later, as an exit. Brazil, hungry for migrant labor ahead of the 2014 World Cup and 2016 Rio Olympics, welcomed Haitians fleeing the wreckage of the 2010 earthquake as refugees. Thousands of Haitians like Mr. Delmas flew to Peru and other nations, where they paid *coyotes* to take them to places like Assis in the Brazilian Amazon region.[3] To better regulate the influx, Dilma Roussef's government lifted the quota on humanitarian visas, distributing them to Haitians in Port-au-Prince and in border towns like Assis.[4] In 2016, a sort of Olympic hangover set in, and Brazil's economy began to slow down, leaving many Haitians out of work and ready to undertake the return hike through the Amazon, the trek through the world's largest rain forest that Mr. Delmas described. By 2016, local news reports indicated that "caravans" of Haitian migrants were crossing into Peru, and even clashing with border guards in the Assis area.[5]

The arduous trip had hollowed out Mr. Delmas' frame. The child . . . we'll call her Victoire, was two or three years old. She might have been one of our children at that age, sucking on a pacifier stamped with a yellow teddy bear, nestled between her father and her mother. Yet she had just survived a trek that not even professional survivalists would take on. Her father rubbed her cheek. At first, Victoire looked at us with doe-eyed confusion, a look that asked the same questions her parents vocalized: "Who are you? Where are we going in the taxi? To Colombia?"

Once her father was at ease with us, so was Victoire. Her smile was a powerful demonstration of the security provided by the family unit. You might imagine that a displaced child like Victoire would be in a state of trauma after such a long and uncertain journey. You might imagine that her parents would have lost their will to support her. But the child gave the parents a reason to be strong, and the parents' strength was all the child needed to feel secure. The Trump administration recognized the sustaining power of the family with the ultimate "deterrence," the child separation.

Still stroking his daughter's cheek, Mr. Delmas looked at us and asked, "Does it get easier in Colombia? Is the rest of the way easier?"

We had to be honest: Colombia, we said, might be a little easier. But Panama was going to be rough, we warned.

It was hard to believe that taxi drivers could look at Victoire and see an opportunity for a profit. Years later, the source of their hardheartedness became clear. There are so many families like Victoire's on the *camino duro* that the taxi drivers would ruin themselves if they began providing charity. We would talk to taxi drivers just like them all along the *camino duro*, even as far as upstate New York.

The Colombian border crossing was reminiscent of the US-Mexico border at Laredo, with the bridge itself helping to demarcate the border. There was a two-hundred-foot purpose-built bridge with entry signs for the two nations on either end. On the near side, there was a large Ecuadorian customs center, and on the far side, an even larger Colombian center.

There was one big difference between this crossing and the Laredo border bridge: the taxi driver did not stop. Police officers around the bridge directed traffic rather than stopping it. The driver just rolled right over the bridge and pulled into the parking lot of the Ecuadorian center. Like the Brazilian border post at Assis Brasil, the physical infrastructure on this border was largely a theater set from the point of view of the migrants. Ecuador and Colombia were going through the motions of migration control, but the sub-text of the performance was a clarion message to migrants: "keep moving and we will not trouble you." As the Ghanaians had discovered, migrants were sometimes stopped elsewhere in Colombia by police checking for the papers processed at these customs centers. Processing the paperwork was a "buyer-beware" optional situation. People crossing the border at Tulcan-Ipiales could stop and process their paperwork, or they could move forward without it, and risk apprehension.

Another thing our ride with the self-catering migrants revealed was how little they knew—or could know—about where they were on the path to the US and what lay ahead. Later that day, we would meet a particularly footloose and carefree Ecuadorian migrant who had not even consulted a map before setting out. We shared a taxi back to Tulcan with the man and his significant other. As he recounted a tale about his arrest to the taxi driver in a loud and charismatic manner, we assumed it was some late-night escapade. Gradually, it became clear that he had traveled to Colombia and was boarding a flight to Panama City when he was pulled off the flight. Far from embarrassed, the man found the whole situation hilarious, and wondered aloud if he was the only one who didn't know about Panama and its visa demands.

When we asked him about his situation, the Ecuadorian man told us he was determined to take another run at going north. He asked us earnestly what other countries and visas he might have to worry about between Panama and the US border.

At the Colombian border, the taxi drivers dropped us straight into another

FIGURE 4.2. On the Colombian side of the Ecuador-Colombia border, between Tulcan and Ipiales.

mosquito cloud of money changers and taxi touts, seeking a piece of the self-catering crowd's budget. It was difficult to get our bearings.

"So we're in Colombia?" Mr. Delmas asked, as we gathered the luggage.

"Yes," one of us said. "I think so?"

There were several passenger vans—*colectivos*—loading up in the extensive parking lot. We were about to climb into one but diverted to the cafe attached to the Colombian border post. It was not the kind of subterfuge any of us had imagined when crossing an international border without paperwork. The money changers hovered, some attempting to tell their own stories about migration from the Middle East. Their attentions added to the harassed, confused state of our party.

We could tell the Haitian men were upset with us, but it took us a long time to figure out why. They were appalled that we had paid for the taxi from Tulcan.

"How much?" one of Mr. Delmas' friends, who had formerly been quiet, demanded. "It would be one thing if I didn't have any money myself, but I have money. How much?" he demanded.

The Colombian money changer who had ripped me off earlier inserted himself between us, misunderstanding the demands: "You need money?" he said to the Haitian man. "I got money right here."

"Look," we said, ignoring the huckster as best we could, "You helped us. So we wanted to help you."

The money changer pulled us aside. He had a salesman's gift for cloaking flattery and greed in a simulacrum of honesty and philanthropy.

"You speak Spanish," he said. "You have to help them. They are going to be picked up by control if they go on the *colectivo*. They have to get a special taxi . . . I know a guy . . . but it would be $30 each. You've got to tell them."

It was impossible to verify the information. We presented it to Mr. Delmas and his friend but added a note of skepticism. A yellow taxi came and stopped by the money changer. He held the door like a valet, ushering us in. We eventually waved him off. As we climbed into a *colectivo* to Ipiales, the nearest Colombian city, the Haitian group was moving into the cafe.

At that time, the official border bridge between Tulcan and Ipiales was another back door into Colombia, and it was still wide open. Both Ecuador and Colombia were still approaching border security as a question of maintaining flows. As long as the migrants kept moving, the authorities washed their hands of them.

In Tulcan, we visited Milton Riofrio, a public defender for the state of Carchi, who handled a lot of the immigration cases. His office complex looked like a shopping mall, complete with a multi-story foyer. He was flattered by the attention from North American journalists. Mr. Riofrio's dapper, somewhat primped appearance, suggested to us that he had used a mirror before admitting us to his office. He made hand signals to his assistants, dispatching one to a vending machine, and another to snap a photograph.

In contrast to US officials we would interview, however, Mr. Riofrio expressed his sympathy for migrants. As an ambitious man, it was clear that he would also like to hold *coyotes* more stridently to account. As it stood, his hands were somewhat tied by national Ecuadorian policies. Most of the dragnet-type cases he shared with us followed a similar pattern. The police raided one of several local motels and rounded up a group of migrants and their *coyotes* (who generally posed as migrants themselves during the arrests). Local *coyotes* were hard to prosecute because the migrants refused to testify against them. The migrants, who included Nigerians, Congolese, and Nepalis, were formally charged and brought to court. A technicality was raised in court, and—almost invariably—the migrants were released with instructions to keep moving.

We later visited one of the motels Mr. Riofrio mentioned. The place was not just tacky, it was 1950s Atlantic City tacky, all orange, green, and plastic: the Motel California.

Mr. Riofrio showed us mugshots of some of the roughly two hundred people. Most of the pictures he showed us were of Haitians: "These people don't have papers, don't have passports, only application for refugee status in Brazil."

The language barrier was something that plagued self-catering migrants all the way along the *camino duro*, but it also created a loophole to bypass immigration control. The Ecuadorian constitution insists that officers must read suspects their rights in a way that's comprehensible to the suspect. Riofrio interviewed the police when he first encountered the Haitian cases and found they were using Google Translate to render the Spanish rights into Haitian Creole. He has repeatedly challenged the practice in court and has succeeded in having most of the deportation cases thrown out. Once the suspects are released, he assumes they proceed to Colombia.

CHAPTER 5

Gulf of Urabá

The Two Faces of Paradise

Passengers disembark the bus from Medellin to Turbo on the dusty street outside the central bus station of the rundown northern Colombian port. Turbo is an industrial port known more for record-setting drug busts than cruise ships and tourists. Until recently, it was largely neglected by the Colombian state, leaving paramilitary forces to control its geostrategic position as the hub of the Gulf of Urabá, the South American doorway to the Caribbean and Central America. The line of old cargo hulks at the port, some with hammocks strung up on deck, are reminiscent of abandoned warehouses being taken over by squatters in some old industrial city—a floating rust belt. For independent migrants like Kidane and Jane Mtebe, Turbo is where you can find smugglers offering transport across the gulf and through the infamous Darién Gap.

In the absence of clear migration policies, many northern South American and Central American governments hand out *salvoconductos* and other transit passes that permit migrants to move legally through the country but exit within a certain number of days. With these transit passes, migrants moved through northern Colombia with relative ease having their pick of entry points to the Darién Gap.

Ms. Mtebe arrived in Turbo at about 7 a.m. one day in early August 2018. She was traveling with two Ghanaian men who she'd teamed up with at the Cali bus station and Gloria, the woman with whom Ms. Mtebe had left Ghana.

The agent approached the group and told them to follow him, quickly, before the police showed up. He took them to a safe house he'd rented for the purpose of facilitating travel north. There was no furniture, except for "tiny, tiny" mattresses on the floor. There, they met with six other Cameroonian men. This was to be the traveling party for the hardest part of the *camino*: the crossing of the Gulf of Urabá to Capurganá and onward passage through the Darién jungle in southern Panama.

The agent, a man in his forties, opened negotiations with Ms. Mtebe's newly assembled group. After some back-and-forth, they settled on a price of $550-per-person for the whole section—two night boats and a guide through the jungle for the trek that could take a week or more.

The agents often divide the groups along national lines. This way someone like Kidane—as was often the case in his group—can act as a group interlocutor with the smugglers, conducting negotiations and passing on any logistical information to the rest of the group. The nationalized groups also reflect efforts by the organized criminal groups who govern the *camino* to set "manufacturer-recommended-prices" for different nationalities, carefully calibrated to be as much as families back home could bear to send.

Despite these price guides and the steep language barriers, there's a surprising amount of negotiation between migrants and smugglers. Kidane made clear that his group was never willing to pay prices they considered exorbitant, even when they were negotiating with their backs to the wall. Both sides view their relationship as a business transaction, but the migrants' vulnerability to robbery (a constant risk when dealing with smugglers), the highly lucrative nature of the trade and the often graphic plight of the migrants make this a business transaction with unique inputs of fear and humanitarian mercy.

Ms. Mtebe's group was to leave the same night. The group was told to pack light for the jungle hike. Ms. Mtebe gave the smuggler a pair of sneakers and some new pants she had purchased in Ecuador so he could give them to his wife, who he had told the group was home with their children some distance from Turbo.

At about 8 p.m., the man led them to the docks, two-by-two, on bicycles. To avoid raising suspicion, they even took a different route each time. Ms. Mtebe said it frightened her to cycle after the smuggler through the dark streets.

"Since I wasn't alone, I was like 'OK, let's see how it goes,'" Ms. Mtebe said.

They were led through a small family home to a hut by the water. There, they were told to turn off their phones so as not to draw attention with lights. Police patrol boats could be passing by, the smuggler told them. They were watched by a nine-year-old boy while the smuggler and the boys' older brothers collected the others.

> The small boy was asking for money. He said if we don't give him money he'll go and call police. And the Ghanaians said, 'Okay, go to the police.' It was a very tense situation. When the big boys came, we told them. They said he's not supposed to ask us for money. And they took the small boy out of the room.

The Turbo docks are the gritty side of a gritty town, the underbelly of the underbelly. The fish swim among plastic bags in the grimy gray waters between the boats. Fishing boats and cargo ships with chipped paintwork, open-topped cabins and rusty hulls are docked at close proximity, hemming one another in so that it's hard to tell the working ships from those under construction or abandoned altogether. When we were there, one of the waterfront boarding-houses was padlocked shut.

If you go with one of the agents, hustling for custom on the dock, between the parasol-covered fish stalls, it costs about $30 for the tourist boat, to travel the roughly fifty miles across the Gulf to Capurganá. With its powerful engine, the tourist boat takes two and a half hours. For migrants like Kidane and Ms. Mtebe traveling by fishing boats powered by smaller outboard motors, it's an all-night trip.

After two hours waiting in the hut, Ms. Mtebe's boat arrived at around 11 p.m. The Turbo smuggler told them he had texted photographs to contacts who would meet them on the beach in Capurganá. They were forty-five minutes out to sea when the engine failed. The boat limped back to the dock in Turbo.

There, Ms. Mtebe's group boarded a second boat. The pilot went full throttle the whole way, determined to reach Capurganá before daybreak. The boat came within sight of the shore at about 5:30 in the morning, just as the sun rose. The arrival was abrupt, to say the least.

"They just tell us to leave, leave: 'vamos, vamonos' . . . 'Where do I go? Vamos, where?'" as Ms. Mtebe described it.

The pilot and his assistant didn't even help with the bags. Ms. Mtebe and her party scrambled ashore. They thought they'd be in sight of the town, but there was nothing around except scrub at the edge of the jungle.

As Ms. Mtebe put it, there was no time to complain, "We were focused on how do we survive."

Her group moved north along the seashore, in the direction of Capurganá. The first man they met waved them off. He wanted nothing to do with them and did not understand English. A younger man approached them and showed them photographs of the smuggler in Turbo. He was there to take them to the safe house in Capurganá. The sense of relief that they had been found soon turned to misery. The path on the verge of the jungle became a swamp. Ms. Mtebe had prepared herself for the legendary rigors of the Darién. But the only thing harder to hike than the mountainous jungle is the tight-weave skirt of mangrove swamps at the foot of the forest. Clambering through mangrove roots is like tussling with a million-legged wrestler, intent on catching you in a pincer grip. Finally, Ms. Mtebe could not walk any further. One of the men traveling with her carried her on his back. They arrived at the safe house a couple of hours later.

A Lucky Break

For Kidane's group, the arrival was even more perilous. The first boat they boarded, on the night of July 8, did not have a powerful enough engine. A few miles out to sea, the engine cut out, and they were lucky to muddle back to port in Turbo.

Describing the route of the second boat trip, Kidane wriggled his arm as if impersonating a disoriented fish.

> After one day we changed into another boat . . . a little bit bigger. But, starting the journey, the boatman didn't have a compass.
>
> He was also afraid because some sea [patrols] were there. We knew that sometimes, he had to double back to avoid them, doing like this [Kidane made a zigzag motion]. Finally, the man didn't know where we were. He was lost, totally lost . . . he turned off the motor and just looked around. We asked him, "Why are you sitting like that?" and he told us he'd lost the direction.
>
> We gave him our mobiles. We were supposed to leave our phones off, so they wouldn't give off any light and get us caught. But we couldn't take it. We turned on the smart phones, hiding them under blankets so nobody would see. When we showed him the direction, he went by the highest speed. It takes about three or four hours from Turbo to Capurganá . . . we left 9 p.m. and reached there 6 a.m.

The night boat to Capurganá is a race against the sun. Kidane's boatman had lost the race. With the gray dawn creeping ahead of them, the risks of capture for everyone on board were rising. The boat dropped anchor before it reached the beach next to the Capurganá docks.

> The helper said "better drop them in the water." I can swim. So I went first. I was checking first how deep is the water. We had lifejackets but I can swim. I entered the water and it was up to my waist, then everyone went in together.

Even in the shallows, it was dangerous for non-swimmers because of the waves, which could be several feet high.

> For the people who couldn't swim, we helped them to the coast. The waves pushed us to the coast. Our bags were sinking but the waves pushed all of our bags onto the shore. No one lost anything. We had already put plastic inside our bags so they didn't get wet.

The police intercepted Kidane's group on the beach. When local or border police caught migrants at sea, we learned, they typically sent them back to Turbo. But Kidane's group was lucky. After forfeiting a bribe, he and his group were quickly released and sent on their way. Before they could reach the hostel arranged for them, however, the group was stopped at another police checkpoint. Fed up with the Colombian police and their extortionate demands, Kidane and the others initially refused to pay anything at the checkpoint. Even when the police brought up the idea of returning to the station, some of the migrants wanted to call their bluff. Finally, the police at the checkpoint settled for a total of $150, and the exhausted migrants made their way to the hostel, a ten-minute walk from the main harbor, near a fishing jetty. Later, Kidane found out just how lucky he had been.

> The people who were coming after us, another group, told us that one son, and father, an Indian man were in the boat in Capurganá. The boatman said, "Get out and hurry up," and they hurried up because they were afraid. They jumped into the water, the father couldn't swim and he sank. He didn't have a chance. The son didn't have a chance to bury his father . . . all the people left.

On July 10, 2018, Kristina, the American to whom we had been introduced when we expressed interest in the migrant question, told us that there were some Eritrean men staying nearby. It was the kind of morning that people in wet climates think of when they imagine paradise—just enough breeze cutting the warm sunshine to rustle the palm leaves. Right next to our guesthouse, we observed a group of young men checking on the clothes they had hung on the railings of their hostel. We could tell that emotions were running high. Learning that we were writing about migrants' experience, some of the men initially wanted to talk to us. They loudly condemned the actions of the Colombian boatmen and the Colombian police. One man interceded, warning his friends not to trust us, suggesting they refuse the cigarettes we offered. We stepped back, hoping not to spark a row among them.

One man, wearing a gold Arsenal jersey and a short beard, called us back. He did not want a cigarette. He understood what we were trying to do, and he wanted to help us. His name, he said, was Kidane.

Kidane was able to tune out the raised voices, the soaked clothes, and the recent trauma. He carefully explained the scant and stark choices that were available to him as an Eritrean. He told us calmly about the group's current predicament, waiting to be whisked off to the jungle at what could be a moment's notice, some time, he thought, in the next forty-eight to seventy-two hours.

We checked in with Kidane frequently during that time. With little money and a warning from the hostel owner to be ready for a move at any moment, he and his friends were generally sitting in the shaded area between their hostel and the waterfront, with a view of the harbor down a slight incline. As with the Haitians at the Colombian border, we were struck by how little information was available to him ahead of the next leg. There were rumors that the group might leave the night of their arrival, but that did not happen.

Dueling Travel Industries in the Beach Town that Became a Global Migration Hub

The tourist boat to Capurganá from Turbo is an over-sized speedboat with a powerful engine and bench seating for about forty people on the open-topped deck. It wends through the ship cemetery of the harbor, then picks up steam in the coffee-colored headwaters of the Atrato River. Gradually, the memory of the fetid Turbo waters are washed away by the fresh breezes and rolling white caps of the ultramarine Caribbean.

Most of the boat's passengers are tourists, but when we took the ride, there were several locals for whom the ferry served as the only link between their jungle-locked communities and the outside world. One of the passengers told us about his time as a teacher in one of these Afro-Colombian villages on the fringe of the Darién, which he was returning to visit. Locals lower their packages down to the *lanchas*, which take them to docks too small even for the midsized boat. The villages are obscured by the thick vegetation that comes all the way down to the shoreline.

For the last section of the journey, the boat hugs the coast, passing a series of steep headlands with spidery mangroves at their feet dipped into the water. On most boats, the eyes are drawn out to sea, and the passenger feels their heart tighten with a sensation of infinitude as they gaze. On the boat to Capurganá, it is the imposing hills that draw the eye. The palm trees near the shore give way to taller trees as the forest climbs hillsides. This forest, we knew, teemed with lost souls, like the Greek underworld.

Finally, in a tiny nook between two of the headlands, a few bright swatches of color become visible, like a small flock of parrots coming into view in the midst of a vast empty forest. Capurganá is hours away from the rest of the world by boat or mountain trail, and, long before COVID-19, even these fragile links were periodically severed. It's hard to shake the impression of a tenuous existence that could be swallowed any day by the wilderness.

Capurganá has the sleepily festive atmosphere of seaside towns all over the world. Souvenir shops, scuba-tour operators, restaurants, hotels, and hostels line the narrow main street a block from the main dock. Wooden fishing boats, many painted in the Colombian colors of red, blue, yellow, and white, are racked side-by-side on the short, steep beachfronts. The day's catch is served in cafes with deck seating and the distinctive drumbeats of cumbia music in the background. The restaurateurs and store managers are a mixture of white Colombians, overseas visitors who couldn't bring themselves to leave, and Afro-Colombians, the main inhabitants of the Urabá Gulf area. Further inland, donkeys dragged rubbish carts around humble houses, while teenage boys played open-ended soccer matches on an open square.

The demeanor of the paradisical Capurganá can change instantaneously, like a cherubic toddler flying suddenly into a tantrum. Black-tinged clouds appear from nowhere and people scatter before the drubbing rain. The rain churns up the unpaved streets, and leaves the square unplayable for an hour or two.

The cement and pebbled streets only go a few blocks in any direction before they give way to mud tracks and hooting jungle. If the sea around Capurganá is ungovernable and full of treacherous undercurrents, the jungle is even more so. In mountain camps above the town, according to our sources, live the paramilitary groups who control drug and people smuggling through the isthmus of Panama. The public face of Capurganá is tourism and fishing, but neither seem to be the town's main industry.

Backpackers and bag-rollers from all over the world find their way to Capurganá, but there is a third type of bag visible. It's the *mochila*, the type of bag carried by Kidane and his friends. The *mochila* is the mark of the *extra-continentale* migrant recognized in much of Central and South America. A *mochila* is roughly equivalent to a schoolbag, far smaller than the backpackers' *equipaje* or the tourists' *maleta*, but larger than the *carteras* and *bolsas*, the hand luggage carried by Latin Americans out for the day. On Kidane's route, the migrant needs a bag that can be packed in moments as soon as the signal is given to move, a bag that will not slow them down when moving on foot or swimming to shore.

As in Quito's Mariscal, many of the businessowners in Capurganá are serving a dual set of customers who could hardly imagine each other's daily existence. Some have even jumped into the vacuum left by the weak state presence in the region to provide humanitarian services.

With the half-board and self-catering options, the standards and pricing in the shadow travel industry are necessarily loose. But Capurganá, like an established resort in the conventional travel business, has more fixed price ranges and protocols. The paramilitary group known loosely as the Clan del Golfo reportedly charges tolls to small-time smugglers around Capurganá near the Colombian border with Panama, and monitors the rates they charge, according to a person we spoke to who was familiar with the business.

When Nicaragua closed its border with Costa Rica in late November 2015, it caused a domino effect of border closures and migration bottlenecks that would extend south to Capurganá. The closure caused an improvised refugee camp to emerge in Peñas Blancas, at Costa Rica's northern edge. After arranging airlifts to El Salvador for migrants (for $555 per person), Costa Rica then closed its southern border with Panama in March 2016. In turn, Panama followed suit by closing its border with Colombia on May 9, 2016. Thus, the Nicaragua closure exposed a fatal flaw in the transit pass approach to immigration policy—that it only works with neighboring countries permitting mobility in unison. It also showed the overarching influence of US-controlled regional geopolitics.

When migrant flow is blocked, as in the case of Panama's closed border, it not only creates a bottleneck of migrants along the border of the country to the south, it provides financial incentives to groups who can circumvent the state. In northern Colombia, it is the paramilitaries and drug traffickers who can provide such passage.

The Capurganá migration business reflects local power struggles rooted in Colombia's long civil war. During the violent conflict between the left-wing guerrillas such as the Fuerzas Armadas Revolucionarias de Colombia–Ejercito del Pueblo, or FARC, and right-wing paramilitaries in the 1980s and 1990s, most groups entered the drug and human trafficking businesses to amass war chests. The political civil war has ended, but the businesses survived and are still fighting over territory. Control of the Gulf of Urabá and access to the Darién Gap was recognized as a strategic asset for these smuggling businesses. The drug cartels viewed the land-and-sea route through Capurganá and the Darién much as conventional industries view the Panama Canal, a chokepoint that must be kept open to their trade at all costs. One historically right-wing group of what's known as *narcoparamilitares*, the Clan del Golfo (also known as Los Urabeños), has been the dominant criminal paramilitary group in the Turbo/Capurganá region since 2007.[1] But clashes between the Clan and leftist rivals such as the ELN still occur in the state of Choco.

We witnessed the control exercised by the paramilitaries on our second night in Capurganá. There had been no power in most of the town all day, a common occurrence. The restaurants had used humming generators to keep the lights on and the fish dishes sizzling. In rapid succession, the generators stopped buzzing, and the grills stopped sizzling.

Suddenly, the sleepy town had the atmosphere of Dodge City after a lookout had spotted an approaching posse of gunslingers. Everyone was shutting up shop, retreating to their rooms or getting out of town. The main street, whose string of restaurants had bustled with tourists and locals just an hour earlier, emptied out, left in silence as the generators ground to a halt.

Three South Asian migrants stood on the deck of one of the closed restaurants. A smuggler sat next to them, backpacks at his feet. It felt like the town was under an evacuation order. One merchant was hurriedly putting up shutters nearby. She advised us to go home, to get out of the streets. Something was happening, she said. It was not safe. Every street seemed to have a lookout posted on the corner. We heard the rumor the next day: the paramilitaries had come to town. One of the smuggling-boat captains had not paid the toll (roughly $50 a head) for their *pollos*—the migrants. The paramilitaries, we were told by people with knowledge of the business, had shot him dead.

The next night, we saw a man wearing a sidearm, sitting at a table with a view of the side street through the house's open front door. The tourists went about their merry business, but the rest of the town was on edge.

On the day we left, about thirty migrants, mostly from India and Haiti, were thronged around the police station near the harbor. Their boat had been

FIGURE 5.1. A group of migrants, intercepted by border police on a boat off the coast of Panama and returned to Capurganá.

intercepted on the way from Capurganá to the coast of Panama. It had clearly been a long night. Everyone in the crowd looked despondent, their t-shirts and baggage sodden with tropical rains, as they waited for the police to book them, or, for all they knew, lock them up. They would be sent back to Turbo, where, if they were lucky, their contacts would make another attempt. More than likely, they would have to pay. This kind of chutes-and-ladders progress is an expected part of doing business.

Several months later, in January 2019, the Clan del Golfo allegedly stopped all maritime smuggling from Capurganá when a boat capsized and killed nineteen migrants.[2] This incident, reportedly caused by a drunk crew that had not paid the Clan, brought unwanted attention to the migrant smuggling, disrupting the uneasy balance with the state and international society.

It is widely reported that the increasing securitization of international borders only increase the profit of smugglers able to escort migrants across.[3] In the United Nations–backed 2018 Global Study On Smuggling of Migrants, the authors estimated that the business of smuggling migrants from Mexico and Central America to the US had a value of about $7.4 billion per year, about the same as what a major multinational corporation like Amazon.com generates in net income. That was based on estimates of 800,000 migrants from all origins crossing the Mexican border.

What is less known is how much the industry profits further to the south. With each new US-influenced policy, such as the increasing securitization of Panama's *flujo controlado*, or the anti-drug logic behind Nicaragua's *muro de contención*, the earnings of the migration industry promise to grow. In 2018, Medellin's *El Colombiano* newspaper cited official estimates of between 4,000 and 11,000 undocumented immigrants passing through the Capurganá region per year.[4] Those estimates likely do not include large groups of Punjabi migrants, who, we were told by someone with direct knowledge of the smuggling industry, stay in camps controlled by the paramilitary groups in the mountains above Capurganá. That person estimated that the number of people passing through Capurganá is closer to 24,000 a year, which would represent $720 million in smugglers' revenue at the going rate. And that's before accounting for the extortionate interest rates—estimated by the UN's International Labour Organization to be an average of 30 percent in Nepal—at which that money was borrowed.[5]

To call the smuggling operations along the extra-continental trail a unified industry, like oil or even illegal drugs, would be a stretch. There are immense differences between the intermediaries of Quito and Capurganá. For instance, the migration-restaurant nexus that we observed in Quito functions according to national or regional associations, even if commodified for profit motives. No such affiliation exists in the impersonal relations of Capurganá's industry. In both cases of Quito and Capurganá, however, the brokerage work of agents maintain power inequalities.[6] In movements through Ecuador and northern Colombia, social differences of region, nationality, class, race, and gender created differential and vastly unequal passages. Thus, working in the shadows does not challenge the unevenness of status quo global inequality or promote subaltern solidarity between migrants.

Escorted vs. Independent Migrants

Walking around Capurganá, the class division between migrants was apparent. While some migrants, mostly African, seemed to be free to move around, others were under constant watch. This latter group of escorted, mostly South Asian, migrants was consistent with our observations in Quito and Tapachula where the higher price of travel entails tighter control of everyday activity.

The difference between escorted and independent migrants could be seen in the disparate housing options in Capurganá. Whereas the latter stayed in hostels in the middle of town, the former were more likely to be in more private safe house-like structures on the outskirts.

A couple of blocks inland from the main street, we noticed an open door to a hostel room with about eight bunk beds squeezed into it. On almost every bunk sat a South Asian man, with the expression of someone in a waiting room. On the staircase next door, another South Asian–looking man checked his phone.

"Buenas tardes," we said.

A stocky man emerged from a third doorway.

"Buenas tardes!" he said, muscling in on the conversation before anyone else could answer.

He had the craggy features, forbidding glare, and stiff chest of a middle-aged enforcer in a mafia film. Slung over his shoulder was a sheet and other bedding items, but you got the sense that he was not recruited as the group's dorm mother for his laundry skills. Later, we were informed that he was an ex-member of DAS, Colombia's controversial intelligence agency started under President Uribe in 2002 and disbanded by President Santos in 2011.

We later ran into two of the residents of the house in one of the little shops in town. One of them had a tattoo on his forearm. It said "Punjabi." Like Akashbir Singh, he was from the northwestern rural region of India. The man with the Punjabi tattoo said his phone had gotten wet. We helped him inquire about a new one.

When asked how he came to Capurganá, his reply was uncannily similar to that of Akashbir Singh, the man we met in Quito and later talked to in the US.

"Oh, we are tourists. We are going back to Turbo, then to Quito, and then home."

Clearly, there is a script and the *coyotes* had trained the migrants to stick to it. This is true almost exclusively of the South Asian travelers, however. Migrants from other countries, like Kidane, tend to show less deference to the smugglers. This dual treatment appears to align with the nationality-based pricing demanded by agents. If you are on the white-glove, door-to-door plan, there is a certain decorum expected of you.

Kidane and his group of about a dozen Eritreans stayed in a hostel opposite one of the patches of beachfront where the fishing boats put in, sheltered by a small section of sea wall. The hostel was a bare-bones place. You could see the beds packed together in the dormitory through the doors to the shaded area below the wrap-around wooden balcony where they all hung out. No chaperones were present at the hostel that we could tell, although at times, Kidane would indicate that he couldn't talk as freely, presumably because one of the people nearby was an agent.

Many travelers are familiar with the state of "hurry up and wait" that

FIGURE 5.2. Waiting for the coyote's signal.

Kidane and his group endured in Capurganá. The mood was akin to a group of airline passengers waiting for the time signal on the "delayed" screen to be updated. On the *camino*, however, waiting times are often measured in days rather than minutes, and the "go" signal often gives people seconds to respond.

When we first met Kidane and his friends, he told us they were under instructions to be ready to leave within twenty-four hours. With little money to spare, restaurants and bars were out of the question. They did not want to stray far from the hostel in the evening, in case the signal to move was given. They spent most of their time in the covered porch, or just in front of the hostel, chatting. Seventy-two hours later, they were still on benches overlooking the fishing beach, waiting for the signal. The last time we asked, Kidane admitted that he was not sure what the cause of the delay was, or how much longer it would last.

Ms. Mtebe had the opposite problem—too much rush, not enough waiting. After she reached Capurganá through the swamp, she was taken to a safe house. The mother of the family welcomed the group, cooked for them, and spoke to them warmly.

Then the news came that they were shipping out again, at seven that night. After the previous night crossing and the trek through the swamp at the edge of Capurganá early that morning, Ms. Mtebe's group was exhausted and bedraggled even before they climbed into a boat, bound for the coast of Panama. They were joined on the boat by three or four Bangladeshi men, Ms. Mtebe said.

After a bewildering couple of days in the jungle, during which time she became repeatedly separated from her group and was conned into handing her bag over to a guide who subsequently abandoned her, Ms. Mtebe was intercepted by a Panamanian soldier and taken to a cell.

She explained that the relief at surviving the jungle was soon extinguished by the sudden register of everything she had lost. It was only now that her pounding heart had time to slow down that she realized what the guide took when he robbed her *mochila*. By taking the bag, he had robbed her of all of her money, her phone and all of its contacts, of all of her clothes, and— it seemed—of all hope to complete her journey. There was only one thing between her and the pits of despair: a line of graffiti on the wall of the cell.

"A Cameroonian has been here: don't be afraid."

The Panamanian officers told her that they would take her to Panama City, which was some consolation.

"They lied," Ms. Mtebe said.

When the military boat came, it took her to La Miel, the tiny beach community just over the border from the Capurganá area, in Panama. Like Capurganá, La Miel is inaccessible by road. A white sandy cove, snuggled between steep jungle hills on each side, La Miel has the ultimate Caribbean desert-island feel. On the day that we visited, Belgium was playing France in the semifinals of the World Cup. Sophisticated young travelers were wandering the beach, muttering comparisons to other far-flung paradises they had discovered. The only television on the beach, in one of several palm-thatched cabana-style bars, could not be plugged in because the cabana was locked. For the first half of the match, fans watched the horizon, waiting for the owner's son to return in a boat. Fans would rise to their feet, then punch the air in dismay, as a speck in the horizon turned out to be a seagull. The wait for the owner's son in his boat turned out to be more exciting than the match.

Ms. Mtebe could not believe what the Panamanian military were telling her as she disembarked: they were bringing her back to Colombia.

The only land crossing of the border at La Miel is a tourist track running to Sapzurro, a mirror image of the Panamanian beach community on the Colombian side. Viewed from the hills above, Sapzurro bay is like a jaguar's jaws. A steep wooden stairwell winds up out of La Miel and peaks at the border post, which consists of a hut manned by a couple of Colombian soldiers and painted wooden signs to delineate the crossing.

FIGURE 5.3. A view of Sapzurro and the Panamanian border on the trail from Capurganá, Colombia.

When Ms. Mtebe reached the top of that hill, she must have felt as if she were beginning the descent into Hades. She had not eaten a proper meal in days. She was feeling betrayed by her guide and her group. She had no prospect of ever seeing Gloria again. She just wanted to go home.

This is where the two sides of the Capurganá area meet, where tourists hiking up to the top of the hill meet apprehended migrants being marched back down again. And this is where Ms. Mtebe found the one thing that separates the *camino* from hell: the kindness of strangers.

The Underground Railroad

The first small act of charity came from an unexpected source: a Colombian border guard. The man, struggling to locate the words in English, gave Ms. Mtebe a pep talk. He told her, frankly, that she would have to go back to square one. The only way to attempt the jungle journey again was to return to Capurganá.

The border guard gave Ms. Mtebe full use of his cell phone to call anyone she liked (She had nobody to call; her female Cameroonian friend's phone was not working.) She would need money, just to get the boat back to Capurganá. The guard asked passing tourists if they had any to spare. One man—"a white boy," Ms. Mtebe said—claimed he didn't have any cash but managed to come up with just enough in Colombian pesos.

Ms. Mtebe went into a bar in Sapzurro—there are only a couple of establishments in the village. It turned out to be another stop in the informal underground railroad that had sprung up in the area. The owner spoke a little English and was sympathetic. First, he helped her orient herself—she wasn't sure how far she had to go to reach Capurganá, and was relieved to hear it was just a short boat ride around the headland. The bar owner reassured Ms. Mtebe that many migrants had gotten turned around just as she had done.

He wasn't just saying that to make Ms. Mtebe feel better: while we were in Sapzurro, we met two men and a woman from Gujarat, India, who entered a restaurant trying to pay for their food and drink with US$20 bills. They were wearing green waders, as many of the migrants we met in the area did, the better to slog through the swampy jungle. The woman told us that they had hiked into the jungle from Capurganá more than two weeks earlier. Although initially escorted by a guide, they were abandoned by their group—again, recalling Ms. Mtebe's experience—and had proceeded alone. Relieved to meet English speakers, they asked us "which way to Panama?" We were forced to tell them they were a mere ten-minute boat ride from Capurganá, no closer to Panama City than when they began their trek. The same shock and despair as Ms. Mtebe had experienced registered on their faces. The three told us they would return to the Darién, in the vain hope of seeking asylum in Panama.

We implored the Gujarati group to wait until they had spoken to a Sapzurro local. They hated the idea of going backward and were determined to press on. Before we could connect them to someone, they had disappeared into the forest.

The Sapzurro bar owner gave Ms. Mtebe food and water. He gave her enough money for the boat passage.

"He told me in the evening, this place was not good for women to just be walking like that. He gave me the money, and I went to the police station in Sapzurro," said Ms. Mtebe.

The police took her to what appeared to be one of the officer's grandmother's house. For a small sum, she got a place to sleep and a sink to wash her only set of clothes—the ones on her back. The police returned in the morning to take her to the Capurganá boat.

At the docks in Capurganá, a man was advertising his services as a guide to the Panama jungle. Ms. Mtebe was not ready for that, nor did she have the money. She didn't know whether she should talk to the police or the immigration services, as people were advising.

The underground railroad kicked in again. A man with a "fair complexion" approached her and asked her if she needed to find onward passage. She told him she had no money, and he asked her to accompany him to his place of business. There, he explained, he could offer her a loan—no interest, merely a humanitarian offer of extending credit to someone in need. Unfortunately, the idea stalled when the man found out she was Cameroonian. He had just been burned by another Cameroonian and was loath to take another risk. He did, however, know someone who might be able to help Ms. Mtebe.

The fair-skinned man asked Ms. Mtebe to walk some distance behind him, so that immigration officials and police would not know that he was helping her. He brought her to a house owned by a woman who was helping migrants. Kristina knew everyone in Capurganá, and everyone knew her. When we arrived, we started asking around about migrants in town, and we were soon directed to her doorstep.

Born and raised in upstate New York, Kristina has settled in Colombia and started a family there. She had learned the theory of human rights in college. As a stranger in a strange land, she had a natural affinity for the migrants around her. Kristina's career in Latin America is intertwined with the migrant trail. She started as a bartender in La Miel, at a time when the border with Colombia was porous. As the US and Nicaragua hardened their policies, and the effects rippled through Central America, La Miel changed. By 2016, the tourist crowd was displaced by a temporary refugee camp by the beach, holding three hundred people at a time. For a month, Kristina said, La Miel turned into a Cuban beach party, with "a ton" of salsa duro music. Photographs taken at the time show a packed campsite, hard to reconcile with the desert-island feel of the beach when we visited.

In mid-2016, Panama, under pressure from the US, sent troops to seal its border with Colombia. The La Miel bottleneck shifted back to Capurganá, which had been little more than an overnight stop on the *camino* up to that time.[7] The camp at La Miel closed and Capurganá filled with hundreds, and sometimes thousands, of migrants from South Asia, Cuba, and Africa, waiting for a new path north to open up. One hostel, on the outskirts of town, called the Calypso, looked like a small American vacation camp, with huts and open-air grills. At one stage, Kristina said, hundreds of people were staying there with no running water, and no bathroom facilities.

Around this time, Kristina opened a bar in Capurganá, in the style of Caribbean cocktail shacks, complete with rope-swing seats at the bar. The bar was popular with tourists but also with the Gujarati Indian, Ghanaian, and Cuban migrants that were flowing into Capurganá. She held a Cuban night; she held an African night. Some of the Gujarati customers complained, saying they didn't like Cuban music or African music. So she held a Gujarati night.

From her studies in human rights and her informal interviews with migrants, Kristina realized that many legitimate asylum claims were not being considered by the Colombian government or the US. She lobbied local immigration officials.

Soon after beginning her informal support work with migrants, Kristina realized the particular dangers faced by women going into the Darién. The nonprofit group Medecins Sans Frontiers opened a clinic in one of the Panamanian migrant camps in the Darién in May 2021. By early August, the group had treated eighty-eight women who had been raped in the jungle. Kristina met women who abandoned the trek after suffering sexual assaults, and she gradually discerned that the risk of such assaults were higher with certain smuggling guides than with others. One of the roles she assumed was warning women off the guides with whom they'd run the greatest risk of sexual assault.

Kristina began to welcome migrants like Ms. Mtebe into her house, out of humanitarian goodwill. Six African guests stayed for about six months. Kristina decided to convert her house into a low-cost hostel, where she would waive charges for the poorest refugees.

Kristina also acted as a custodian and a banker, filling a void in those areas in Capurganá. With the risk of robbery astronomical on the route, as Jane had already discovered, Kristina's services included safeguarding money and possessions, then sending them on to the migrants once they had reached the relative safety of Tijuana or the US. In her PayPal account, Kristina received transfers from the families of people like Ms. Mtebe, and even held the money for the migrants until they reached the US border. She also held vital documents, critical to their asylum claims.

She talked to the migrants and gathered their stories. She met Ghanaian men who had been convinced by con artists that they would be greeted in Costa Rica by a professional soccer team seeking their services.

She spoke with journalists from national Colombian newspapers who were seeking information about the *extracontinentales*. The journalists promised to protect her identity, but "American woman who owns a bar" did not qualify as anonymity in Capurganá. Soon, there was a knock on the door. The representative of one of the paramilitary groups paid Kristina a visit and told her to stop talking to people about the migrants. The message was clear: Kristina's humanitarian activities were bad for business.

At one stage, Kristina said, two bleary-eyed Irish tourists for whom she arranged a trek in the jungle were apprehended by the paramilitaries, who were convinced—due to blue headwear—that the two young men were United

Nations officials snooping on a jungle camp. (For their troubles, these young men were rewarded with the most prized of souvenirs in Ireland—a story to tell.) At other times, relations were more cordial. Kristina attended meetings the paramilitary leaders called of local business owners and community representatives to discuss issues like changes in Colombian laws that made it more difficult to provide lodging to undocumented migrants, Kristina said.

Kristina lowered her public profile but continued to have strong links with the migrants. By 2018, when we arrived, the bottleneck had unclogged somewhat. People were moving. But Kristina said there were still incidents such as intermittent attacks on migrants by the Panamanian army in the mountains nearby.

Ms. Mtebe, the Cameroonian migrant, could not believe the hospitality she encountered as soon as Kristina answered the door.

> She acted like she's met me before. She was cooking there. She gave me food to eat. Beans and plantains the first night. She encouraged me not to worry. She said I was not the first who had got lost or left behind. It happened to others and that I could continue with this journey. "You should not be discouraged," she said. "Do you want to go back to Cameroon and die? Why don't you go to Europe if you don't want to continue the journey?" She was really welcoming. She boosted my spirits . . . she told me she'd give me a room with a bed to stay as long as I want . . . I should not pay any money.

Through an American friend, Ms. Mtebe's family sent her $300. Kristina gave her some cash and held the rest for her, to be sent on when she reached Tijuana. Kristina's experience with the underground railroad gave her a unique perspective on the journey.

Ms. Mtebe had started to make efforts to resume her journey. The trauma of the first jungle crossing stayed with her, however. She visited the woman at the safe house in Capurganá, who had been so hospitable on her first day there. The woman acted like she'd never seen Ms. Mtebe before in her life. She met the Ghanaian migrants whom she had lost in the jungle. They asked her if she wanted to go back with them, for a second try.

"You're the ones that left me in the jungle," she told them. "I'm not going with anyone."

Migrants like these young men were often chosen by their families precisely because they were so physically fit, and more likely to complete the journey, said Kristina. Such groups were impossible to keep up with, and frequently left people behind (the Gujarati Indian migrants in Sapzurro had a similar experience). If Ms. Mtebe wanted to go back into the jungle, she should travel with one of the family groups that sometimes passed through, Kristina advised her.

One afternoon during the week that Ms. Mtebe stayed with Kristina, four families with young children, three from Angola and one from Congo, passed by the front door of the house. "This group is the group I have to follow," said Ms. Mtebe.

Departure

The split experiences of the escorted and independent migrants also played into how they left Capurganá for the Darién. The first option out of Capurganá is to pay guides who lead migrants straight into the roadless Darién Gap jungle. This is one of the most treacherous hikes imaginable. Authorities have smoothed the way for tourists on the first part of this hike, from Capurganá to Sapzurro and La Miel. Even on that short section—little more than a couple of hours—it was hard to gain purchase on the steep, slick path in places. No matter how much water we drank, it could not replace the sweat drawn by the humidity. Howler monkeys growled from the trees.

For a higher price, migrants can take a boat into Panamanian waters and start their hike through the jungle at a more advantageous point. That was the route that Kidane and his Eritrean friends had chosen. A smuggling boat would take them to Pito, a small settlement on the Panamanian side of the border. From Pito, the military camps where Panamanian transit papers and passage to Costa Rica were available would be a four-or-five day hike, the Eritreans had heard. That was if nobody was taken ill or injured. One of the Eritrean men told us his brother, who had gone a few months ahead of him, and was now seeking refugee status in Canada, had been stuck in the jungle for more than a week because of an injury to one of his party.

On Thursday, July 12, 2018, the power was still out in Capurganá. We happened to be passing near the hostel where the Eritreans were staying, when we saw movement. We took cover in the shadows and observed the following scene:

Roughly a dozen people jogged out of the hostel in uniform lines of four, each with their bags held over their heads. We only saw them because of the flashlight that someone, presumably the safe-house owner or an associate, was holding behind them. The group of migrants took cover by a harbor wall nearby. The holder of the flashlight began to make signals out to sea.

He also whistled a couple of times. Shortly thereafter, a fishing boat, about twenty feet long with a brightly painted rim, glided silently into the beach. The boatman also had a flashlight, with which he returned the smuggler's signals. The migrants boarded quietly, and the boat glided back out to sea, propelled by the engine on a very low, almost inaudible setting. Only when it was about five hundred yards from the shore did the engine start to blare. A second boat arrived, and the operation was repeated in a matter of seconds.

The military precision was remarkable—up to a point. One of the migrants must have been on the toilet during the operation. A smuggler came running out of the hostel and began whistling to the second boatman, who had just left the harbor wall. When that did not work, he began yelling.

The second boat slunk back into port, again without a sound. A moment later, it started chugging out to sea.

With that, Kidane and his friends were gone, spirited away into the night.

CHAPTER 6

The Darién

The Land of the Dead

Just as Deadly a Land as It Was in 1513

Even at the fringes of the Darién jungle during a dry spell, the paths are treacherous. Flat is seldom seen here. The path varies between steep sections and steeper sections. The narrow lane is constantly obstructed by thick roots, as if the trees amused themselves by sticking out a leg to trip unsuspecting hikers.

The first people we ran into on the trail between Capurganá and Sapzurro were a single file of about twenty weary-looking migrants, many carrying the *mochila* backpacks associated with *extracontinentales* and wearing ponchos and gumboots. Most of the migrants appeared to be from parts of South Asia or Africa, and we later learned they had been intercepted in the Darién and marched back to Capurganá by Colombian migration officers.

When the clay is wet, it turns slick and slippery, developing a red, shiny surface. Like chewing gum, it sticks to everything, and it instantly doubled the weight of our shoe soles. There are cobwebs dangling over the path, bringing the hiker eye-to-eye with sizable spiders. The path bristles so extensively with insects that it's like the site of one vast, recently overturned stone. The hoots of birds and the rustle and howl of monkeys give the impression that hidden jungle fauna stalk the hiker along the path. In Texas and much of the US South, any exposed piece of food will almost instantaneously be engulfed in nibbling insects; in the Darién, the same is true of the human body. In the jungle, insects of all sizes hydroplane onto the hiker's sweaty face; if everything else is doused in repellent like deet, the insects land on the sweat in the hiker's eyeballs and try to bite the pupils. Thanks to the mosquito anesthetic, it's a good idea to periodically slap exposed skin; the odds are good the hiker will splat something with each slap.

It's impossible to tell how far you've come or how far you have left to go because every eye-line is thatched by trees and vines. The humid air Saran-wraps the hiker in a layer of sweat, so that each sip of water only maintains the unquenchable thirst at a bearable level. There are no sweat patches; clothes are uniformly soaked. A mile trudging in the Darién feels like three in more hospitable country.

From the bay of Pito, the most common point of departure for the migrants we talked to, it's roughly twenty miles as the crow—or macaw—flies west to migrant camps such as Bajo Chiquito, Lajas Blancas, and La Peñita. These camps are maintained by the Panamanian military, who use the camps to process migrants and control the onward passage by river or truck to the nearby road system. From Pito, the route crosses mountains with near alpine gradient—the highest is near as tall as anything in the US east of the Mississippi; a swamp comparable to a vast pit of quicksand; and a major river; with all ground in between covered by tangled, thorny, viper- and tarantula-riddled forest. In 1972, a team of sixty-four British scientists and engineers took weeks to cross the Darién Gap—and they had access to Land Rover jeeps and boats. On foot, it's almost impossible to cover more than seven miles a day, and that's if the migrant is fortunate enough not to get lost in the labyrinth of unmarked trails. Whatever their luck, the minimum a migrant can expect to spend in the treacherous Darién is two nights.

The physical jeopardy faced by migrants through the Darién has grown in correlation to the legal jeopardy faced by the boatmen who bring them there, and to the drug kingpins who oversee the route. For years, according to one knowledgeable source in Capurganá, boatmen caught by the Panamanian police or military with migrants on board got little more than a slap on the wrist, seldom serving more than a year in jail. It was effectively a bureaucratic, boat-licensing issue. So the boatmen, who would only move drug cargo in the dead of night because of the onerous prison sentences that resulted from interception, saw the migrant business as lower risk. For years, the boatmen conducted migrant transportation more or less in broad daylight, said Kristina, the American hostel owner who worked with migrants in Capurganá. In 2016, under pressure from the US, Panamanian authorities began prosecuting the boatmen under a human-trafficking law designed to stop exploitation of children, a law that mandated ten-to-fifteen-year prison sentences. The risk calculation was flipped on its head.

"If you're caught with a ton of cocaine, you get five years," said Kristina. "Anyone caught with migrants on board gets fifteen years."

When the business was less risky, the boatmen used to take the migrants to Puerto Escocés, a boat ride of several hours from Capurganá. After the crackdown, they started dropping migrants at Puerto Obaldía or Pito, which are "a lot easier to go to," but represent much more dangerous entrance points to the jungle, said Kristina. For the migrants, that wasn't even the worst part of it.

"Before, when risks were low, smugglers would accompany groups most of the way" through the jungle, Kristina said. Now, migrants are lucky to have a guide for half of the trail. Guides routinely leave stragglers behind, abruptly disappear, or even turn on their customers.

Migrants expect to encounter cartel criminals in Mexico, and to contend with gangs, the *maras*, in Honduras. But our reporting suggests they are just as likely to be robbed or assaulted in the Darién, which is a lesser-known hub of Latin American crime networks. One reason that Kristina started to provide advice to women like Jane Mtebe were the accounts she heard in Capurganá of women returning from the jungle traumatized by sexual assaults on the trail. Many migrants meet armed smugglers, and all feel the indirect effects of the paramilitary groups' activities. Freight shipping lines often provide limited passenger service, but passengers who avail themselves of this service board the ship with the understanding that the crew's priority is the cargo. In the same way, the Colombian paramilitary groups are primarily in the cargo business. Migrants like Kidane are left waiting for days and, sometimes weeks, after paying for passage through the Darién. This may be partly based on maneuvers of Panamanian and Colombian coast guard. But our reporting suggests that the paramilitary groups' priority is keeping the drug supply chain open.

Kidane's group entered the jungle in July 2018, in the depths of the rainy season, when the risk of death is at its greatest. Yet they traveled almost entirely without the assistance of either local guides or maps. Much as nineteenth-century sailors who navigated the deadly waters of Cape Horn relied solely on the memory of a hand that had sailed the route before, Kidane's group relied on the digital grapevine of Eritrean migrants.

Once the boat glided away from the fishing dock in Capurganá, and out of our sight, Kidane's group of eleven Eritreans and three Ethiopians had a relatively smooth ride to the beach at Pito. Another group of Cameroonians landed on the beach at the same time.

The boatmen just dropped us there and left. On the beach waiting for us were three people, naked, except for short pants. At first, we were afraid of them. They had primitive guns, shotguns. At first we were trying to hide from them, hide in the trees, the jungle. It was me, I went to them and said, "What do you want?" They said, "We can guide the way . . . for $50 each." We argued with them. There were thirty-eight people, mostly us and a lot of Cameroonians.

Kidane's guides reassured the party that the guns were for hunting purposes. They led the migrant group on a narrow path, using flashlights to guide the way. It was a hilly route. Even in the darkness, they could tell that the terrain became even more mountainous ahead.

We walked on foot for three hours with these guys. They were guiding us. I don't know how they knew the way. It was very small. They had flashlights. Almost everyone was wearing gumboots. My gumboots were lost so I had to wear normal shoes. It was lost maybe in boat. We walked for three hours. Then the guys leading us told us to sleep.

It was impossible to sleep properly, Kidane said. Everything around them seemed to be alive.

The ground was wet. We were sleeping on a river bank. We were also afraid of snakes. We'd be flashing the phone light all around if we heard something. Everybody feared everything. But they were very strong. In your mind, you think to yourself: there are men and women here. You think physically this woman is weaker than the man. But she keeps going. Then it energizes you to [keep] going.

When they awoke from this fitful rest, the men with the guns were gone. From now on, the only guides Kidane and his group had were the digital and physical footprints of those who had gone before. They consulted text messages from friends and compatriots who had followed the same route, which provided vague descriptions of landmarks and turning points. Otherwise, they relied on the clothes that migrants tied to trees to mark the path.

They put everything in texts. They gave out all information. If we [lost the path and] wanted to find the way again, we looked at the texts, or the recordings they had sent. Some of them were in Mexico. Some were elsewhere along the route. They just used their memories. If one crossed, they put it on their mind . . . "when you reach this place . . ."

We were checking the texts, constantly. Even when we climbed the mountain. "At the end of the path, you get to the waterfalls. When you see the waterfalls, turn right." We knew the path from signs of people crossing. You've got many things along the path . . . clothes, trash . . . all these things can act as a guide. Even clothes, you don't just throw away. If I couldn't carry my clothes, I tied to a tree . . . put them as a sign. Other people coming after us can use [the markers] as guides. In the jungle, there aren't any road signs. It can be confusing.

You also see footprints. In front of us people might be one day, two days ahead. You can still see their footprints.

The other signs that migrants look for are human bones.

There are no solid estimates of how many people have died on the trek through the Darién jungle in the last ten years. It seems safe to assume the tally is more than one thousand. Colombian journalist Juan Arturo Gómez Tobón, who is based near the Darién region, documented a flash flood that carried away between ten and twelve Cuban migrants.[1] Kristina has advocated searches for the remains of those lost in the jungle, as mothers of disappeared migrants have searched the deserts of Mexico.

More than a dozen people interviewed about the trip for this book have described the Darién as an extended brush with death. Anyone who makes it through the roadless section of the Darién jungle—the section known as the Darién Gap—counts themselves lucky to be alive. The journeys taken by the migrants like Kidane are life-shaping in their contours. They are the kinds of experiences that grandparents tell incredulous children. Some of the migrants we interviewed were eager to talk about all their experiences. Others were more guarded. But the Darién is one of those experiences that human nature makes it difficult to bottle up.

In southern Mexico we met a group of Nepali migrants—two men and four women. They didn't want to give their names, as their handlers had warned them against talking to anyone about their trip. They didn't want to talk about anything. But it seemed none of them—and least of all one young woman who we will call Yuki—could resist talking about the Darién.

"It was an incredible experience," said Yuki. "I could not believe it. We saw snakes, we heard jaguars. We saw dead people."

One of Yuki's male companions described the shock at seeing the body of a pregnant woman.

For African migrants who have considered migrating to Europe, the Darién is understood as an American version of crossing Libya, the most treacherous part of the Africa-to-Europe journey.[2] Much like post-Qaddafi Libya, many parts of the Darién function beyond the state's control.

A History of State Failure

There are many vast areas of Latin America cut off from road and rail transportation, in Venezuela, Brazil, Guyana, and elsewhere. The unique aspect of the Darién is the longstanding tension between its status as a wilderness and its status as a thoroughfare for international traffic. Partly, this landscape is untamed because its fecund mountains are practically untamable, tangled forests and tumbling rivers presenting a formidable challenge to any engineer; partly, it's untamed because its wilderness serves a purpose to the powers that be. The natural ferocity of the Darién has been harnessed by the Panamanian state and its US ally, serving as a natural tollgate on the *camino duro*. The Darién is employed like a transitory version of the island wildernesses on the fringes of the Roman empire or the British empire's Van Diemen's Land—a natural gauntlet that migrants like Kidane are forced to run; an impenetrable forest handed over to the criminals who can do as they see fit with Indigenous locals and visitors; a place of banishment, where the map is left blank, except for a "here be paramilitaries."

The first *extracontinentale* migrant to cross the Darién was the conquistador Vasco Núñez de Balboa, a piratical character who helped establish the first permanent European settlement on the mainland of the Americas, Santa María la Antigua del Darién, on the Caribbean side of the jungle less than two decades after Christopher Columbus's arrival in the hemisphere. Hearing rumors of gold deposits, Balboa mounted an expedition into the Darién jungle in 1513. Having to fight multiple battles against interior chiefdoms, the mission lost most of the 190-strong party to fatigue and illness. Eventually, they stumbled on what he called the Mar del Sur, the body of water that Ferdinand Magellan would later rename the Pacific Ocean. In 1517, Balboa retraced his steps with an even more ambitious expedition, attempting to hike over the Darién mountains with ships broken down into components like kit cars. (Balboa's Herzog-esque heroics overshadowed the governor of the Darién, which was almost certainly a factor in the conquistador's 1519 arrest and execution.)

Since Balboa's traversal of the Darién, would-be colonizers and state forces have had little success in asserting control over the region. Prior to colonial arrival, the Darién was home to the Indigenous group Kuna. The first out-siders to arrive in the Darién in large numbers were African escapees from enslavement in Colombia's Chocó gold mines.[3] They were followed by Euro-pean settlements in the early seventeenth century consisting of military forts and mission posts along the river basins. The Kuna rebelled success-fully against the Spanish in 1725, but the colonizers responded by recruiting Indigenous people and Afro-Colombians from the adjacent Chocó region of northern Colombia to displace and, ultimately, replace the Kuna. The Span-ish, however, could not maintain control for long, eventually abandoning the region by 1783.

Since that time, the Indigenous and Black populations have cohabited the Darién, often keeping one another's settlements at arm's length. The Chocó Indigenous, consisting of Emberá and Wounaan groups, settled along the tributaries upriver whereas the Black communities (known as the Darienitas, Chocoanos, and Libres) tend to occupy towns on river confluences serving as mediators with the state and markets to the north. The Indigenous maintain what one ethnographer describes as a "retreat and controlled engagement" with the state.[4] For most Panamanians, the Darién is "out of sight, out of mind"—recognizing just the fringes of the jungle with the goal of controlling the border, reducing malaria, and regulating resource extraction.[5]

The dynamics between the Indigenous and Black populations with the central state shifted in 1968 when military commander Omar Torrijos gained control of Panama through a populist coup. As part of his nationalist pro-gram, Torrijos promoted the consolidation of Indigenous villages, reorga-nizing them around newly built schools and health clinics in the name of "development." Even as the state assailed Indigenous culture, it recognized the groups' land claims for the first time. Torrijos, who ruled until his death in 1981, struggled to exert the tight control he had over the rest of the nation in the Darién province. Hoping to capitalize on the region's lumber resources, with the help of the US, he attempted to extend the Pan-American highway through the Darién beginning in 1973. The project was halted two years later when a US court injunction raised objections over the lack of environmental and cultural impact statements.[6] Undeterred, the Panamanian state contin-ued to invest in the region in the early 1980s, recruiting Afro-Colombian locals to expand work on highway construction. The highway has never been con-nected to the South American spur that ends in Colombia—leaving a sixty-six-mile "gap"—but it did reach the remote Darién town of Yaviza in 1984, bringing with it the state's plans of large-scale development, migration of land-hungry "colono" ranchers, and widespread deforestation.[7]

Wary of the state's actions, the Indigenous groups organized politically to demand land rights, leading to the establishment of the Emberá-Drua Comarca, or autonomous zone, in 1983.[8] Along with the Darién National Park, created in 1980, the new zones formalized the buffer between the Indigenous and the state, itself marked by the Panamanian military installments near the highway now used to process migrants. The creation of the autonomous zone, and the impenetrability of the forest to visitors mean that the Emberá and Wounaan people have retained some of their pre-Columbian traditions, including dugout canoes and jagua-fruit-juice tattoos.

The state's retreat left a vacuum for guerrilla forces to fill. As Colombia's civil war raged in the 1990s, the FARC established camps in the remote Darién. In 1997, the right-wing Autodefensas Unidas de Colombia attacked the FARC, beginning a rivalry over the drug trade in the region.[9] The Clan del Golfo, the criminal group that often provides paramilitary muscle to right-wing causes, established the Darién as a regional headquarters so they could control the movement of drugs and, to a lesser extent, migrants, through the vital choke-point. Little goes up the nose of a partygoer in Manhattan that has not passed through the Darién Gap. Even after the 2016 peace agreement with the Colombian state, the FARC challenged the Clan del Golfo for control of the route and the loyalty of the local communities. Vestiges of FARC forces still occupy parts of the Darién, leaving the Indigenous groups in the crossfire between the paramilitary groups—often literally, as seen in video of Emberá people dodging bullets near the Darién in early 2020 that was posted to the Internet.[10]

The migrants we talked to are not the first to have crossed the Darién Gap on the way to the US, but they are the first to do so in such large numbers. Since the Spanish colonial era, people have recognized the isthmus as a narrow bridge between North and South America. A succession of national, industrial, and paramilitary powers have tried to control passage of goods and people through the gap. During the second half of the twentieth century, most of the smuggling in the region was narcotic rather than human. As a treacherous border zone, the Darién has always been a consideration for the shadow travel industry in the Americas, presenting both an obstacle to business and an opportunity for higher profit-margin guided packages like that undertaken by Kidane. Even South American migrants on the *camino duro* seldom braved the jungle.

It is only in recent years that *extracontinentale* migrants started crossing the Darién in large numbers. One account identifies an arrest of Chinese migrants traversing the Darién by boat in 2006.[11] In 2010, the first year the Panamanian government kept a tally of the "irregular transit of foreigners" at the

Colombian border, Chinese migrants accounted for 268 of the 559 recorded.[12] Chinese have since disappeared from the records, as migrants from South Asia, the Caribbean and Africa accounted for 99 percent of the rapidly grow-ing "irregular transiters" during the 2010s. As Cuban-US relations thawed and the "wet foot/dry foot" policy looked in jeopardy, the number of Cubans registered crossing the Darién grew exponentially from 1,154 in 2012 to almost 25,000 in 2015, before tapering off in 2017 and 2018 as Central American coun-tries sealed borders. What we're calling the digital grapevine likely contrib-uted to this rapid growth, as the early pioneers left digital footsteps that their compatriots followed. The same pattern recurred with migrants from other parts of the Global South. Only eleven Haitians were registered crossing the Darién between 2010 and 2016. By 2017, they were the largest contingent of irregular transiters, representing the vast majority of those recorded that year with 16,742. (That number was likely eclipsed in 2021 after the assassination of President Moïse plunged the nation into further turmoil. The UN's Inter-national Organization for Migration estimated that as many as 133,000 people attempted to cross the Darién in 2021, with Haitians comprising by far the largest contingent.) Other contingents who have numbered more than one thousand in Panamanian records during one of the last five years include Nepalis, Indians, Bangladeshi, Cameroonians, and Congolese. Eritreans have often numbered in the hundreds.

While the origins of the migrants vary considerably from year to year in the Panamanian records, the growth in overall numbers passing through the Darién is stark. The total number of irregular transiters was tallied at a mere 559 in 2010, the first year Panama kept these records. The total rose threefold to 1,777 in 2012 and seventeen-fold from that level to 30,055 in 2016. Border closures and "deterrence" policies caused a sharp decline early in 2017 and 2018, but the total number of migrants rebounded to 22,102 in 2019. After another dip during the pandemic, the numbers of irregular migrants docu-mented crossing the Darién have returned to all-time highs. In the first four months of 2022, Panama documented 19,092 such migrants, which would be an annual rate of 50,726. That would be equivalent to the entire population of the Darién province of Panama, estimated at 51,000 in 2010.[13] Roughly one third of the 2022 total are from Venezuela. While the number of Haitians is down slightly from prior years, the Panamanian authorities registered 1,355 Senegalese migrants and 934 from Angola.

Surely this surge in migrant traffic through the Darién—swelling the pop-ulation in transformative ways—would prompt the state to re-engage with the area? Quite the opposite. Instead, the authorities have used the autonomous zone and its paramilitary-controlled fringes as a pretext for abandoning migrants. Here, nature is used as a scapegoat for migrant deaths and serves as a low-cost border control. The state has tacitly handed off migrant welfare in this treacherous environment to smugglers and can deflect blame for their brutal treatment. But, as scholars have noted of other migrant "corridors of death," from the Mediterranean sea to the Sonoran desert, the Darién experience is part of a purposeful state agenda.[14]

One telling comparison is the US decision to funnel migrants away from urban border crossings toward the fatal conditions of the Sonoran desert, known as Prevention through Deterrence (PTD). The anthropologist Jason de León interprets PTD as an example of Achille Mbembe's theory of necropolitics, or the state's ability to dictate who should live and die in the name of sovereignty.[15] A necropolitics framework cuts through the doublespeak of hollow justifications (such as "guarding the homeland" or "migrant protection"), and deflections of responsibility (fatalities as an "unintended consequence"), to reframe policy as political violence, foregrounding the human decisions that force migrants into deadly landscapes. As De León writes,

> The terrible things that this mass of migrating people experience en route are neither random nor senseless, but rather part of a strategic federal plan . . . a killing machine that simultaneously uses and hides behind the viciousness of the Sonoran Desert . . . . The goal is to render invisible the innumerable consequences this sociopolitical phenomenon has for the lives and bodies of undocumented people.[16]

In the case of the Darién, the impact of Panama's US-influenced *flujo controlado*, or "controlled flow," policy has made crossing the Darién not only inevitable, but difficult and dangerous. In what De León calls necroviolence, the state's reach extends beyond the moment of death to use corpses as a message to the living.[17] The corpses in the jungle serve a dual purpose: as a Dantean deterrent to the migrants ("abandon all hope . . ."), and as a deterrent to the families back home, who will never see the bodies of those they had helped to send out. Worse, families must go through months of wondering whether their loved ones perished in Panama or are languishing in detention in Central America, in Mexico or the US, incommunicado.

The migrants we interviewed said the message was clear: enter at your own risk, because search and rescue is not a thing in the Darién. Migrants often encountered Panamanian forces in the jungle. But, until they reached the military camps, they were treated as criminals. The migrants were dead to the soldiers in the jungle, sometimes literally. The actions of the Panamanian border forces sometimes saved migrants' lives, but, generally, that was an unintended consequence of a deportation effort. When they do send out an SOS, migrants appeal to the Indigenous residents of the area, not to the troops. However, due to increasing criminalization of smuggling, most locals prefer to stay distant from migrants.

Coping with the absent state, mercurial smugglers, and distant locals, migrants experience a cooperative spirit rarely witnessed along the journey. Migrant connections in the Darién go beyond the use of technology and the digital grapevine. The idea of a "mobile commons" suggests people on the move reciprocate more than just information. They also share care, survival "tricks," services, and expressions of solidarity.[18] Kidane's group figuratively—and literally—stretched out hands to help others. Unlike in the industry and state-controlled sections of the route, which tend to segregate migrants along national or ethnic lines, the Darién is a place where migrant solidarity goes beyond national identities.

Walking among the Dead

Kristina, the hostel owner, once hiked part of one smugglers' route through the jungle with a local man, who we will call Sapo. The two often hiked together, going into the forest with nothing but hammocks and machetes.

"He's one of those old jungle guys that knows every inch of the Darién," said Kristina.

One day, the two smoked a joint together, and, without really planning to do so, started to follow the migrant path.

Sapo knew which trees to check for fruit, and when the fruit was ripe. Most importantly, he knew the dangerous snakes, insects, critters, and plants that lurked in the trees, and the thousand different ways they could injure a person. It had taken Sapo decades to learn the language of the Darién.

Even guided by the sure hand of Sapo, Kristina found the experience terrifying. "It's an extraordinarily difficult journey . . . the walk itself is very difficult, with steep climbs," said Kristina. Measured by "prominence," the mountains in this region are as tall and steep as the Swiss Alps, with many rising more than three thousand feet from the sea-level fringes. One peak on the route is known as the *montaña de muerto*—mountain of the dead. And with good reason. The main thing that struck Kristina about the route were the bones: "there were a lot of bones, a lot of carcasses."

Kidane is an unflappable man. Even sitting on the dock in Capurganá, waiting for a boat ride much like the one that almost drowned him, he emanated ease. He might have been sitting in his kitchen on a quiet evening, rather on a dock in a foreign land, waiting to risk his life. It seems that adversity is to Kidane what water is to a duck's back.

He and the other Eritreans in his group were still joking as they hiked into the unknown with nothing but digital word-of-mouth. One man kept taking off ahead of the group, and so he was given the nickname of Kenenisa after a famous Ethiopian long-distance runner, Kenenisa Bekele.

Even for Kidane and Kenenisa, however, the *montaña de muerto* was almost too much. "There are mountains in Eritrea, but not like this," said Kidane.

The vegetation was so thick and the path so steep that the ascent felt more like climbing a mile-high tree than hill-walking. The tree trunks and brambles blotted out the sky above, Kidane said. The only solid footing was on the tangled roots. To maintain balance on the extreme gradient, they had to climb hand-over-hand on the vines and tree limbs, using the forest around them as a kind of ladder. Kidane compared climbing in such humid conditions to treading water. With no visual aids available to assess progress, it felt like they were hoisting themselves up by the same branches over and over again, fighting with every sinew in the body to stay in place. The twigs and thorns tried to catch them from behind while the heavier limbs pushed down on them from above so that it felt like they were dragging themselves through an endless scrum.

Falling was never more than a snap or a slip away. Every time they grabbed a branch, they counted on it to take their weight and hold its shape. As often as not, a branch would snap, a vine would come loose, or a patch of slick clay appeared underfoot. Everyone fell at some point. And the only place to fall was onto the person behind you. Kidane, who was taking up the rear of the group, kept imagining a scenario where Kenenisa or someone else near the front would take such a tumble that they took the whole domino chain of climbers down with them like a human avalanche.

The *montaña de muerto* was not the only place Kristina saw human remains. The valleys and ravines of the Darién are crisscrossed by rivers the color of thick gravy. They are dangerous enough when you can see them coming. Kristina also saw bones in a gully, a dry riverbed. The way Kristina described it, this riverbed had the contours of a storm drain. Even on this dry day, Kristina said she felt uncomfortable, having seen how flash flooding could occur. The sides of the riverbank were so high that she knew it would be futile to try to get out of the torrent's way.

"I thought, 'if there was a flash flood here, everyone here is dead, there is absolutely no way to survive it,'" said Kristina.

It was in one of these riverbeds, shortly after particularly heavy rains, that locals discovered a dozen drowned migrants in 2018, according to interviews conducted by Colombian journalist Tobón.

"It's a dynamic place, one of the most inhospitable in the world," said Tobón, when we talked to him. "The rivers crest fast and, if you don't know them, you can easily be washed away."

It wasn't just the human remains that shocked and touched Kristina. She also found a trail of personal belongings, similar to the one that Kidane used as a trail marker.

Overpacking is not generally a problem along the *camino duro*. While visiting migrants in camps and hostels around Capurganá, Kristina sometimes had to talk people out of entering the forest with wheeled luggage or open-toed shoes. But very few migrants carried more than a backpack into the Darién. Still, the detritus Sapo and Kristina saw suggested that no traveler could pack light enough to cope with the weight of the Darién experience.

At the start of the trail, the items were castoffs you might expect—clothes and cookware. Further along, Kristina said, migrants had dropped children's toys, family albums, and wedding pictures along the route. To Kristina, the changes mapped out the spiraling fears of the migrants, their descent into desperation.

Kidane witnessed a similar desperation in two Ghanaian women who joined his party. In the Darwinian world of the Darién, where all loyalties are tested and where most groups disband somewhere along the way, the Eritreans refused to leave anyone behind. The two Ghanaian women struggled to keep up the pace set by Kenenisa. But the young Eritreans did all they could to keep the two women with the group.

[They] were totally exhausted. They couldn't carry their bags. We helped. In Eritrea, when people come, we help them. We didn't know the Ghanaian people but we helped them. Finally they couldn't go on. They threw the bags away. They couldn't carry, couldn't tolerate them any further . . . we were moving very fast because we expected that we had to cover a long distance.

The Nightmare: Lost among the Dead

The most disorienting part of the Darién journey for many of the migrants is the behavior of the guides. Like forest sprites, the *coyotes* appear and disappear unpredictably, abandoning their groups without any hint of the way forward or the way back. In Capurganá, Kristina saw it as her duty to warn migrants that smugglers' promises of an easy trail were empty (she also tried to direct migrants toward the smugglers with a humane reputation, and away from those she suspected of rape and extortion.)

Without Kristina's support, migrants set off on one of the deadliest treks on the face of the planet under the false impression that they were embarking on a guided tour.

"This was a nightmare," said Amiri Tumwine, a thirty-two-year-old Ugandan man we met in Tapachula, Mexico, referring to his week in the jungle.

In the Global North, the word "nightmare" is often invoked to describe experiences like a long day home-schooling or a particularly bad traffic jam. Mr. Tumwine's experience sounded much closer to the experience of night terrors. He described fumbling around in the darkness of an infinite maze, with death stalking every step. As in a nightmare, Mr. Tumwine's slog through the Darién had a quotidian rhythm, violently interrupted by terrifying sights and sounds. As in a nightmare, these shocks could set off a staccato, panicky rush through the woods.

The most nightmarish quality of this world, one that jibes with Dante and Homer's vision of the underworld, is the proximity of other people, living and dead. While the forest, even at the fringes, feels like an empty wilderness, most of the trails are now heavily trafficked. It's not just the remains and the detritus; migrants often hear or see other groups, or what might be other groups. Faces or voices can appear from the void at any moment. Like ghosts, these people cannot be approached. Smugglers do not allow groups to mingle. Even guides in the conventional travel industry are protective of their services, policing groups to make sure nobody is getting a free tour. In the Darién, the stakes are much higher, and the policing more brutal, with guides often carrying rifles. Add in the fact that migrants are often traveling at night, surrounded by monkeys and other tree-shaking animals, and the sense of a nightmare is complete.

Mr. Tumwine encountered dozens of people outside of his own group. But each was in their own personal hell. Mr. Tumwine's group met with one man who was selling passage through a limited area by horse. He would only help those who paid for the horse. He refused to answer questions to the rest of the group. For the guides that take parties from one end of the jungle to the other, exclusion is even more critical.

Even an infectiously sociable man like Mr. Tumwine could not find a way to bridge the gaps between the groups.

A fit young man, Mr. Tumwine tried to help others in his group who were less prepared for the ordeal. One man demanded that he be left to die. Mr. Tumwine said the man even posted a Facebook farewell to the world. Mr. Tumwine stayed with the unfortunate man long enough to see him and other vulnerable members of the group picked up by Panamanian border forces. Our reporting suggests that such humanitarian acts by state forces were the exception rather than the rule. If the security forces do go out of their way to rescue a migrant on the jungle trail, the migrants were summarily deported rather than taken back to the military camps. Only those who make it on their own power are accepted in the camps. This discourages the migrants from seeking assistance from the authorities, except as a last resort.

Late one evening, Mr. Tumwine lost the group he was following. He had to follow footprints, which was almost impossible. The light was failing and it was hard to tell the fresh prints from older ones.

"I got lost for almost six hours in the jungle in the middle of the night," said Mr. Tumwine. "I sat down and said 'God, please send an animal to kill me . . . let a person kill me.'"

Mr. Tumwine cited the Ugandan tradition of warmth and positivity by saying, "if you go to Kampala, you will have a friend before you leave the airport." Even by these standards, Mr. Tumwine is an exceedingly warm and positive person. For twenty minutes, the Darién Gap had reduced him to a suicidal state.

"I had no food, no nothing," Mr. Tumwine said.

Mr. Tumwine said his life was saved in a fashion that recalls a Grimm Brothers fairytale. He found some crackers on the ground. Before he did anything else, he sat to devour as much of them as he could. Then he went to find the source of them. He encountered a group of Cubans. Migrants from some countries, particularly those with terrain comparable to the Darién, such as Cuba and Haiti, sometimes take on the hike without assistance from guides. There are also reports that Cubans and others in the area have become guides themselves and set up safe houses along the route.

That appeared to be the case with the Cubans. One of them was armed with a hunting rifle. He pointed it at Mr. Tumwine.

"I'm with them," said Mr. Tumwine, who thought he recognized people sitting with the Cubans. "I paid to go with another group."

"We cannot take you nowhere," said the Cuban man with the gun.

Mr. Tumwine went to look for his party. He stumbled upon a broader path, where he met a group of Haitians.

The Haitian families Mr. Tumwine encountered reminded him of the hardest working families he knew in Uganda. Like these families, the Haitian groups often cover large distances and forbidding terrain with children in tow. The men and women frequently look after the children while carrying large bags on their heads. Months later, Mr. Tumwine still marveled at the endurance of the Haitian groups he met.

"They're very strong," said Mr. Tumwine. "Can you imagine going into the jungle with a bag on your head?"

At another point on the road, a man was collecting tolls. Mr. Tumwine said he didn't need a guide for this section and refused to pay the $2. To pass this point, the man said, everyone had to pay.

Mr. Tumwine met an Indian man slumped on the ground, drinking rainwater that he'd captured in the cup.

"Please don't leave me," the man said.

"What can I do for you?" Mr. Tumwine asked. Mr. Tumwine took a lump of sugar from his bag and added it to the man's rainwater. The sugar seemed to give the man the energy to clamber to his feet.

Mr. Tumwine followed increasingly wide paths to a rough roadway that led to a clearing and a military camp. There was even a small store where he could buy a bottle of water. He sat outside with some other migrants, all sharing badly needed hydration and all feeling the visceral relief that courses through a person's nerve endings after a narrow escape from death.

But his nightmare wasn't over yet. A man approached the group outside the store. He pointed a gun at Mr. Tumwine and robbed him of all his money.

Recurring Nightmare: Going Back to Square One

The first time Jane Mtebe entered the Darién, before she met Kristina, she was still with her Cameroonian group. Recounting the journey, Ms. Mtebe had a shudder in her voice because the experience still haunted her. The sojourn in the Capurganá safe house was her chance to catch her breath, to screw up the courage for the next leg after the rough boat ride and the clamber through the mangroves. The respite was cut short. The knock on the door came that night, twelve hours after she had gotten to town. She was still exhausted. The smugglers put her group on a boat with two young Bangladeshi men and two Ghanaians for the ride to the Panamanian coast.

As soon as they disembarked, Ms. Mtebe was in trouble. She was not in good physical shape, and immediately fell behind the group. Initially, she thought they'd left her alone in the dark. But the two Ghanaian men came back for her. They warned her she wouldn't survive if she hiked alone. In that case, Ms. Mtebe said, the group should slow its pace so she could keep up. That didn't suit the Ghanaians. They wanted to work a system where she would trail the larger group and they would run back regularly to check on her.

"I refused. I said 'how can I stay here in a dark place and an animal could come and eat me?'" said Ms. Mtebe.

After some argument, the Ghanaians washed their hands of the situation. It would be up to Ms. Mtebe to keep up, they said. As Mr. Tumwine, the Ugandan, and others, explained to us, the urge for self-preservation in the Darién can lead to the kinds of callous acts a person would never consider outside of that setting. Like Mr. Tumwine, Ms. Mtebe—who had some experience with rain-forest terrain in Cameroon—followed her party's footprints. Then she came to a fork in the path.

"There were three roads, [but] all of the routes had footsteps," she said. "So I sat down and started crying."

One of the Ghanians was holding her bag. She didn't call out because the Ghanians were supposed to be calling for her. She sat at the fork in the path and cried and prayed herself to sleep.

Ms. Mtebe had an electric flashlight. She awoke to noises in the bush next to her. She shone the flashlight in the direction of the noise and was startled to see two "red eyes" right next to her. She thought it might be a bird, but she wasn't taking any chances. She ran for it and heard the creature shaking the trees behind her.

"I can never forget that," Ms. Mtebe said.

The path she took led to a hill. On the slope ahead, with the help of her flashlight, she saw some of the clothes that Kidane had described, the ones the migrants tie to trees and mangroves to mark the way for those that follow. She soon lost the trail of clothes, however, and realized she was completely lost. Fortunately, her experience in Cameroon taught her a protocol for this situation. She decided to look for a water source and follow it wherever it led. In this way, she would either reach the seafront, where it would be easier to navigate, or a village, she believed. Following riverbanks is a common practice, but also a treacherous one, as Kristina had found when retracing migrants' steps.

The only thing more dangerous than traversing the Darién jungle is traversing the Darién in the rainy season when the rivers are raging. Another Cameroonian woman told us that an Eritrean man in her group would swim a little downstream as a precaution, using his arms as a net to catch anyone in danger of being washed away.

Ms. Mtebe soon located a stream and hiked along the bank, clambering over stones and around trees, when necessary. While following the stream, Ms. Mtebe stumbled upon her group.

"I saw a group of people sleeping," Ms. Mtebe said. "I pointed a torch and I looked . . . it was my group. They said they came and looked for me and, when they didn't see me, they thought I was with a different group. I had taken a different route from them."

When they awoke, a second smuggler-guide relieved the first team. This man offered to take Ms. Mtebe's bag from the Cameroonian man who was carrying it. Then he demanded an extra $100-per-person fee.

"Everybody was like, 'how can we give you the $100? We paid the man in Turbo . . . that was supposed to take us out of the jungle.' He was like, 'give me $100, or if not, I'm leaving you here.' So we paid him another $100."

This kind of extortion happens on every leg of the journey, but it's particularly rampant in the Darién where guides have the upper hand in a mostly stateless landscape.

The new guide walked with the group for an hour. At that point, he stopped and told them to shelter in place while he went ahead. Soon, the group's suspicions grew that the man had simply conned them.

"The boys were like if we stay something would happen, we should go, we should find our way on our own," said Ms. Mtebe.

The group hiked down to the coast. In theory, it made sense: as long as they hugged the coast and headed north, they were assured of reaching Panama. In practice, it's a roughly one-hundred-mile hike through the grasping mangroves, along the crenulated coastline to Puerto de Carti, the nearest point on the coast with any sort of road connection to Panama City. Even the rare tourist motorboats that go from Capurgána to Carti take the best part of a day to get there under full speed. It's a painful truth that groups who survive must accept: the only realistic chance to get out of the jungle and the mountains was to go deeper into the jungle and higher up the mountains. The only way to the Panamanian road network was west and not north.

Ms. Mtebe lost her group once again. This time, she fell into the company of a Venezuelan man who she'd met on the way to Capurganá (he had carried her bag, for a fee, during their slog through the swamps at the edge of town). Without any means to pay guides, the Venezuelan man had hiked into the jungle alone, hoping to find his own way.

Now, both were hopelessly lost. They were fortunate to run into a Panamanian military detachment. The troops took them to the jailhouse near the border with Colombia, where it began to dawn on her how circuitous her route had been.

It turned out that Ms. Mtebe's first grueling trek through the Darién was an almost perfect circle. When she was picked up by the Panamanian military, she was almost in sight of Capurganá, much closer to the little Colombian town than she'd been two nights earlier when the boat deposited her on the beach.

Ms. Mtebe's experience is cruelly common, particularly for female and vulnerable travelers. As previously observed, the Gujarati trio we met in Sapzurro had spent nearly three weeks walking through the jungle only to end up several hours north of where they started in Capurganá. They were distraught. We begged them to return to Capurganá where we could help them regroup. But they would not hear of it. They could not bring themselves to go back to square one. They turned around and went straight back into the jungle. How far they made it, we will never know. It's hard to fight the suspicion that they were not finished moving in nightmarish circles.

Kristina had seen this many times before: migrants returning to Capurganá, looking as dazed as a mortal after a tour of the underworld. She recognized Ms. Mtebe's situation from the expression on her face. It's not hard to imagine the torment that Ms. Mtebe and the Gujarati trio were feeling.

Anyone who has become lost on a wilderness trail will appreciate that feeling. There's the initial stroke of terror when you look around and realize that you are not going where you intended to go. That terror must be suppressed before it sends you rushing around in panicked circles. Then comes the creeping hope as you try to navigate your way back to your appointed route. Some promising sign will have you rejoicing, almost erasing the suppressed terror altogether. And then you will see it—Square One, the very point where you realized you were lost in the first place. An hour is gone, and all your terror, hope, and navigation was for naught. You have to start all over again.

Now imagine the wrong turn lasted two days. Imagine the wilderness was squirming with snakes and pitted with quicksand. Imagine there were people waiting in the wilderness with guns to take whatever you had left after they took everything the first time.

That's how Ms. Mtebe felt when she arrived at Kristina's hostel.

In desperate circumstances, a human being needs to know that someone else has been in their shoes and came out the other side. Perhaps because of all the adventures and traumas that she has survived, Kristina has a manner of calm authority. When she recommends you not do something, like trying to visit a paramilitary camp, she makes the thing sound impossible. When she recommends you do something, she makes failure to do it sound impossible.

As we noted before, Ms. Mtebe was utterly despondent when she met Kristina. Kristina convinced her that she was capable of a successful trip through the Darién. She advised Ms. Mtebe to avoid groups with young men in them. Young men frequently abandoned women and children that stymied their progress.

A week into her stay, a group of four families, three from Angola and one from Congo, came to Kristina's front door. There were nine children, some as young as two years old, in the party, and about ten adults. One of the women was seven months pregnant.

After some days of counsel with Kristina, Ms. Mtebe knew what she would do. Rather than a group of fit young men, led by a fast guide, she would go with a group of other vulnerable people with a more patient guide.

Kristina said the choice of guide, something migrants told us they hardly thought about, made all the difference. Some guides were notorious for abandoning their charges and others for robbing and raping. Kristina knew some of the more scrupulous middlemen, including a Cuban man, who Ms. Mtebe said acted as a liaison finding her group reliable guides and boatmen. This Cuban man spoke to us by WhatsApp message and was very friendly.

He strenuously denied that he had ever worked in the smuggling industry. Ms. Mtebe said she paid him $100 for the agency service. This Cuban man has remained in Central America, and in late 2020, nearly two years after he helped Ms. Mtebe, he told us he was near the border of Costa Rica and Nicaragua. He put his extended stay in Central America down to bad luck with visas, and said he worked in the service industry to make ends meet.

The Cuban man's evident distaste at association with the smuggling business was not just secrecy. All the *coyotes* we interviewed rationalized their work differently. Mr. Guerrero, the Venezuelan man who drove the Punjabi group from Quito to Colombia, was eager to see his name in print. It was our decision to protect his identity rather than his request. We can only conclude that he did not recognize anything morally—or even legally—wrong with the job he did driving the migrants. Another man we met further down the *camino* seemed to recognize the illicit nature of the work. But he behaved in the excitable fashion of a small-time drug dealer, lacking any of the discretion of the career criminal. From what we could tell, the Cuban man seemed to think that whatever he did in Capurganá, he did to survive, and not as a business.

On Ms. Mtebe's second trip to the jungle, the pace was, perforce, very slow. She walked alongside the pregnant woman. Nobody was left behind. The trip was pleasant, she said. The resourceful group even "had pots to cook with," she recalled, and prepared tasty meals.

But the travails through the jungle had taken their toll on Ms. Mtebe's body. Chafing between her toes that dated back to her arrival in Capurganá had developed into an abscess. Now, after eight days hiking with the African families in the jungle, the pain of the abscess was unbearable, and the infection began to spread, causing her foot to swell. Ms. Mtebe may have developed "trench foot," the fungal infections that afflicted World War I soldiers whose feet were incessantly drenched.

The group decided Ms. Mtebe could go no further. Two of the men went ahead to look for a village.

The Indigenous Emberá and Wounaan have a complex relationship with the migrants, and with border authorities. They provide some boat transportation and other services, but generally keep their distance. In a pinch, however, migrants frequently seek out their assistance.

Waiting for the two men who had gone ahead for assistance, Ms. Mtebe's group ran out of food. The children were crying from the hunger. What if the men became lost, as Ms. Mtebe knew from her own experience, was so easily done? What if one of them was taken ill himself? If the group tried to move now, the rescue party might not be able to find them.

As it turned out, one of the men *was* incapacitated, so exhausted that he required medical attention. But he made it as far as the Emberá village, where the other man stayed with him.

Fortunately, the two men were able to provide accurate directions to the Emberá villagers for the clearing where they had left Ms. Mtebe and the rest of the group. Two villagers, a father and a young son, located the group, bringing them bread, milk, and other supplies.

Ms. Mtebe limped as far as the villagers' canoe. It was a different design to the boats she was used to in Africa. Emberá use hollowed-out slender hardwood trees to make durable twenty-five-foot long crafts.

The Indigenous Panamanians cut the boot off Ms. Mtebe's leg, which had swollen to three times its usual size. They used herbal cures, rubbing the leg with crushed leaves. The military oversaw the settlement, and Ms. Mtebe said the local commander was shocked when he saw her leg.

"Why didn't you take care of this foot earlier?" he said

A policeman helped her to the local doctor, who, with the help of the policeman, squeezed the puss out of the abscess. The doctor discharged her with medication, and instructions to return if the swelling recurred.

The swelling recurred the very next day. So Ms. Mtebe went back to the doctor's office, only to be told that he was not working that day. She later found him drinking outside the local store. He was apologetic and, the following day, fixed the dressing on her foot. It slowly healed. Ms. Mtebe and the others in the group paid $3 a day per person to stay in the villagers' houses, a slightly different arrangement to the military-run camps.

A Brush with Death

When they awoke after the second night in the jungle, Kidane's group discovered they had lost phone coverage. They could no longer look for tips from the compatriots who had gone before. When they encountered areas that did not correspond to the recordings and text messages, they were truly flying blind.

Consulting the texts and following the shirts and towels left hanging on trees, they pressed on, moving as quickly as they could. The texts had promised that they would run into guides along the way. But, for most of that day, the group did not see anyone.

They stopped briefly at the rivers and streams to drink and splash water on their faces. Kenenisa never stopped for long. He had already crossed one shallow river when he cried out in pain.

Kenenisa stood on a large grey snake, likely a fer de lance or Bothrops asper, which bit him in the leg, just above the ankle. The Bothrops asper is the deadliest reptile killer in Panama, where incidence of snakebite is among the most prevalent in the Americas. There are fifty-five snakebites referred to health centers in Panama per 100,000 people a year, according to one epidemiological study, almost ten times the Americas-wide average of 6.1 per 100,000, and more than twice the rate of the second-most afflicted nation, Guyana.[19] Kenenisa was one of the few hikers who, like Kidane, lacked the gumboots that would protect against a snake bite. Two of the Cameroonian men, familiar with exotic animals, chased the snake with sticks and their machetes. But the snake got away before they could catch up with it. Kenenisa was using a bit of rope as a belt.

He actually removed the rope, and tied it on his leg. He automatically cut the place where the snake bite was, trying to remove the poison. The Cameroonians, in their culture, they have one thing when you cut someone . . . a liquid antidote. They told us that would help. He wanted to cut the poison out with a razorblade.

Kenenisa asked Kidane to do the cutting. Kidane couldn't bring himself to do it. So they just tightened the tourniquet until nearly all the blood was cut off to his foot. The leg swelled like a balloon and turned a funny color.

Kenenisa could hardly walk in this condition, even with assistance from Kidane and others. Fortunately, a few minutes later, they saw some Indigenous Panamanians with some canoes nearby. The canoe was a hollowed-out log about twenty-five-feet long with a pointed tip fitted with an outboard motor. Representatives of the group rushed to seek their assistance. After some negotiation, the Panamanians agreed to take them by canoe to the village.

We told them, "This guy was bitten by snake . . . we must go very fast. We can give you the money."
He couldn't tolerate his pain. Blood cannot pass the tourniquet. If we untied the rope, he could die. After three hours by boat, we reached a military camp.

The soldiers sent traditional doctors, who gave Kenenisa herbal remedies. While the remedies didn't seem to be much help, the doctors were able to examine Kenenisa and inform him that he had been bitten.

Kidane and Kenenisa were lucky. Another group in the Panamanian camp, an Indian party, showed Kidane a smart-phone video. It captured the moment that the group, while hiking along a riverbed, was hit by a flash flood. On the video, the group watched, helplessly, as one of their party, a young woman, was carried away by the torrent to her death.

Although the camps provide a brief respite from the physical threats of the jungle, they also mark the re-entry into the surveillance and management conditions administered by state authorities. In the subsequent travel from the northern tip of the Darién to Guatemala's border with Mexico, migration policy and practices of each Central American state shift according to geopolitical winds, often dictated by US overreach.

CHAPTER 7

Central America

Controlled Flow

Recovering from the Nightmare in the Panama Camps

After his athletic friend Kenenisa was evacuated for snakebite treatment, Kidane and the rest of his friends stayed for a few days in a military camp. It's one of several camps maintained by the Panamanian army near the jungle towns of Metetí and Yaviza, where the road to Panama City begins.

The relationship between locals in the Darién and the military national border service, SENAFRONT (SErvicio NAcional de FRONTeras), is an uneasy one. According to the anthropologist Nanneke Winters, SENAFRONT occupies every corner of Metetí from the health post to churches, restaurants, and shops. Organized as an anti-drug operation, SENAFRONT is also charged with stopping migrant smuggling, an activity often conflated with locals offering any kind of support to migrants. As a result, some are afraid to offer help.[1]

Like the US border patrol, SENAFRONT also takes on humanitarian needs when migrants enter the country with health risks. At worse, they collect corpses from the jungle. Although the Panamanian government has provided funding to build additional migrant shelters, Winters notes that construction has been abandoned due to protests from residents demanding their own needs to be met first.

La Peñita shelter, one hour south of Metetí, is where migrants are counted, checked, and vaccinated. At times over the past half-decade, there have been more migrants than local residents around La Peñita. During the 2020 pandemic, at least 2,500 migrants were trapped in the camps. The vast majority were kept in La Peñita; about ninety, who had tested positive for COVID were quarantined in nearby Lajas Blancas for roughly fifty days.[2] These camps have makeshift huts for sleeping and large huts for communal meals. During some periods, the military provided food for all residents; during others, the migrants were given cooking facilities but had to provide their own food. At another shelter, Bajo Chiquito, in lieu of a state-sponsored shelter, locals rent out houses to migrants, while retreating to farms downriver.[3]

Kidane experienced the Panamanian camp as something of a respite after the ordeals of the jungle, finding the beds relatively comfortable and the food palatable. Others experienced the camp as a kind of prison. Amiri Tumwine, the Ugandan man who was robbed on the fringes of the settlement, received a cold welcome that set the tone for his experience of the camp.

"I saw one of the guys who stole our money. I saw him changing the money. I said, 'I know you . . . you stole my money.' He said, 'I don't know you. . . .' He kept the stuff," recalled Mr. Tumwine.

Mr. Tumwine believed the man was attached to the Panamanian military. How else would he be allowed to arm himself in the jungle, Mr. Tumwine wondered.

The way Kidane, Mr. Tumwine, and others describe the Panamanian camp, life there is reminiscent of *M*A*S*H* at best and *Bridge Over the River Kwai* at worst.

Mr. Tumwine hated the Panamanian camp. In his opinion, the guards showed bias in favor of Cuban migrants, with whom they had more in common than they had with migrants from non-Spanish-speaking parts of the world. The Cubans, in Mr. Tumwine's experience, often received seconds of the food, while leaving other migrants with short rations that did not fill the void.

> They give you food, but it's not enough. If you were sick, you would die. If you were sick, they say "we're not here to help you, we're not here to treat you. We're just here to protect our country." We're not here for you guys.

Mr. Tumwine's experience was echoed by that of migrants interviewed by Reuters in the summer of 2020 at the Lajas Blancas camp, where they were quarantined for months after some of them had tested positive for COVID-19. More than one of them told the Reuters reporter that shoddy food had given them diarrhea. Throughout the COVID-19 pandemic in 2020, about two thousand migrants were trapped in the Panamanian camps, according to the UN High Commissioner for Refugees. The camps are essentially steamy waiting rooms. The migrants have little to do but swat away the biting flies as they anticipate the order to move on, which could come at any time.

There is no good reason from the Panamanian perspective to hold the migrants in these camps for weeks at a time, as happened in the case of Mr. Tumwine. The Panamanian approach to migrants is, essentially, an outsourcing of American border policy—another hurdle to slow the flow of people reaching the US border. Not only are the Panamanian authorities turning a blind eye to the death toll in the jungle, they use the treacherous terrain and forbidding camps as an extension of the US policy of "deterrence."

Migration policy for Central American nations is part of the diplomatic *paso doble* all must dance with the United States. Unlike Mexico, which maintains a complex love-hate relationship with "Gringolandia," smaller Central American states tend to swing between explicitly pro- and anti-American governments. Some US allies, like Costa Rica, have established humanitarian migrant policies while keeping the interests of their key allies in mind. Others are more prepared to do American dirty work, in exchange for economic rewards.

Since the Panama Canal's construction in 1903, and especially since the 1989 ouster of Noriega, US policy has had an outsized effect on Panamanian politics. However, the Trump administration's crackdown on immigration added a new layer to the US-Panamanian agreement. A PhD student in anthropology, Caitlyn Yates, has followed the extracontinental trail for years, and is among the few scholars who has visited the military camps in Panama. In Yates's research, a key turn in Panamanian policy came with the US training of SENAFRONT officers and the $8 million (an 800 percent increase from the previous year) in funding and equipment in 2018. In exchange, the Panamanian forces collect biometric data on migrants and submit it to the BIT-MAP (Biometric Identification Transnational Migration Alert Program) system established in 2018. This information sharing provides, as Yates argues, an "invisible form of border security outsourcing, targeted primarily at the extra-continental migrant population."[4]

To trek the length of the *camino duro* has always been to pass through the eye of the needle. Under pressure from the US, Panamanian authorities carefully—and often brutally—titrate the width of that eye.

In 2016, two years into President Varela's tenure, there was a spike in the number of Cubans passing northward through Panama, as they rushed to preempt the end of the US "wet foot, dry foot" policy. The closure of the Nicaragua-Costa Rica border, justified in part to stem Cuban northward movement, led to an overnight "crisis" in immobile migrants, especially Cubans. Officials from the Obama administration convened meetings with senior delegations from Ecuador, Colombia, and Panama, aimed at slowing the Cuban rush.

Varela's response to the Cuban influx was the policy of *flujo controlado*. Panama would process migrants in the camps, taking a sort of running census of the number in transit at any given moment. It was as if the nation were a giant train station, with a conductor clipping tickets at the gate until the latest train grew full. Migrants would be released from the jungle camps and hastened to Costa Rica, with no more than one hundred leaving per day. The policy may have been reasonable, if the enforcement were not so harsh and inhumane. *Flujo controlado* was one of those migration-policy euphemisms that could cover a range of sins. The Panamanian military periodically sealed the border with Colombia, enforcing the action with live fire, according to Kristina, the hostel-owner, who said she heard the shots in the jungle hills above the Colombian town and met migrants who told her they were fleeing the gunfire.

When the Trump administration took power in 2017 and demanded more action from allies on migration, such incidents became more common, according to Kristina. The migrants we talked to, additionally, almost always described rough treatment at the hands of the Panamanian military.

Under the *flujo controlado* policy, Kidane stayed about five days in the Panamanian camp, as migrants were bussed out in groups.

> We saw officers, gave them our fingerprints. They took our photo. They gave us our papers, and told us to pay them some dollars for transportation. They sent us by bus to Costa Rica. We got to the border of Costa Rica at seven or eight evening time. They made us sleep at one place near the border in a shelter.

The bus is subsidized, with migrants paying about $40 for an express bus through Panama to the Costa Rican border at Los Planes de Gualaca.

The Panamanian authorities also tried to control the Colombian border under *flujo controlado*. Traditionally, the transportation of migrants was treated as a minor infraction. The boatmen and jungle guides who ferried people to landing spots in Panama such as Puerto Escocés, roughly twenty miles north of Capurganá, received little more than a slap on the wrist for carrying passengers without a license. When the *flujo controlado* crackdown came, the smugglers were prosecuted not for operating crossings without a license but for human trafficking, which carried a sentence of as much as fifteen years, according to Kristina.

The boat trips became more crowded, dangerous, and shorter. Kidane experienced as much—not only with the skittish boatman who refused to land at Capurganá, but with his boat trip from Capurganá to Pito, which is only about halfway between Capurganá and Puerto Escoces.

Prior to *flujo controlado*, Panama had sought to keep migrants on the move. In one example, Panama provided an airlift to Mexico for stranded migrants. However, all the migrants we interviewed who passed through the nation after 2016 noted the rough treatment and bad reputation of the Panamanian authorities.

Asked what the worst part of his journey was, apart from the jungle travail, Mr. Tumwine, the Ugandan man, cited the Panamanian camps.

"What we saw was just a complete breakdown of any kind of guarantee of human rights: both Panama and Colombia realized, if they broke UN rights conventions, the US would not do anything," said Kristina.

Migrants who were returned to Capurganá spoke of Panama denying them the opportunity to file asylum claims. In further violation of human rights laws, Panama implemented a creative circumvention of obligation while removing migrants. Out of fear of disturbing Colombian officials and undermining international law, officials would send apprehended migrants to La Miel, a small beach town on the Panamanian side of the border, referenced in Chapter 5. Although technically in Panama, La Miel's geographical position makes it virtually impossible to walk anywhere but back to Sapzurro or Capurganá, Colombia, effectively creating a form of voluntary self-deportation.

In Colombia, the police in Capurganá often sent these migrants back to Turbo where they gain *acción tupelo* papers, or right to constitutional protection, from the Colombian state. In actuality though, they sign voluntary removal forms—giving them ten days to self-deport—an easy sleight of hand given that the vast majority of migrants do not read or speak Spanish.

Most followers of migration policy and smuggling trends see an unintended correlation, where increased securitization of international borders leads to increased profit of smugglers able to escort migrants across. The migrants we spoke to were keenly aware of the slightest shift in the policy wind, even in smaller transit nations like Panama. They were fully prepared to change their budgets and itineraries as smugglers adjusted to these shifts.

The only other way around Panama is by boat. While we were in Capurganá, we met a swashbuckling Spanish sailor of about fifty years of age who we will call Pedro. Pedro carried himself with the bemused sangfroid of a lifelong adventurer. His features were as tough, sun-worn, and varnished as a ship's deck.

Pedro's main business was skippering a chartered yacht between the Colombian coastal city of Cartagena and the San Blas islands on the Caribbean coast of Panama, two major stops on the *Lonely Planet* map of the adventuresome world. While he had often been begged by migrants to transport them out of Cartagena, the only time he complied was when about a dozen Cuban migrants approached his boat on the dock at a time when he needed the money badly.

He described a comic scene. Pedro had charged the going black-market rate—several hundred dollars each for about two dozen passengers—but he felt somewhat conflicted about charging such an exorbitant sum. To separate himself from more extortionate operators, he decided to provide the Cubans with a large supply of liquor to amuse themselves on the voyage. He had underestimated the shock of the heaving seas and heeling craft. Almost all his passengers were soon retching over the side into the towering waves, which were lofty even by the experienced captain's standards.

To keep their minds off seasickness, he had persuaded them to fish for tuna off the side of the boat. It turned out to be a bonanza. Amazed at the ease and size of their catches, the drunken fishermen ceased to worry about the rough sea motion.

By the time Pedro dropped them off at a port near Panama City, they were delighted with their catch, one of the best hauls Pedro had ever seen on the route. Between the fish and the booze, Pedro felt their trip may have paid for itself.

In February 2019, Costa Rica and Panama revised their pact. *Flujo controlado* had now become a bilateral policy providing for more shelters in Panama, with an emphasis on stopping smuggling of migrants.

Costa Rica: Place of Refuge?

The distance from Panama to Guatemala is not much further than that from one end of Colombia to the other. Much of Central America has similar rhythms—of music, speech, and geography. The peck and rattle of meringue and cumbia music are never far away. In the highlands, the Spanish spoken is often of a *tranquilo* diction while many lowland speakers are staccato.

The highlands often feature spectacular mountains, including volcanoes. Almost all Central American countries boast beaches and reefs fit for the poster art in travel agencies and the home pages of travel websites. For most visitors, the differences between the countries are subtle.

Yet the experiences for migrants in each Central American country are radically different, revealing how domestic and foreign policy shape the *camino duro* as much as the physical route. Compared with the ordeal of crossing Panama, Costa Rica feels like a bed of roses. Costa Rica has long cultivated an image as the Switzerland of Central America, and it is one of the only nations in the Western hemisphere without a standing army.

The Costa Rican authorities were the first people who offered Kidane and his friends a chance to apply for asylum. This is an extraordinary fact, given the oppressive regime Kidane was fleeing.

> The Costa Rican police woke us. Costa Rican immigration took fingerprints . . . took photos. After taking fingerprints and photos, they sent us to a small camp, a Red Cross camp. We had soap, toothbrush. Also the food was good. There was a place to sleep. They were treating us very well. Everybody got the same treatment [no matter where they were from]. The paper in Costa Rica said we can stay for twenty-five days . . . within twenty-five days they wanted us to leave.

"I never saw Panama City," said Mr. Tumwine, the Ugandan migrant. "They take you to the Costa Rica border. In Costa Rica, they are very good people. They processed papers the same day."

One Cameroonian woman who passed through in 2019 said the Costa Rican immigration officials were "very nice," and remembered how they gave her the option of applying for asylum there.

But even Costa Rica can be seen as complying with a larger anti-migrant shift in regional geopolitics. Two anthropologists familiar with Central American migration, Nanneke Winters and Cynthia Mora Izaguirre, have found that Costa Rica's self-mythologizing as a "humanitarian transit country" is an oxymoron. The act of moving people on, no matter how humanely, is by definition refusing them refuge, they argue.[5] They note, "On the one hand, Costa Rica juxtaposes its own, supposedly humane treatment of transit migrants with the neglect of these migrants elsewhere in the region," while on the other, it adopted some of the registries and security measures used by the US and Central American nations where it "externalizes" its migration policy.

Costa Rica's shift toward securitization is evidenced in the increasing number of sanctions, detentions, and deportations of migrants since 2010.[6] In a catch-22 scenario, migrants need proof of health care insurance to become regularized but need to show regularized migratory status in order to obtain insurance.[7] The Costa Rican policies foreshadow the Trump administration's twisting of loopholes in humanitarian laws to create nooses for migrant families.

Instead of regularization, most migrants opt for the PIT (Permiso de Ingreso y Tránsito), which, according to Winters and Mora Izaguirre, provides the state a "certain measure of control on this largely undocumented and largely undeportable migration."[8] Implemented in late 2015 to document the flow of Cuban migrants, these transit passes—comparable to *salvoconductos* in Colombia—became available to all migrants in June 2016 after at least twenty-five days of registration in the country and provision of personal information and biometric data. It allows migrants access to the country's reception centers at no cost.

Costa Rica's humanitarian image was additionally damaged by periodic border closures that affected some of the migrants assisted by Kristina. Thousands of Cubans and African and Asian migrants became stuck in Peñas Blancas, an improvised refugee camp erected by the Costa Rican government along the Nicaraguan border. The camp became extremely overcrowded and replete with inhumane conditions. In response, Costa Rica then closed its border with Panama in March of 2016 to stem future pileups.

Border closures added to smuggler incentives to find circumvented routes. According to a 2016 report in *El Pais*, a boat carrying about twenty-five African migrants ran aground in Nicaragua after a desperate attempt to make it all the way from Costa Rica to Honduras by sea. The smugglers abandoned the migrants, many of whom were suffering from heatstroke and exhaustion.

In 2019, Costa Rican police broke up a thirty-six-person people-smuggling organization, which it alleged was facilitating the boat travel and the overland route. Among the women arrested was a woman known as "Mama Africa," Ana Yansy López Martínez, who had allegedly recruited migrants from Africa and Asia for the smugglers. According to some reports, the smuggling ring charged up to $20,000 per person for passage from Costa Rica to the US.

Yet the reporting of others suggests López Martínez was part of the informal "underground railroad," consisting of individuals, mostly female, who develop a connection to the migrant trail for reasons other than pure financial gain. Without joining any formal aid groups, women like Ms. López Martínez provide crucial humanitarian support for the most vulnerable migrants, unaccompanied women like Ms. Mtebe, in the most treacherous areas.

Kristina said she often gave migrants the contact information for a woman in Nicaragua who fits Ms. López Martínez's description, illustrating how the loose network may function.[9] Among the other female-led humanitarian efforts along the route are women we would visit in Southern Mexico, and a Central American nun working in McAllen, Texas.[10] Kristina had heard that women faced the same risk of assault on the Nicaraguan border that they encountered in the Darién region, and believed Ms. López Martínez was working in a similar capacity to her own. Ms. López Martínez was also reportedly married to a Ghanaian man. Like another woman we were to meet further along the *camino duro* who was given the name of Mama Africa, it seems likely that Ms. López Martínez had a more complex relationship with migrants than straightforward exploitation. In the vacuum of state support, she claimed to provide humanitarian assistance.

Nicaragua and Honduras—The Vacuum

If the experience in Costa Rica provided some respite from the brutality of Panama, Nicaragua was a rude reminder that the worst was not yet over. Even before Kidane left the camp, Red Cross officials warned him about the dangers of crossing Nicaragua. "'Please be careful,'" they said. Rather than the de facto deportation, the migrants were allowed to leave on their own recognizance, albeit with instructions to proceed to the Nicaraguan border.

> We paid for our bus and our food with our [own] money. They gave us some maps where we could get buses, and told us how much it costs. They also gave us information for the bus, a timetable. Starting from the border, we took a bus to San Jose City for about $15.

From San Jose, Kidane and his friends took a bus to La Cruz, the small border town in the north. From there, Kidane walked across the border to meet with Nicaraguan smugglers in a car.

"In Nicaragua, no matter who you are no matter how poor you are . . . you must pay $150 . . . every man woman and child," said Mr. Tumwine, the Ugandan.

Kidane used almost every conceivable mode of transportation to cross

Nicaragua. The smuggler at the Costa Rican border took a photograph of Kidane so that the coyotes elsewhere in the country would be able to verify his payment. It was not a good situation.

> We walked three hours from the border . . . then went by boat. The boat [was] very safe not too large.
>
> When we came down from the boat, we went about twenty minutes on foot. Some cars were waiting for us. I had the money for the cars with me: about $3,500 for the group. The others gave it to me when we reached Nicaragua. They sent my photo to the Nicaraguan smugglers.
>
> It was at night. They shone a flashlight and looked at me. When they saw my clothes, they knew it was me.
>
> We started our journey 6 or 7 p.m. They drove us for about three hours. We even felt that we might crash. The drive was very speedy. I was sleeping on the open side of the pickup truck. My friend was in the front seat . . . so he saw how fast they were going—two hundred kilometers per hour. Our friend told us that, if they hit some rock or something, they could have turned the pickup over. The road was good.

After that hot ride, Kidane's party was met by a group of smugglers under a bridge. They had three horses with them to help transport children and adults who were sick or exhausted. The group walked for several hours, arriving at the Honduran border just after sunrise. There, they had to cross a narrow river by boat.

Kidane said this part of Nicaragua struck him as the driest landscape he had seen since leaving Bolivia. The verdant surroundings of the Andean highlands and the equatorial jungles were gone, replaced by scrub and arid pasture.

Nicaragua was also the only country that did not even pretend to process the migrants. The only encounter with the state any of the migrants we interviewed remembered there was the vague sense of the smugglers paying police at a roadblock. Many of the states on the camino have ceded some responsibility for migrant flow to the shadow travel industry. In Nicaragua, the state has outsourced border control almost entirely. This makes periodic crackdowns feel even more arbitrary.

Most of the erratic changes in Nicaraguan treatment of migrants are designed to aggravate the US rather than please the nation. For the migrants, the effect is the same.

In 2016, there was a violent confrontation between the Nicaraguan police and a group of African migrants as witnessed by the Tamarindo community in southern Nicaragua.[11] Historically known as a Sandinista stronghold and pro-Ortega, the community was shocked by the brutality of the police against migrants. One person claimed the migrants were treated "worse than animals." Another referred to it as a "war" of beatings and bullets exposing the hypocrisy of Ortega's government claiming to be "Christian, socialist and in solidarity."

Nicaragua's *muro de contención* (containment wall), justified to stop Cuban migrants, as well as drug and human trafficking, had come to mean militarized force against all migrants. Nicaragua's periodic attempts to seal its border created a domino effect of closings and humanitarian crises to the south, but it also internalized border enforcement. Ironically, however, the policy benefits both the United States, Ortega's apparent enemy, and human smugglers, the policy's professed target. The former gains by adding another barrier to migrant movement, while the latter benefits by being able to demand more pay for crossing Nicaragua.

The Nicaraguan activist Martha Cranshaw has noted the contradiction of a supposedly leftist government complying with US policy, stating "there's no logic or thought to their agreement with the US." She added that the country's treatment of migrants stands contrary to the history of Nicaraguan hospitality, insisting that "the people will continue to help openly or clandestinely." Moreover, 11 percent of the country is itself living in foreign countries as migrants, a number that is second only to El Salvador in Central America. Like Nepal, a significant portion of the country's GDP is based on migrant remittances.[12]

In one particularly egregious case, Marie Frinwie Atanga, a Cameroonian national residing in Belgium, was arrested for trafficking when she came to claim the body of her dead son.[13] In 2017, her son was shot dead in southern Nicaragua in an alleged clash between a border patrol and a group of *coyotes*, who were transporting migrants from Costa Rica to Honduras. Atanga was detained and accused of belonging to an international migrant smuggling ring, and, at one stage, faced up to twelve years in prison. Gonzalo Carrión, a lawyer for the Nicaraguan Centre for Human Rights, viewed the judgment as an example of "legal and moral barbarism of Nicaragua against migrants."

The absence of migration officials in Nicaragua contrasts with an abundance of officials and long bureaucratic waits in Honduras. That does not necessarily make for safer journeys. The vacuum Kidane found in Honduras was one of law enforcement.

Honduras is where migrants like Kidane begin to hear cautionary tales about the *maras*, the tattooed members of criminal gang such as MS-13. This is no myth. Honduras has one of the highest per capita murder rates in the world, and it's especially dangerous for women. For Kidane, the main sign of the gangs was the eerily strict curfews in the city of Tegucigalpa. He was shocked to find the city shut down around him as night fell, with every single shop and restaurant shuttered until the only place to go was back to the hotel where he and his friends were staying. He would also meet, as we have met, Honduran migrants who were forced to flee their homes, their families, and their businesses because they could not keep up with the *maras'* extortion.

For Gabriel Aguilar, who built a business in his home of Tegucigalpa, the *maras* were a much more palpable threat. In 2019, his mobile-phone store was one of many businesses in the city extorted by gangsters running a protection racket. The Honduran president from 2014 to 2022, Juan Orlando Hernandez, allowed criminal operations to flourish. After leaving office, he was arrested and then extradited to the US where he awaits trial on drug-trafficking and firearms charges.

When Mr. Aguilar said he could not afford the latest price increase, the gangsters threatened him. In October, he returned to his store one evening to find it had been shot to pieces by an automatic weapon. There were bullets everywhere, Mr. Aguilar said. The *maras* probably thought he was inside. He didn't want to give them another chance. That very night, he fled for the Guatemalan border to reach Tapachula, where we met him in the town's central plaza in January 2020.

The danger of becoming targets for the *maras* in Honduras and neighboring El Salvador is one reason that migrants from the region began banding together in "caravans." The practice originated as a simple calculation of "safety in numbers." Honduran journalist and social agitator Bartolo Fuentes grasped the power of these traveling groups at a time when the migration trail was an obsession of global social media. He helped to unite the small groups traveling in this way into the mass pilgrimages that captured the world's imagination.

It's easy for border police in Guatemala, Mexico, or the US to apprehend an individual woman using physical force. It's easy to separate an individual family without fear of pushback. With the whole world tracking the progress of a long train of women and children, such actions would have to be done in public. The caravan forced the world to see what the Trump administration's criminalization of migration entailed. Apart from the security angle, the migrants in the caravan had reason to hope that border guards would find it harder to say "no." To paraphrase an old mass protest saying, "they can't detain us all."

What Mr. Fuentes likely did not anticipate was how the anti-immigrant lobby in the US would cast the mass march in traditional xenophobic terms of an "invasion." Right-wing media figures such as Glenn Beck also made unfounded claims that the caravans were funded by billionaire George Soros's Open Society Foundation. Like many other philanthropic and religious organizations, Mr. Soros's nonprofit does support charities working with migrants in the Americas. But there's no evidence that it had anything to do with the caravans. In one migrant shelter, we found a newsletter sponsored by Open Society, one of the few printed sources of information for—and about—migrants available anywhere on the route.

Mr. Tumwine, the Ugandan migrant we met near the Guatemalan border with Mexico, is a charismatic and resourceful young man. When he arrived in Honduras in 2019, several caravans had already made global headlines. He was still traveling with the roughly one hundred people who had been released by the Panamanian military through Costa Rica under the *flujo controlado* policy. There was no welcome for them in Honduras.

"The police chased us with guns and tear gas, shooting bullets in the air," said Mr. Tumwine. Inspired by Mr. Fuentes's success, Mr. Tumwine not only rallied his own group to stick together, he tried to recruit other groups. As he relayed his efforts to us, it was easy to imagine the draw of his buoyant energy to crowds. By his account, Mr. Tumwine's caravan grew to three hundred strong that night on the border between Nicaragua and Honduras. They managed to cross the river together. To his regret, the crowd then broke up.

In Honduras, Mr. Tumwine slept on the streets while he waited for his paperwork. With or without a caravan, the road north is always hard.

Guatemala: Gateway to Mexico

The cellphone was central to Kidane's experience on the *camino duro*. It served as a headlight on the boat lost in the Gulf of Urabá, as a means of verifying payment to Peruvian and Nicaraguan smugglers, and, above all, as a vital link to friends further along the trail. During previous great migrations, people designed their trips, to a large extent, according to letters they had received from those who had gone ahead of them. The cellphone has made this process an instantaneous one.

When we reached Guatemala, they said the police were not allowing people to cross. But a smuggler was also there. The people ahead of us had told us what he looked like, with long hair. "He will wait for you, and just ask him for help to cross." We got off the bus and found him.

He was trying to take us through the jungle for about an hour. He asked us to give him $20 each. He made us lift a fence and scramble underneath. I remember walking through some field. The farmer asked him not to cross this place unless he paid . . . They communicated . . . I think he gave him some money. Finally, he came back and told us what was going on. My friends paid $10 to the farmer.

From there, Kidane and his friends boarded a "chicken bus," one of the brightly painted vehicles, often decommissioned American school buses, that are a major means of Guatemalan transportation. It's a common sight along the *camino duro*: a conductor hanging out the door with a fistful of quetzales or pesos, while a load of burlap bags and livestock totter on the roof. They settled in for the bracing ride through the mountainous spine of Guatemala.

Roads aside, for Kidane and other migrants with whom we spoke, the passage through Guatemala was relatively easy and devoid of the checkpoints and security concerns in other Central American countries. That might be changing.

In recent years, Guatemala, like Panama, was pulled into the Trump administration's anti-migration projects. As part of the administration's larger strategy to end asylum in the US, Guatemala and the US signed an Asylum Cooperation Agreement (ACA) in July 2019. A practice common among North American and European countries dating to the 1980s, ACAs allow states to transfer asylum seekers to a "safe third country" through which the seeker has previously transited.[14] Thus, all non-Guatemalan asylum seekers who passed through Guatemala on their passage to the US could now be transferred back to Guatemala.

Pushed by the threat of US cuts in aid, outgoing president Jimmy Morales agreed to US Attorney General Barr's certification of Guatemala as a "safe third country" in November 2019. This paved the way for 939 Salvadorans and Hondurans to be transferred to Guatemala City between November 21, 2019, and March 16, 2020—in spite of the country's documented inability to protect asylum seekers.[15] Due to the pandemic, the transfers were suspended in March 2020, but the the Trump administration had intended to expand the program to El Salvador and Honduras to "share the burden."

When the Spanish established a colony in Central America, they called it Guatemala and built their capital in the center of the modern-day nation. Over the cobbled streets of Antigua, the sun sets in layers of violet and fuchsia behind snow-capped volcanoes. Tropical flowers in iridescent pastel colors twine around the fringes of the arched colonnades and belfried churches. The new capital, Guatemala City, has none of this serenity. It's a conurbation of aging high-rises and roads crammed with honking traffic, with a few islands of wooded hills, too steep to be incorporated into any phase of the city's development. The brutalist architecture creates a stark juxtaposition of the natural and the manmade.

In early 2020, about fifty people lined one of the streets in Guatemala City's diamond grid. Eli Sanic, twenty-five years old, had come for an appointment at the passport office. Mr. Sanic came from a farming community in Tecpán. He was recruited by other Guatemalans who came to Tecpán looking for people willing to work in Canada.

For four years previously, he had spent half the year in Saint Rémi, just outside Montreal, on a seasonal work visa, "picking onions, carrots, anything that's going."

"It's all legal," said Mr. Sanic. "It's easier than trying to go undocumented. They have invited us, so we can get papers. If you just come and ask for papers, they don't give them to you."

North of Guatemala City, the road winds gradually down from altitude and the sun grows steadily stronger. The verdant cloud forests slowly give way to lower-lying palm trees and banana plants. At sea level, nestled between the mountains of Guatemala and Chiapas are the coastal lowlands drained by the Suchiate River.

The Guatemalan town of Tecun Uman is the gateway to Mexico. Pedal taxis squeak around the undulating streets with wooden buckets full of tourists and passers-through. In the center, the palm-lined streets have the unmistakable feel of the water's edge. When the cyclists run out of momentum on steep patches, a local invariably reaches out an arm to hoist them on their way.

Long the very definition of a porous border, with rafts of migrants ferried across the Suchiate in broad daylight, within sight of Mexican border posts, the crossing at Tecun Uman was all but shut down in 2020. The ferries still carried migrants, but only at night. In 2018, when Kidane crossed, the official border crossing was still open, but not available to him and his friends.

At the [Guatemala] border with Mexico we got a bicycle rickshaw to the river [Suchiate]. The river was full, we needed a boat. It was an innertube with wood attached. We rented the boat and used a stick to move across the river. It cost $5. It was nighttime, not a legal crossing. The legal crossing was at a bridge.

By 2020, in the ultimate act of outsourcing migration policy to Central American allies, the US had effectively moved its border with Mexico 1,500 miles to the south. The eye of the needle had all but closed.

CHAPTER 8

The Waiting Cell of Tapachula

Happy to Wait

Each category of waiting—the doctor's office, the pharmacist's counter, the Department of Motor Vehicles—has its own blend of excruciation. Among the most suspenseful and maddening wait of them all is the customs line. Here, the mundane agony of lugubrious red tape is combined with intermittent nightmare flashes of legal jeopardy. Will they reject the visa because of that minor slip on the application form? Will the immigration official stretching the passport over that barcode reader see a lifetime of transgressions on that obscure screen of theirs and refer you to the local secret police?

Imagine that feeling extending for days, weeks, months—even, in some cases, years, and you will have some idea of migrants' life in Tapachula, southern Mexico.

For Kidane, the tortuous wait at borders, and the tenuous life in suspended animation, was routine by the time he reached Tapachula.

He remembers the town, and his fifteen days there, waiting for a transit visa, fondly. If he was trapped in the town the US media nicknamed "Trapachula," it was a propitious trap, like Circe's island. Those happy memories are almost entirely because of another member of the underground railroad, the loose network of women who help people along the *camino duro*.

Etelvina Hernández López, seventy-one years old, has lived her whole life

FIGURE 8.1. The multilingual markings of Mama Africa's.

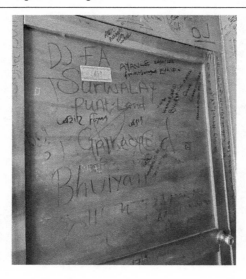

in Tapachula. She showed us the building where she hosted Kidane and his friends, on a busy side street near the palm-fringed Zocalo of the city. The street is a staple of Mexican towns and cities—a terrace of hardware stores, barbers, and restaurants, each with a large opening in place of a store window and a sign painted right onto the wall in primary colors. Ms. Hernández López's original location was a sliver of a premises, little more than a roofed alleyway, hardly wide enough to squeeze a table into with chairs at either end. She had since moved her restaurant to a larger, adjoining building, and the narrow premises was now a retail outlet, with either wall lined by shoe displays. On the doorpost outside were the faint remains of a menu painted onto the wall in English, Arabic, and Tigrinya scripts.

Kidane had urged us to visit this tiny premises, and he told us to look for the notes that migrants had scrawled on the wall. Ms. Hernández López helped us remove one of the shoe stands, and there they all were: messages in Tigrinya, Arabic, Bengali, Nepali, Spanish, and English. The messages were addressed to compatriots that had not yet arrived, and to compatriots who had already left.

This space—appropriately a gap between two larger spaces, like the Darién or the no-man's land between two nations' border fortifications—was one of the few on the thirteen-thousand-mile *camino duro* that was reserved for the Global South migrants.

Above all, the messages were addressed to Ms. Hernández López herself. "Te amo, Mama Africa," read one.

Almost all Eritrean migrants know that Mama Africa awaits them in Tapachula, said Kidane. He had heard the rumor himself but couldn't believe it was true.

Here, in an alien land, with an unfamiliar, stifling climate, was a place where Eritreans could finally taste home-cooked Eritrean food. It had been almost four years since Kidane sat with a group of his compatriots and eaten dishes like doro wat, a mixture of chicken and eggs, with injera flatbread. Coming to Tapachula was not coming home, but it was a brush with home. Ms. Hernández López embodied, for Kidane, the spirit of hospitality he had experienced in Bihat, and which had been so hard to find on the *camino duro*. As Ugandan migrant Mr. Tumwine observed, there is a racial and ethnic pecking order for migrants on the trail, with Black, non-Spanish speakers often treated with the most contempt and suspicion by officials and citizens alike.

That made the experience at Mama Africa's all the more welcome for Kidane. He never called Mama Africa's a restaurant; it seemed to mean much more to him than that.

After June 2019

Kidane's relatively short and enjoyable experience in Tapachula contrasted with the conditions that we witnessed in January 2020. When he traveled through in 2018, the Mexican government was issuing exit permits (*oficio de salida del pais*), colloquially known as *salvoconducto*, which give migrants twenty to thirty days to leave Mexico. Such documents were typically granted to citizens from countries lacking consular representation in Mexico or that do not accept returned migrants.[1] The permits documented migrants, allowing them to buy plane and bus tickets to cities bordering the US border. Kidane stayed in what he described as a comfortable house while he waited for his paperwork to be processed.

A year-and-a-half later, Tapachula had become a twenty-first-century Casablanca, a liminal home to thousands of migrants stuck in transit. We found migrants living in a semi-permanent condition of limbo, much closer to the migrant experience along the US border than the transit-oriented conditions in Central America. We observed the small southern Mexican city coping with the kind of dangerous crossings, militarized border control, overcrowded detention centers, violent flareups, bureaucratic waits, and threats

FIGURE 8.2. A group, likely border dwellers with permits, crossing the Suchiate River from Guatemala to Mexico.

of deportation long associated with border cities like El Paso/Juárez, Laredo/ Nuevo Laredo, and Brownsville/Matamoros.

We entered Mexico at the nearby border town of Cuidad Hidalgo, crossing a bridge over the Suchiate River. Adolfo, who transported us on a bicycle rickshaw, pointed out the improvised truck-tire rafts crossing just east of the bridge, as we jingled across. Most of their passengers on these rafts were now local Guatemalans with permits to go back and forth, he told us, but the rafts had long been the primary way for overland immigrants to enter Mexico. He also showed us the spot, just west of the bridge, where truck-tire rafts were lying stacked on the banks. Here, he said, was where the immigrants now crossed, in *la madrugada*—early morning hours. You could spot "them," he explained, by their *mochilas* and sometimes, by their children.

It was the dry season, and the Suchiate River was low, with almost half of its silty bed exposed in places. On the way back, we saw people wading across. If it were not for the banana leaves and thick vegetation on its banks, it could have been the Rio Grande somewhere in West Texas.

A week after we left, on January 21, an immigrant caravan tried to cross the river on foot at that same spot. On that attempt and on other occasions, they were blocked by the Mexican national guard.[2] Footage sent by our sources shows immigrants flinging rocks at security forces, and the forces flinging them back. The Mexican authorities rounded up and deported hundreds of people in brutal scenes that echoed the anguish of the US-Mexico border.

"We've been locked up here for hours," said one Honduran woman on a recording sent to us from a make-shift dormitory in what our source told us was a Tapachula immigrant shelter. "They say that buses are coming to take us to Tabasco, but there's been nothing so far." More than two thousand people from the caravan were eventually deported, many in flights from Tabasco to Honduras, according to a press release from the Mexican immigration service.

The number of immigrants showing up at the US border had fallen by tens of thousands at the end of 2019, but that was partly because Mexican authorities were now doing the dirty work for the Trump administration. Soon after winning the presidency in 2018, Andrés Manuel López Obrador, known as AMLO, made good on campaign promises to reform immigration policy by increasing humanitarian visas and lowering deportations.[3] The reforms didn't last long. Threatened with US tariffs in the late spring of 2019, the Obrador administration agreed to increase deportations, detentions, and stop the distribution of exit permits.[4] As a result, thousands are stuck.

For migrants who are apprehended at the border or wish to be documented in Mexico, they must first commit to a three-week stay in Estación Migratoria Siglo XXI detention center in Tapachula. Conditions in the Siglo XXI sound grim; the Associated Press has reported on chronic overcrowding there, up to double its 960-person capacity. At least one migrant has died in custody.[5] "It's not detention, it's a prison," said Amiri Tumwine, the thirty-two-year-old Ugandan man who we first met outside the detention center. He said he had to share a cell with seven other men. The only way he could get seconds of the paltry rations in the detention center, he said, was to pretend he was Cuban.[6] Mr. Tumwine said his papers expired while he was being treated for a medical condition in Tapachula. He had returned to the detention center to seek an extension, but was convinced that he'd be locked up again while they processed his request. According to a report by the Black Alliance for Just Immigration, some migrants have been detained up to six times at Siglo XXI.[7]

Siglo XXI has historically served, like other detention centers, as what one anthropologist has called a "sorting center" to control flows and meter transit.[8] But, the halting of exit permits didn't control flows, it stopped them. Exit passes were now only granted to exit via the southern border to return to Guatemala. If one wished to stay in Mexico, they needed to apply for humanitarian visas or asylum. Although Mexico grants temporary or permanent status to a majority of asylum applicants (71 percent), the growing caseload at COMAR (Mexican Commission for Refugee Assistance) has greatly extended decision times.[9] While waiting, immigrants can apply for humanitarian visas (*tarjetas de visitante por razones humanitarios*, or TVRH) via the Instituto Nacional de

Migración (INM), which allow one to work. Many of the migrants we met were reluctant to apply, even for the temporary humanitarian visas since it would require staying in the state where one submitted their application—in Chiapas. Moreover, they worried that it would reduce their chances of receiving asylum in the US. Instead they were planning trips through Mexico without papers. For unlucky others, they are sorted for return. In October 2019, for instance, 311 Indian migrants were deported on a chartered flight to New Delhi.[10]

But perhaps the main reason for skipping visa applications was the bureaucratic nightmares they entailed. One head-numbingly hot afternoon, hundreds of people queued outside the main Tapachula INM office, known for its location in the "Las Vegas" neighborhood. Some were seated with their backs against the center's wall, while most stood in the shade, all facing the barricades at the end of the cul de sac. The combination of the skin-frying heat, the interminable waiting and the barricades gave the crowd a restive atmosphere.

The only movement in the line came when a police vehicle rolled down the street, parting the stragglers and iced-drink vendors. The people in the crowd came from Haiti, from Honduras and El Salvador, from Uganda, and from Cuba, among other countries, all bearing their plastic folders of paperwork. At 2 p.m. Mexican marines advanced to the barricades with their helmet vizors down and riot shields raised. The troops' stance did little to diminish the adversarial tensions. Between the marines' shields, immigration officials read out names from the headers of stapled-together papers—the elusive transit papers. The crowd surged forward as people strained to hear the names being called. Two groups of Haitians, one on either side of the barricades, yelled at each other. It felt as though violence was at hand.

"Are you a journalist?" said a voice, in an American-English accent directly out of the Midwest.

"Yes. Does this happen a lot?" we asked, nervously.

The woman laughed.

"It's an everyday event," she said. "Monday to Friday."

Jackie Ortiz knew all of this all too well. She was born in El Salvador but was raised in Wichita, Kansas, where she spent about eighteen years until she was deported. Like Dorothy, Ms. Ortiz was picked up by a whirlwind and dropped in an unrecognizable land to start a surreal journey. Now, she is waiting. She has filed for asylum in Mexico, hoping to work in Cancún or Tijuana, where her English skills will come in handy. She should have been a shoo-in for Mexican residency, but immigration officials denied her initial

FIGURE 8.3. The daily "ritual" at the Las Vegas immigration office, Tapachula.

application when they saw her tattoos. They conflated the stars and other decorative images on her body with the brands of the *maras*, the very people she was fleeing in El Salvador. Now, she waits in the daily scrum to see if her appeal will be accepted.

"I can't go back and I can't go forward so I'm stuck in the middle," said Ms. Ortiz. She was speaking for the thousands of immigrants that make up an increasingly large percentage, ten percent by some estimates, of Tapachula's population of half a million.

Although we learn in geography class that borders are defining lines in the sand, scholars have come to think of them as performances, rituals, and spectacles like we witnessed at the Tapachula's immigration office.[11] As an inherently liminal space between two states, borders are open to instability and uncertainty. The state obscures this vulnerability through repetition to naturalize its power over the border.[12] While the repetitive and bureaucratic nature of the crossing drama might signal cosmopolitan prestige for the upper class North American arriving at Mexico City's airport, for the transit-seeking migrant arriving at the Tapachula immigration office it traps them in an ambiguous space in between legal and illegal.

Down one of the dusty streets adjoining the INM, we found a torn set of papers. It was an immigration document, or *tramite* as they are called in Mexico, of some sort—the precious papers for which the crowd had clamored.

It identified the Haitian owner of the *tramite*, using a photograph, a passport number, and a bar code newly created by the INM. Other than that, the papers, which the man had signed in crude handwriting, outlined the terms of the man's stay in Mexico. The papers granted him ninety days to stay in Chiapas.

Further down the street, there was a bodega selling water, chiclets, and basics. The owner said he sometimes heard the cries of migrants from the INM's office. There was a rumor that one man had died in captivity there.

As a result of the June 2019 deal with the US, migrants now have to wait for as long as nine months in Tapachula to obtain humanitarian visas which allow them a right to stay in, but not leave, Chiapas. It's a strange, suspended state of existence, as if they've pulled into a highway rest stop for so long that there's a dry and rainy season.

Mexico's Arterial Borders

Although the Obrador government's acquiescence to Trump's demands appeared to be a U-turn in Mexico's immigration policy, it should be understood as a continuation of a long history of the externalization of US border policy.[13] The northern influence on Mexico border/immigration policies reads like a primer in recent US history, as the logics of the Cold War and subsequent wars on drugs and terror were extended to anti-migrant deterrence.

The US recruitment of Mexico as an anti-immigration partner started in the 1980s when migrants were fleeing the violence of US-supported right-wing governments in El Salvador and Guatemala. Ideologically positioned on the "wrong side" of the Cold War, migrants were deemed "economic migrants," not refugees, by the US.[14] In particular, the 1989 Operation Hold-the-Line trained Mexican personnel to stop Central American migrants moving through Mexico before they could reach the US and apply for asylum.[15] At the same time, Mexico's contested election of Salinas de Gortari in 1988 ushered in an era of neoliberal reforms, culminating in the 1992 NAFTA agreement, which propelled the US "War on Drugs" initiatives into anti-migration practices. In the name of "free trade," Mexico increased border "control" efforts to make it appear safe for multinational investment, resource extraction, road construction, and megadevelopment projects.[16] Any cross-border movement contrary to this image, such as drugs and undocumented migrants, became linked as security problems.[17]

As the war on terror took precedence after 9/11, Mexico increasingly followed the US deterrence agenda. The Plan Sur, 2001–2008, started under President Vicente Fox, mimicked US securitization efforts by doubling the number of detention facilities and increasing deportations in Mexico. Additionally, following the US reorganization of immigration control from the Department of Justice to the newly created Department of Homeland Security, Mexico followed suit in 2005 by repositioning the INM within its security branch of government.

The subsequent Calderón administration (2006–2012) further securitized immigration by subsuming it within its anti-cartel agenda. For Calderón's signature Mérida Initiative in 2008, the US gave US$2.5 billion in equipment, training, and intelligence to Mexico to fight drug trafficking. Such military support led to increased violence between the state and cartels (150,000 deaths and 42,000 disappeared), which in turn, justified the circular logic of expanding security measures to stem "violence."[18] The alignment of Mexican and Central American security goals with US policy led Alan Bersin, Obama's Assistant Secretary of Homeland Security, to famously boast in 2012 that "the Guatemalan border with Chiapas is now our southern border."

The 2014 Programa Frontera Sur of President Nieto (2012–2018) used Mérida funding to further "protect" migrants by increasing deterrence efforts. The Mexican government collected biometric and biographical data, increased deportations, and closed the la Bestia train routes to the north. Rather than protecting or deterring migrants, the increased securitization and militarization of anti-smuggling enforcement has exacerbated their vulnerabilities, particularly for women and children.[19] Instead of removing cartels from the migration business, the increasing danger made buying their protection essential.

Throughout this history, Central Americans have remained the main target of anti-immigration initiatives. They have been forced into what some have called a "vertical" or "arterial" border, a relentless web of state and informal barriers pushing migrants into increasingly dangerous and expensive clandestine routes.[20] Traditionally, the issuance of exit permits exempted Asian, African and Caribbean migrants from the arterial borders of Mexico by allowing them to travel directly to the US border with documentation. As one journalist described it, "the border of Guatemala with Mexico is a hell for Central Americans, but for Africans it is the final step of their odyssey."[21]

After June 2019, the "other" migrants increasingly experienced the same "hell" that deterrence has inflicted on the Guatemala-Mexican border. As asylum application numbers at the US border declined for Central Americans, but increased for other nationalities in the latter part of 2019, it seemed the dual-nation project of border securitization turned its sights toward other nationalities. The Trump administration's acting CBP commissioner Mark Morgan identified a shift in US focus toward "extracontinental migrants" at the southern border, particularly those belonging to the category of "Special Interest Aliens," a vague classification that is often mistakenly conflated with "suspected terrorist."[22] Although there have been no known terrorist attacks or plans linked to southern border crossers, the vestiges of the war on terror are still used to militarize the region against immigration.[23]

Multi-continental migrants must now face the arterial border conditions of Tapachula, but often without the language or cultural awareness that their fellow Central American migrants possess. The result is an indefinite stay that extends the prison-like conditions of Siglo XXI to the entire city.

Tapachula as a Waiting Cell

Signs for "Mexico," as the national capital is known here, can be seen throughout Tapachula. Without the legal right to mobility, the directions to northward destinations remain teases.

There were two agents waiting in vain for customers in the Xiinbal travel agency, which sells airplane and bus tickets to northern border towns. Business is dead, said the owner, whose partner had quit shortly before.

"There's no movement," said the man. "Many come inquiring, very few have the documents." When migrants came without visas, he tried to explain that a plane ticket was useless without the documents. When they insisted, he reluctantly sold them tickets, knowing they would likely return for refunds when stopped at the airport, bus station, or at checkpoints down the road.

There are roughly two dozen bus-ticket offices in the streets near the open-air market at the center of town. They are almost identical—one-room shops with just enough space for a person behind a make-shift desk, flanked by bright posters for the myriad bus lines, and a destination menu. Mexican tourist destinations, like Oaxaca and Huatulco, were never on the menu. Those destinations were served by a more up-market bus depot on the other side of town, with its own electronic display. The posters at these agencies advertised bus rides to cities like Tijuana, Ciudad Juárez, and Nuevo Laredo, towns along the US border forty-eight hours by road to the north. To stick out in the minds of migrants faced with so many options, the bus agencies even advertised using bus names such as Betzy and Mary—much as whalers

FIGURE 8.4. Bus agencies in Tapachula.

in Melville's Nantucket drew sailors with affectionate ship names. Like the street markets around the corner, these agencies are outside the formal Tapachula economy. They are the shop fronts of the shadow travel industry.

It costs about US$100 for a bus ticket to Nuevo Laredo, but, according to one Salvadoran woman, smugglers were now charging US$10,000 for the same trip. Up until the deal with the US in June, business was brisk, the bus agents told us. The migrants would jump on these buses after the three-week wait for transit visas. One Bangladeshi man told us that, instead of waiting around Tapachula for months, he had tried his luck boarding a bus without a visa in December 2019. He didn't even get out of the bus station before the immigration police nabbed him. It was back to the detention center for what he told us was his third month-long stint.

In August 2019, several months after the Mexican policy shift, African migrants in Tapachula started protesting against their immobility and deplorable living conditions. When state authorities countered with violent measures, even putting one migrant unconscious, they organized an "Assembly of African Migrants in Tapachula." The Assembly organized an encampment outside of Siglo XXI, consisting of seventeen African nationalities.[24] They issued a press release demanding exit permits, the ability to apply for asylum, and humanitarian assistance. Several months later, they joined a Central American Caravan moving toward the capital in a sign of inter-migrant solidarity.

The protests did lead to an agreement supporting mobility for some Africans.[25] However, for the rest of the Global South migrants, little had changed. Denied the right to move, they were forced to make do in an unwelcoming city.

Like many other chokepoints on the long road through Central and South America to the US, the city of Tapachula has been transformed into a kind of landlocked port. Interspersed with the rotisseries, pharmacies, shoe shops, and hardware stores that typify mid-sized Mexican towns, there are many small, bare-bones hotels catering to the immigrants.

Not far from the center of Tapachula, we happened upon a multi-story boarding house where dozens of Cuban immigrants appeared to be staying. A girl in her twenties sat on a stoop outside the hotel, looking at her own phone and crying. We had come looking for Mr. Tumwine, the Ugandan migrant. The property manager, who appeared to be Cuban himself, reclined on the couch in the lobby grinning at his texts. He thought he recognized Mr. Tumwine's name and waved us up. On the second-floor landing, several migrants had gathered to chat. They were friendly and gave us a room number to try. It felt as though we were popping our heads into a boarding house in the Five Corners of New York during the Industrial Revolution. Mr. Tumwine was not there, but at least three young men were sitting on their bunks, and there were berths for three more. One man cooked eggs on a tiny gas camp-style cooker.

Everywhere we went, we recognized migrants by the plastic folders they use to carry their paperwork. They waited on park benches around the central square, they waited in the hallways of boarding-houses, they waited in long lines outside the detention center and even longer lines outside the refugee office. They waited for their number to come up, waited for the situation at the US border to change, waited for the US presidential election.

For the migrants, the whole city of Tapachula is a penal experience. Movement is extremely limited, the wolf of hunger is never far from the door, and migrants must constantly account for their activities to armed guards. Such surveillance extends to denied jobs, poor service in restaurants, and inflated prices for housing.[26] Much like descriptions of Cueta, the Spanish port on the northern edge of Morocco, where exits are blocked and migrants are under constant surveillance, Tapachula had become a holding cell.[27]

Mr. Tumwine spoke of the prison conditions of Siglo XXI extending to all of Tapachula. He reported stories of being harassed by private security guards who were protected by state authorities and did not want to listen to migrant complaints. "Here," he explained, "we have no one to talk to. We come from beautiful countries, from good families. We want to stay in our land, no one wants to leave their country. No one wants to leave their country without papers. We didn't have choices."

Many migrants do receive temporary work permits through a program organized by the municipal authorities of Tapachula. Like a prison labor program, the work is menial and underpaid. Mostly, the city employs the migrants to sweep the street, or gives them permits to sell water on the street. The Spanish language seems to be a quasi-requirement for these jobs as we observed mostly Cubans, Hondurans, and Salvadorans working them.

With the exception of a few barbershops, restaurants, or hotels, it seemed few of the local businesses in Tapachula employed migrants. Disturbingly, one help wanted sign specified that applicants must present Mexican citizenship identification, the (somewhat) polite version of "no immigrants need apply."

"We have no money but we're not allowed to work," said Casiona Fiorista, a Haitian immigrant seeking papers for herself and her family, which includes a newborn child. "It's impossible." Without the ability to work, a sense of frustration takes over the migrant experience while waiting for papers. A group of six Nepalis, two men and four women, had met in Tapachula after a grueling month to half year journeys from Kathmandu. Having been released from Siglo XXI one week prior, they were settling into a Tapachula routine while they pondered many unanswered questions. Would they receive asylum in the US? Would it be easier in Canada? How long would they be in Mexico? How would they get to the US border?

When asked about their daily routine, they explained "sleep, wander around, and hang out in the park." They visited Mama Africa's restaurant for lunch and dinner, but were starting to find the food monotonous, and to complain about the dal, occasionally preferring the Chinese take-out next door.

The boredom is compounded by an overwhelming sense of surveillance. The police patrol the central square and migrant-heavy streets on a regular basis. But, for this group of Nepalis, it was not state surveillance that froze their actions, but rather the constant watch of their agents. During our final meeting as we were saying our goodbyes, several of the Nepalis whispered to us to meet them for tea the following morning as they had "things to tell us," but worried about being seen talking to us. They never showed.

The sense of surveillance separated the Spanish-speaking and non-Black Latino migrants from the others, particularly the Haitians and Africans. Migrant stigma is thus not only nationalized but also racialized. Alain, a white Cuban who had been in Tapachula since April 2019, spoke of avoiding Haitians and Africans to not be identified (and thus, discriminated against) as a migrant. He lived on the periphery of town to try and blend in with Mexicans. Others openly spoke disparagingly of the "*morenos*" (Blacks) who they said brought disruption to the documentation-seeking process. "They bring disorder," said one Salvadoran migrant. A shopkeeper near the immigration office spoke of a *moreno* who he heard had attacked an official during the summer protests, causing him to be hospitalized for twenty-three days.[28]

As Ms. Ortiz and other Central American immigrants acknowledged, the many African, Haitian, and South Asian immigrants have it even tougher than they do in Tapachula, thanks to the language barrier and racism.

One Haitian migrant, Patrice, who came to Tapachula from Chile where he had lived for three years after leaving Haiti in 2015, explained his role as a Spanish interpreter for many of his compatriots. He left Chile due to the low pay as well as overt racism he experienced there. His immediate plan was to join his wife in Tijuana. She had gained Mexican refugee status from the embassy in Chile and came directly. Patrice, without such status, had to travel overland with their two-year-old son. His ability to speak Spanish provided him a first-hand account of the discrimination against migrants, particularly against those who couldn't speak Spanish. He lamented that Latins are not "fiel" (loyal).

A small but growing minority of the immigrants in Tapachula, including Ms. Ortiz, have given up on the American dream, and are seeking asylum status in Mexico. The wait is slightly less tortuous, at about six months—if accepted. Even with a residents' card, however, there's little hope of a comfortable life. One Salvadoran man told us he made about $100 a week working a grueling job at a Guadalajara recycling warehouse.

However, for groups like the Nepalis, staying in Mexico was not an option. They told us, "We don't know Spanish, we don't want to stay here." However, unable to continue on their journey, staying in Tapachula is their only option for the moment. As one migrant-advocacy publication put it, "They're in limbo. . . . The Mexican government doesn't allow them to finish their voyage to the U.S. . . . . At the same time, it doesn't offer them a real alternative of employment or even a return to where they've come from."[29]

Mama Africa's: The Heart of Tapachula's Southern Cosmopolitanism

While state policy keeps migrants stuck in limbo, it does not—outside of the mandatory stay in Siglo XXI—provide any sort of housing or shelter, which opens an overlapping private market of assistance that is both humanitarian and profiteering. As scholars have shown, humanitarian efforts often reproduce governmental agendas, patriarchal conditions, and structural inequality.[30] While the humanitarian work of Tapachula entails a mixture of motivations and perpetuates inequalities, the relationship between global migrants and local service providers has also fostered an unexpected cosmopolitanism.

As mentioned earlier, Ms. Hernández López has never left Tapachula, but she has seen the world through her small restaurant along Octava Avenida, the one that Kidane remembered so fondly. She has run the restaurant since around the time she separated from her husband in the early 2000s. At that time, the bonds of Catholicism and the hierarchy of machismo reigned in Mexican family life. It took great courage for Ms. Hernández López to strike out on her own. She initially served classic Mexican dishes, based around tortillas, beans, and rice. When migrants started coming to town in large numbers around 2013, her restaurant grew in popularity.

One day, some Bangladeshi customers approached her with a frank confession: "We don't like this food. Do you want to learn how to cook our food?" Ms. Hernández López took up the challenge, hiring a Bangladeshi man named Sadek. "He said, 'Let's go shopping.' I went to the market with him and he picked out the stuff." As Ms. Hernández López's son, Daniel, who runs the kitchen now, put it, "It's all the same ingredients as Mexican cooking, just prepared differently."

The other tradition Mexico shares with other parts of the Global South, as Kidane found, is hospitality. Ms. Hernández López tours the tables of her restaurant more assiduously than a New York maitre d', and has a joke or a word of encouragement for almost every diner—often in their native language.

Ms. Hernández López listed off about a dozen countries—from Cuba to Ethiopia to Yemen—whose cuisine is available. She has also learned phrases, such as "do you like chicken?" and "please, sit down" in about a dozen languages. She sang a Somali hymn. In turn, migrants have given her maternal names, Mama Africa by Eritreans, Nani by Bangladeshis, Amma by Nepalis, Mamasha by Somalis.

When we arrived at her restaurant, she was stirring the contents in the chafing dishes in the center of her restaurant, a range of dishes including Indian dal soup, Bangladeshi-style fish, and a Somali chicken in sauce. A multinational crowd gathered around her, viewing the evening's offerings. Her face was suffused with maternal warmth as they greeted her, some with hugs.

"When they come, it gives me animation—'Nani'—it's like, when they say it, it gives me strength and makes me feel better," she said. "They tell me sometimes, 'there's no other person who understands us, no one who helps us, no other person who will give us food.'"

The restaurant is a microcosm of the *camino duro*, a multilingual bottleneck where the lines between customer and cook, traveler and resident, smuggler and smuggled are constantly shifting. While we were there, many of the regulars passed freely through the narrow hall that separated the restaurant and the kitchen. On the wall, somebody had scrawled "agent" and a phone number. Once we had returned to the US, we figured out that the number was a landline somewhere in rural northern India. When we called, the man on the other end was somewhat upset. He spoke very little English. From what we could make out, he seemed to say that his phone number was used as a sort of clearinghouse, that he passed messages from one caller to another but took no part in their business.

Ms. Hernández López attends an evangelical church, and she clearly sees her outreach to the outcasts of Tapachula as a religious mission, in addition to being a business. While we were there, we paid $3 a plate for the multiethnic buffet, but Ms. Hernández López told us she never turns people away for lack of money. She had been feeding one Eritrean man, whom she called Franco, for about four months. Like Kidane, Franco had spent a few weeks in Tapachula in 2019 and had eaten regularly in Mama Africa's. He then trekked north, where he managed to enter the US. Franco did not last long there, however, and, to Ms. Hernández López's surprise, reappeared at her restaurant a couple of months after he had bade her farewell.

Ms. Hernández López follows a tradition of women in Tapachula who have nurtured the migrants. In the 1990s, Olga Sánchez lived close to the tracks of La Bestia, the freight trains that the desperate jump to travel north to the US. She saw migrants wounded during their attempt to jump the train and left for dead by the tracks. Ms. Sánchez carried some of these people back to her home and procured prosthetic limbs for them, eventually opening a shelter. La Bestia no longer passes Tapachula (a Mexican artist has constructed a wooden statue of a coyote and its cub where it once ran). Now Ms. Sánchez and two other administrators give room and board to hundreds of migrants in the facility, Albergue Buen Pastor, which is about the size of a rural American elementary school. There were about four hundred people there when we visited and it seemed overcrowded, with throngs of people gathered in the entrance courtyard. It's hard to imagine the conditions in early February, when an official there emailed to say there were now seven hundred residents.

It is not uncommon for support to be maternalized along the migration trail. In the camps and hostels of northern African transit cities, workers are referred to as "madres" who administer an "uneasy mix of coercion and charity" on behalf of the Spanish state.[31] Similarly, accounts of China-to-US smuggling have referred to the gendered cultural expectations of migrants to assume female guides (or "snakeheads") to be more reliable and trustworthy.[32] In southern Mexico, Mama Africa represents not just a maternalization of humanitarianism, but also its global outlook.

References to other Mama Africas have emerged in multiple descriptions of the route. One research project, based on interviews with African asylum seekers in the US, describes a reference to another "Mama Africa" who helped migrants cross Nicaragua.[33] Other journalists have identified the name also used for a hotelier in Tapachula known to house African and Haitian migrants.[34] References to "Mama Africa" connect with the term's meaning in the African diaspora where, as one scholar put it, "the idea that Africa exists as a nurturing spirit inside every black person."[35]

The nurturing spirit of the migrant Mama Africa is complicated by the profit-seeking of the shadow travel industry. There is the phone number on the wall. Sadek, Ms. Hernández López's first Bangladeshi apprentice, went on to start his own restaurant and travel agency one block away. He has since closed his business, disappearing near the same time that the leaders of a smuggling ring were arrested in Houston and Monterrey.[36]

Ms. Hernández López said she doesn't know where people go when they leave her restaurant. But, she does keep track of people who have been forgotten. When one of her regular customers, a Nepali man called Sagar, suddenly stopped coming some years ago, it played on her mind. In the local newspaper, she read an account of a Nepali man admitted to the hospital. Following a maternal instinct, she went to the hospital. Sure enough, the man, who had been robbed and beaten, exacerbating his mental illness, was Sagar. Mama

Africa helped arrange for Sagar's return to his family. "He never washed [at that time], but the day they told him 'you're going home,' he scrubbed up very clean and did his hair."

When we met her, Ms. Hernández López's main concern seemed to be Franco. Franco is an Eritrean man haunted by the ghosts of the migration trail. He stands in the doorway of a nearby hotel and gesticulates in the air. So many migrants find themselves in a strange state of suspended animation on the *camino duro*, and that's particularly true in the vast waiting room of "Trapachula." For Franco, this state of limbo may be permanent.

He was immaculately dressed in a red polo shirt and understated gold jewelry, and he seemed to have some attachment to the boardinghouse near Mama Africa's where he was so often hanging around. When we asked him how he was doing, he was very positive and animated. Once we stepped away, a sadder, more laconic shadow passed over his face. He seemed keen to hide his troubles, to hide what Ms. Hernández López told us was a very precarious existence. But Ms. Hernández López told us Franco had nowhere to go at night, that he slept on the street. She had set up a bed for him in the restaurant but he refused. She goes frequently to the opening at the front of her restaurant and looks down the street to where Franco stands, with the inimitable look of a perturbed mother.

"You'll help him, right?" she asked us, on the verge of scolding.

We arranged to meet Mr. Tumwine at Mama Africa's one night. When we had started to describe a local restaurant catering to African tastes, he instantly recognized the description. As it turned out, Mr. Tumwine was thinking of another African restaurant in town. "You went to Mama Africa's, but I was at Papa Africa's," as Mr. Tumwine said later.

After resolving this misunderstanding, we accompanied Mr. Tumwine to a fried chicken restaurant near the Zocalo. There, he recognized a woman who appeared to be Mexican or Central American. He signaled to her and proceeded to make a plate to give her. "I know what it's like to be hungry" he explained when returning to the table.

The signs posted on the lampposts around Tapachula demanded a similar memory from the community: "When did you forget that you are an immigrant?"

CHAPTER 9

The Road Trip to End All Road Trips

In Mexico, the long-distance bus ride carries some of the cultural freight of the US cross-country car drive. The nation's roadways might have been designed as a test course for the modern bus, and Mexican bus drivers pride themselves on pushing their machines to the limit. Setting off from the main Tapachula station, the bus wends up from sea level through the semi-tropical mountain forests of Chiapas, down to the marshes of Veracruz, and back up the Veracruz hills to the semitropical mountains of Puebla and the nation's central plateau.

Curran has traveled much of the route through Mexico to Texas by bus. A passenger usually hopes an overnight bus will allow them to arrive at their destination refreshed. This is akin to bedding down to a nap in an unstable washing machine. The ups-and-downs and switchbacks are so profuse in southern Mexico that it makes the passenger wonder if the cartographers had erred and left out entire mountain ranges. If the passenger sleeps long enough to chance a dream, that dream will have to incorporate the jarring lurches of the seat, the painful creaking of the suspension, and the roars of protest from the engine as the driver tries to accelerate on the uphill. The rhythm of the gears becomes so ingrained in the consciousness that the sleeper eventually preempts the bus's jolts. The only advantage provided by the overnight bus is an inability to see the road. When the sun rises, the passenger realizes that they are a participant in a three-dimensional game of chicken, as the bus driver dares oncoming rivals and sheer ravines. On the rare stops, the gas-station forecourts are filled with passengers fumbling tortas with the kind of dazed expressions normally seen on rear-ended drivers.

In the mountainous parts of Latin America, piloting a car, or even riding a bus, is an experience more akin to operating a speedboat or a plane than cruising along an interstate. The traditional driving cues of visibility and road signs are seldom available and even more rarely reliable. The narrow mountain roads in Bolivia, Ecuador, Colombia, Guatemala, and Mexico seldom have protective barriers, even as they skirt precipices. Ms. Mtebe, the Cameroonian nurse, found the roads in Colombia almost as terrifying as her trek through the jungle.

> Bad roads in Colombia, some terrible roads so scary. . . . One group had [an] accident on [a] Colombia road, some group that was coming behind us. They had their bus fall. They had injuries. There was a wound [above one woman's] eye. She had the wound [in] Tijuana. Then she had a bandage I think her arm. Some people died in the bus in Colombia.

Roads are constructed with an almost abstract sense of design, as perfectly paved surfaces give way to rubble without any discernible pattern or internal logic. A widening or flattening of the road is usually a tease, and, often, a sort of trap, lulling the driver's adrenalized awareness just long enough to make them prey to a sudden plunge or virtual disappearance of the road.

The speed bumps, known variously as *acostado* (short for supine policeman); *lomo de burro*—donkey's back; *tumulo* (tombs); and in Mexico *tope*, seem designed to disable speeding cars rather than encourage safe driving. The bumps have the surprise placement and formidable shapes of booby traps. Even this approach is futile as bus-drivers in the region have mastered the art of approaching the obstacles at speed and only breaking stride long enough to finesse the bump, after which they resume their careering pace with an indignant roar of the engine.

Only once the volcanoes Popocatépetl and Iztaccihuatl come into sight can the passenger look forward to smoother roads, as the mountains flatten out on the central plateau. The smoky, snow-capped Popo and its sister "the white woman" sit either side of the Paseo de Cortes, the conquistadors' entrance to the valley of Mexico. By the time the bus nears Mexico City, the plateau is 7,000 feet above sea level. Just as ravines cease to be a worry, they are replaced by increasingly crowded roads, and increasingly impatient city drivers.

All cross-country bus trips in Mexico lead to Mexico City, whose four major bus stations serve tens of thousands of passengers a day. The largest, the TAPO, looks and feels like a roofed football stadium. If Mexico City is no longer the largest city in the world, it feels like it when you're traveling through on a bus. In America and Europe, highways glide through the outer rings of cities without much change in the vistas on each side. Not until you are some distance into the five boroughs does driving through New York start to feel like being in New York. Going through Mexico City, the bus is at street level the whole way. In European and American cities, a great effort has been made to preserve a "village" atmosphere. The exposed parts are mostly public spaces, such as parks or broad thoroughfares. Traffic is generally diverted away from the densest residential areas.

Mexico City does not hide its multitudes, does not shield resident or visitor from the sensation of being an ant. The first thing you see is the exposed concrete and corrugated rooves of the shantytowns clustered onto the hillsides, the *colonia populares*. The *colonias* are as dense as the smog that often smothers the city, blotting out the tropical sun. The traffic is even denser. Soon, you are surrounded by throngs of green taxis and buses, as countless key-cutting stores, bimbo-bread sellers, and soccer courts scroll by. After an hour of this, you think "this, then, must be the center." And the scroll continues. The concentric rings of Mexico City leave a more palpable imprint on the mental map than those of comparable metropolises in Europe or the US, where highway flyovers conceal the masses. It is hard to sit in the quiet cafes around the picturesque Zocalo without thinking of the rings upon rings of *colonias* in its orbit.

North of DF, as it's known, the vegetation gradually thins out, with palm trees gradually giving way to less tropical cover and rolling ranchland. This part of the central plateau is where some of humankind's first mass settlements originated; and it's where the Spanish built the first great colonial cities of their North American empire—including Queretaro, one of the early capitals of Mexico; and Guanajuato, a city so beautiful its roads were laid underneath the historic center. The bus rider loses count of the colonial towns with their twin-spired churches, bell towers, and cattlemen breakfast places.

Further north, the trees shrink to shrub, and the plateau gives way to the jagged spine of the Sierra Madre. Northern cities like Monterrey glimmer like

FIGURE 9.1. Approaching the U.S. from Cuidad Juárez overlooking downtown El Paso.

mirages in the hyper-bright sun. From the mountains, the bus descends into the Chihuahua desert, a boundless crust of sandy rock and rocky sand the color of burned caramel.

The next stop is the US border.

CHAPTER 10

"Welcome to America"

Zero Tolerance in the Immigration Gulags

When Kidane started the 2018 leg of his journey in Dubai, his destination was as clearly defined as a goal line: the US border with Mexico.

Not long after he arrived in the Americas, he realized the goal posts had moved. By the time we met Kidane's party in Capurganá, Colombia, they had received horror texts from friends about months-long stays in detention centers, waiting for repeatedly postponed asylum hearings.

One of Kidane's friends, the bitter realist of the group, had said it out loud: "We're basically going to prison, right?"

Kidane himself dismissed his friend's trepidation at the time, almost rolling his eyes at the misanthropic overtones. He knew he had a strong asylum case, and he believed the US had a long history of sheltering refugees. Kidane fully anticipated short-term pain in the US, but he saw the sacrifice as a relatively small one given the strong chance that the US would eventually provide a fulfilling life for his young family.

We received an e-mail from Kidane when he reached Tapachula, Mexico, in mid-August 2018. It was a great relief to hear from him after seeing him drift off into the darkness on the overcrowded boat. He sounded excited. He told us he had booked a ticket to the US border, and that he expected to cross into Texas around August 24. We expected to hear from him in a week or two. The tone of his e-mail made it sound like a routine crossing. But nothing is routine crossing the US border.

A month passed and we had heard nothing. We checked the ICE online detainee database, using various spellings of his first and last name and various iterations of his nationality. John Stauffer, the president of non-profit The America Team for Displaced Eritreans, was not surprised to hear we were having difficulty in finding Kidane in the system.

> Kidane may have given ICE three names—the third name is the paternal grandfather's first name and ICE could end up using that as his "last name." (My guess is this is what's happened.) Also, you must have the country of birth. Many Eritreans were born in Ethiopia or Sudan, rather than in Eritrea, so you need to repeatedly re-enter the search using all three countries.

We tried all the combinations we could think of and, as Mr. Stauffer put it, "came up dry." We contacted Carl Rusnok, a spokesman for Immigration and Customs Enforcement (ICE) in Dallas.

In our experience, asking an ICE spokesperson about the well-being of an individual elicits the same kind of jaded impatience as asking a Wall Street analyst or Securities and Exchange Commission regulator about the moral rectitude of a particular trade. Processing 60,000 detainees a month, they gave the impression they'd seen it all. Some guy's unaccounted for at the border? What's new?

This is not to say that Mr. Rusnok was unwilling to help. At his request, Texas ICE officials double-checked data bases of detainees. Nothing.

Kidane had disappeared into the ICE detention system without a trace. This is a common occurrence for migrants on the *camino duro*. When they cross to the US, they may lose contact with their families for weeks or months at a time.

Even if we had found Kidane, we likely would not have been able to speak with him, warned Mr. Stauffer. You can't call detainees, though some centers will allow you to leave a message for them. Usually, detainees were required to have money in their commissary account to cover the cost of the phone call. If Kidane called someone and missed them, he would not be allowed to leave a message.

Perversely, the idea that detainees could be held incommunicado gave us some hope. Perhaps Kidane was still alive, but just unable to reach us. We were Facebook friends with Kidane. He had not posted anything since very early in his odyssey. We tried to contact people who sounded like relatives on his friend list, to no avail. Our next plan was to contact organizations on the border who seek for migrants' remains in the Northern Mexican desert.

Kidane, as it turned out, had flown from Tapachula to Reynosa on the Texas border, with the paperwork he'd gotten at the Mexican immigration office.

> Our papers were good for fifteen days. Five of the group went to Reynosa . . . the rest went to California. Six went to California, including Kenenisa [the man who'd been bitten by a snake]. I don't know where he is now. But we have a Facebook Messenger group. If one guy free from detention, he must say "hi" on the group. Some people had said California is a good place for accepting refugees. That's why they wanted to cross in California. But, at that time, you had to wait on the Californian border for months. That's why I came here to Texas.
>
> We came to the border in Reynosa when we were trying to cross the border, the police officer was asking for papers. When we showed them, they said, "you are legal but you can't cross at this place." We tried to cross, but we could not cross at that bridge. So the options were to wait a week, or, the police told us, we could cross by a far bridge. We went to the far bridge. This was a long bridge that local people only crossed in cars. We went by taxi to the bridge. The taxi driver told us, "if you go on that bridge for four miles, you'll reach the US."
>
> The temperature was very hot, but it was normal for us. I'd prefer to go in the sun than wait. We had walked on foot for about one and a half hours. Then we crossed the border. We knew because there were some signs also there on the border: US/Mexico. We crossed the bridge and showed paper to the immigration officers. The American police were coming by police car asking us our plan. We were told to go inside and we'll inform ICE. Then we reached the immigration office. They had dogs come up and check our bags. They accepted us and then transferred us to Port Isabel.
>
> They were good. They welcomed us with sympathy and did their job.

Somewhere along the way, Kidane had lost our contact information. We had all but given up hope, when, in mid-February 2019, we received the e-mail we'd been hoping for against hope. After more than three months he was out of detention, and his asylum application was under way. He was staying in a Catholic migrant shelter in Houston. The hostel was where Kidane would await a final ruling on his case. He welcomed the idea of us visiting him at the shelter.

We were instructed to hit a buzzer at the back entrance to the shelter building, a metal door set into a larger metal gate. Through the door was what looked like a laundry. The official who answered the door seemed protective of the men's privacy and security and shut it again while he went to look for Kidane.

The shelter was on the outskirts of the affluent Houston neighborhood of Rice Military, on a street dotted with gas stations, storage facilities, and the other markers of the outskirts. The location spoke to the endlessness of Kidane's journey. Even here, past the goal line, there was no destination to reach. Nearly six months after "arrival," Kidane was still living a liminal existence in a liminal neighborhood.

The Casa Juan Diego is one of several Catholic shelters in the city, and one of many in the nation who take in migrants with no other addresses to provide the ICE agents who remove them from the detention centers. Kidane got the name of the place from one of the Eritrean friends who was released just before he was. Few things will bond a group tighter than rushing a snake-bitten member to life-saving care. Celebratory emojis flew whenever one of them was released from detention.

Kidane felt fortunate to have his turn. The Eritrean group that split in Tapachula all faced months of languishing—either at the Californian border or in Texas detention centers. Kidane took his chances on Texas, because he knew more people in Houston.

The Houston sunshine had done wonders for Kidane. The weight of dread had lifted from his features, transferring to his frame, which had lost the gauntness of the long-distance runner. He looked, above all things, American, as if he were a cornfed Hollywood actor who had only been method-acting when we met him in Colombia. His hair was carefully groomed, and the ragged clothes were replaced with a white t-shirt bearing a picture of Sylvester the cartoon cat under the legend "One Bad Cat." And, yet, as we chatted, it became clear that Kidane's view of his odyssey was not as sunny as it had been back in the hazy tropics of Colombia. When he spoke of his time in US detention and, especially, his time before an immigration judge, he grew frustrated.

The ICE agents took Kidane to a detention center in Port Isabel, officially given the bureaucratic title of Port Isabel Service Processing Center. That's where Kidane's faith in the US commitment to human rights was tested. Known since the 1980s as El Corralón, or "the big corral," it was a converted naval base that became part of president-elect George H. W. Bush's plan in 1988 to make asylum more difficult for people fleeing civil war in El Salvador and Guatemala.[1] The new rules prohibited work permits, interstate travel for asylum applicants, and importantly, detained rejected applicants for quicker removal. As the detention center grew in capacity from hundreds to several

FIGURE 10.1. Kidane Okubay in Houston, 2019.

thousand, it became notorious for beatings, sexual assaults, and inadequate medical care.[2]

According to Kidane, the detention center itself was not bad, at least not by prison standards. It's a complex of seventies-style brutalist buildings, painted an unbecoming mustard, with a few palm trees. There was an exercise yard, surrounded by barbed wire, where the detainees could play basketball or take a walk for a couple of hours in the Texas heat. In August and September, the Texas sun turns asphalt surfaces to bubbling lava. Concrete surfaces are so white hot they are impassable in bare feet. The cicadas pine deafeningly for cooler weather.

Inside the Port Isabel center, the air-conditioning made it feel frigid, Kidane said. The place sounds like a prison-of-war camp. There were four units, called, in the military-alphabetical fashion, Alpha, Beta, Charlie and Delta. There were four dormitories in the Charlie unit, and Kidane slept in C3 with about seventy-five other male detainees, all on bunk beds. There was a camera in the dormitory, monitored by a guard who usually sat in the hallway outside. He received three meals a day and had access to a small store. Upon arrival, the guards took his money and gave him a receipt. Whenever he purchased something at the store or made a phone call, the charge was deducted from his cash balance. He could use the phone at any time.

There was no privacy. Everything happened under the eye of the security camera. Even the toilets were on live television.

"You could be using the toilet, [and] talking to your friend like this," said Kidane, gesturing as if there were someone sitting right next to him. He laughed.

Five of Kidane's Eritrean-Ethiopian group were in the dormitory with him. They met migrants from Ghana, Guinea, Congo, and Gabon, but most were from Central America.

At an initial interview with Customs and Border Protection (CBP) near the bridge in Reynosa, Kidane applied for asylum. In the Port Isabel center, Kidane had a "credible fear" interview with another CBP officer by phone. After that, he had to wait for a judge to rule on his application.

This wait is another part of "deterrence." Under the Trump administration, the wait to see a judge had been growing. For instance, while the average period of detention in 2016 was twenty-one days, by 2018 it had become fifty-five days.[3] (However, it should be noted that rapid deportations of some individuals skew this data. It is common for non-citizens defending themselves against deportation to wait longer than six months; one study of ICE detention centers in California found the average stay to be 421 days in 2013.) The ever-increasing periods of detention were designed to send a message, just as the "ice box" and "child separation" policies were. Such anguish is intended to reverberate along the entirety of the *camino duro*, making migrants reconsider their departure, seek asylum in whatever Latin American country they get stuck in, or simply turn back home.

Kidane's separation from his family grew even more painful in the detention center.

"I was trying to call my wife," said Kidane. "But she didn't know how to pick up because the instructions were in English: 'Press one'—she couldn't understand. It's a recorded message."

Imagine the agony on both ends of that line. It's always painful when a technical issue thwarts an important call. But imagine if that call were the only contact you've had in weeks or months with the person you love more than anyone else in the world, a person for whom you would literally cross deserts, continents, and oceans. Imagine Kidane's end, wishing that Hiwet would, somehow, perhaps even unintentionally, hit the right button. And imagine Hiwet's end, knowing, from the English recording, that this was some news from Kidane, but not knowing whether the news was good or bad. They were separated by nothing but a keystroke and the Trump administration's desire to "deter" migrants like Kidane and his family by making the experience as painful as possible.

We were talking to Kidane in a breakfast place in Houston. It was an airy café with large windows, and an affluent clientele who agonized over a chalkboard menu full of avocado and farm-raised poultry dishes. Casual-dining establishments of these cavernous proportions—with these vaulted ceilings, church-scale capacity, and correspondingly monumental servings—do not exist in many cities of the Global South. Could any of these people imagine a life where restaurants were squeezed into the gaps between buildings; a world where you dried your only change of clothes on the railing of an unventilated hotel; a world where the entire café line might crowd onto a boat to speed through the night into the jungle? Could they imagine spending three months locked up with hundreds of other migrants from all over the world? Yet Kidane was as much at his ease in the Houston café as he had been in the Capurganá hostel.

He enjoyed the coffee and the eggs-sausage-patties-and-toast (the only thing Kidane ever let us purchase him were the meals in Houston.) The only time that the pain registered on Kidane's face was when he talked about his hearing in front of the judge in Port Isabel. Kidane had come to the immigration court with the expectation that it was built around traditions of American justice and fairness. That day in the café, he sounded indignant, as if he were raging against the myth of America itself. He addressed the judge, as if he were sitting opposite the man in this court-room sized café.

I don't have any idea why the judge rejected my application. He spoke with me twice. He told me to submit an asylum form. After you fill out the asylum form, he tells you to gather evidence.

Then finally, he gives you an interview. I spoke with a lawyer, and I had a translator in court. We weren't represented by lawyers. If you have a lawyer or don't have a lawyer, it doesn't make a difference. There was a free lawyer. To have a specialist, you have to pay more than $3,000.

When he was judging me, I think there was a breakdown in understanding. I had difficulty understanding what he meant by his questions.

I replied as best I could, based on my understanding. When he summed up the case, he spoke about a few things.

"Did I have a good reason why I fled from my country?" I've never seen my son with my eyes. When my wife was pregnant, I left, and I've been away ever since, until now. I [should have] said . . . "If I was able to go back to my country, if I didn't have a problem there, why wouldn't I go see my family?" [There was a] problem in understanding.

"Did you use government phones and government internet?" He asked me, but there's no private networks [in Eritrea]. "Yes, I used government phones and government internet . . ."

I was using [the] phone in an internet café. I paid money to use the internet. . . . When I was in South Sudan, the internet and phone was private. I paid for myself . . .

The judge understood I was using phone and internet in government offices. But I was using phone and internet in cafes. The company is owned by the government. I was working in government national service, but not using a government office. Not using. I used *my* money to use the internet.

From the beginning the government said that every national must join [national service] for eighteen months. You can't leave.

For my diploma program, you had to join national service. Five years without proper pay. They asked me, "did you work for government pay?" Well, yeah, they paid me service money, but that was pocket money. "Whatever . . . did they pay you or not?"

He appealed to us, as he must have appealed to the judge, imploring us with looks and gestures to listen to reason. This rehearsal of his case was tough to watch. There are people who always act as their own defense lawyers, providing a self-championing view of every situation. Kidane is not that guy. In the four years we've worked with him, he's never asked us for anything—except to publicize his niece's plight in Libya.

It was clear from his tone of voice: the asylum argument was something Kidane had to get off his chest. Kidane was determined that someone would give him the fair hearing that the judge had denied him.

Before he arrived, Kidane had faith in the US and its adherence to the international human-rights conventions that it helped to shape. He believed in a system designed to protect the vulnerable, and refused to believe that it could be repurposed as punitive. When his Eritrean friends in Colombia spoke of Trump's border prisons, Kidane dismissed their cynicism.

It's hard to justify that faith given the US immigration court record. As one legal scholar notes, "asylum outcomes often depend as much on the luck of the draw as on the merits of the case."[4] One study of asylum cases between 1997 and 2008 showed that applicants in San Francisco were twelve times more likely to receive a positive ruling than applicants in Atlanta.[5] Even within the same court, rates vary greatly depending on the judge.[6] In addition to the variability of one's assigned location and judge, success is often predetermined based on nationality. In that same study, applicants from Albania, China, Ethiopia, Iran, Russia, and Yugoslavia had over 50 percent affirmative rate, while Salvadorans, Guatemalans, Hondurans, and Mexicans were less than 10 percent likely to receive asylum. Observers have concluded that decisions depend "largely on chance," while others have identified "ideological" or extralegal factors, such as US military aid or trade, that influence decisions.[7] In a very telling example from the 1980s, Central Americans fleeing violence committed by right-wing states were often rejected as "economic migrants" whereas migrants coming from Sandinista-ruled Nicaragua were much more likely to win asylum cases.[8]

Judge William Hanrahan, who as assistant head of the San Francisco immigration courts oversaw their day-to-day operations, quit in 2021 after just over a year on the job because political directives were forcing his judges to deport sympathetic people. The sway of Immigration and Customs Enforcement prosecutors over the courts was "disconcerting," Mr. Hanrahan said.[9]

One of the judges at the Los Fresnos court overseeing Port Isabel cases, Judge Robert Powell, has made himself famous for saying "No." Roughly 88 percent of asylum applications put before Judge Powell from 2014 to 2019 were denied, compared with a national average of just over 60 percent, according to Syracuse University's Transactional Records Access Clearinghouse (TRAC) database. More than one in ten of the applicants were from Eritrea, a nation that was at war with neighboring Ethiopia for much of Judge Powell's tenure, and where political persecution is still reportedly rife under the dictator Isaias Afwerki. Overall, Los Fresnos court denied more than 80 percent of asylum applications in that five-year period, including Kidane's.

Judge Hanrahan's description of the "soul-crushing" immigration courts and their self-perpetuating misery echoes Kidane's disillusionment. It also echoes the portrait drawn of the Soviet prison system drawn by Alexander Solzhenitsyn in *The Gulag Archipelago*. Solzhenitsyn described the gulags as a hungry beast whose appetite only grew the more lives they devoured. The keepers of the gulag system rehearsed the rituals of justice—interrogations, case files, formal charges—but neither justice nor state security had anything to do with it. The gulags themselves demanded to be fed.

In the same way, the US asylum process has been repurposed as a penal system. The rituals of asylum seeking are observed, but the true search is for a pretext to detain or deport. As Judge Hanrahan observed, clemency is determined by the political winds of the day, rather than the compulsion of case facts.

The criminalization of asylum represents a logical conclusion of thirty years of increasingly overzealous border securitization. For much of the late twentieth century, the Republican Party balanced "border security" with the pragmatism of the "party of business." It was an open secret that South Texan cattle ranchers, Houston homebuilders, and California Central Valley almond farmers could not sustain their businesses without the steady flow of laborers across the US-Mexico border. Their representatives in Congress, mostly Republicans, turned pragmatically blind eyes to the relative porousness of the border.

Border policy started to change in the early 1990s. Although the border patrol started in 1924 and military units were deployed to the border throughout the twentieth century, it was not until its last decade that the border received massive buildup.[10] With the passing of NAFTA and its disastrous effects on Mexican farmers, migration toward the US grew. In response, border patrol strategy shifted from apprehending border crossers after they crossed to militarizing the border to not let them cross.

Starting with a number of urban area "operations" in the early 1990s ("Blockade" in El Paso, "Gatekeeper" in southern California, "Safeguard" in Arizona, "Rio Grande" in South Texas), the US instituted its "Prevention through Deterrence" (PTD) policy, which pushed migration to the rural, and more dangerous, areas.[11] Border patrol spending skyrocketed, from less than $500 million per year in the early 1990s to $3.5 billion per year by 2012. Immigration policing in total had grown to $18 billion—more than all money spent on federal law enforcement combined.[12] Similarly, the number of border patrol agents grew from less than four thousand in 1994 to over twenty thousand by 2010.

At the same rate of physical border buildup, the border wall went "virtual" through surveillance technology, defense, and intelligence resources, not to mention the expansion of border internalization of deportations and detentions.[13] Before 1986, the US averaged 20,000 deportations per year; by the mid-2000s, the number of annual removals had grown to 400,000. Similarly, the passing of Clinton-era AEDPA and IIRIRA laws foreshadowed the marriage of immigration reform with anti-terrorism legislation, effectively criminalizing immigrants through a quadrupling of detention center occupancy from 85,000 in 1985 to 410,000 in 2013.

The World Trade Center attacks extended the war on drugs techniques to the war on terror, expanding the racialized effects of drug enforcement to immigration control. Consequently, the ambiguous criteria of "national security" were used to detain asylum seekers at an unprecedented level. Soon after 9/11, the US implemented Operation Liberty Shield, which required automatic detention of asylum seekers from thirty-three countries. The criminalization of asylum applicants morphed into the Blanket Detention Order of 2003, which allowed for the indefinite holding of asylum seekers. With the creation of the Department of Homeland Security (DHS), and its subsidiary Immigration and Customs Enforcement (ICE), detention and removal became big business. The Obama-era Secure Communities and Criminal Alien Program instituted detention bed quotas, which fueled the growth of private prison companies overseeing 49 percent of detention beds in 2009 to 81 percent by 2018.

The post-1990s buildup was justified in the name of deterrence. But, as we have shown, as border security funding grows, so does the profitability of migration, effectively incentivizing, not deterring, crossing.[14] Indeed, since the early 1990s, the number of irregular US-Mexico border crossings have not only grown, but so too have the rates and use of smugglers.[15]

The militarization of the border and criminalization of migrants would take a further turn to the right after the Great Recession of 2008. Particularly during the second term of the Obama presidency, the Grand Old Party platform, driven by figures like then senator Jeff Sessions, became overtly anti-immigrant. It was facile populism from the start, blaming migrants for the economic downturn: a page taken right out of the 1930s rightist rabble rousers' beerhall speeches. It was plain old "coming-over-here, taking-our-jobs" xenophobia. Nowhere in the academic economic literature does anyone suggest that immigration policy had anything to do with causing the Great Recession. Quite the reverse: many economists would say the US grew at suboptimal levels during the Obama recovery because population growth had stalled. Other reasons for the slow grind included advances in factory automation; the complex trade and labor-market currents created by globalization (mostly a case of factories migrating, rather than workers); and the continued concentration of US economic activity in services and intellectual-property businesses.

Of course, the new Republican line that the US should only respect immigrants who follow the letter of abstruse immigration regulations also flies in the face of the party's philosophy that red tape is the enemy of enterprise and personal liberty.

Democrats, too, have played a key role in border securitization and immigrant criminalization. While the Clinton administration oversaw the initial buildup of border security, President Obama became famous for administering a record number of deportations, even earning the nickname of Deporter-in-Chief. However, the partisan differences in immigration policy were starkest in the transition from Obama to Trump. Beginning with the appointment of Sessions as Attorney General, the Justice Department has openly supported the Trump administration's mission to not only minimize crossing of the Mexican border, but effectively end asylum as we know it.

The Muslim travel ban of January 2017 would set the tone for the four years to come. In June 2018, the administration's "zero tolerance" policy would refer all adults apprehended at the border to criminal prosecution, separating them from their children according to the Flores Agreement. At the same time, the Administration chiseled away at asylum. It instituted a dizzying range of reforms, the most damaging including asylum metering, limiting the number of asylum seekers to apply per day; Migrant Protection Protocols (MPP), forcing applicants to wait in Mexico until their cases are heard; barring victims of gender and gang-based violence to apply for asylum; forcing applicants to apply only at official ports of entry; and instituting fees for migrants to apply for asylum. As we discussed previously, one final nail in the asylum coffin came in the form of "safe third country" agreements with Guatemala, El Salvador, and Honduras, which allowed the US to return applicants to Central America—or deny applicants for not applying for asylum in one of the countries through which they transited.

All of these policies undermine US and international immigration law and are being challenged in court at the time of writing, as well as gradually overturned by a new Biden administration. Nonetheless, they have achieved the objective of wreaking havoc on the US immigration system, effectively thrusting millions of people into dangerous and inhumane conditions. There remained a sliver of hope for migrants who present a claim for protection under the Convention against Torture (CAT), which often requires detention before one's case is heard. For many of the rest, the strategy was to wait in Mexico until a change in the US presidency.

The Republicans claimed they were tolerant of immigrants because they tolerated immigrants "who came here legally." It was immigration judges like Judge Powell, of course, who would determine what "legally" meant. Kidane had modest expectations for his experience in the US, but he was still deeply hurt by the court's treatment. He came to seek refuge, but the court treated him as a criminal who came to seek a free ride.

Kidane does not contain the ingredients for bitterness. As a rule, his face has an open expression of goodwill. The only time we saw lines of anger and frustration was when he talked about his asylum application. For someone who set high standards of fairness in their own treatment of others, his reception to the US burned acutely.

Although he was denied asylum, Kidane was granted a "Withholding of Removal," meaning he would not be deported, at least not immediately. According to the America Team, up until September 2017, the US government was not deporting Eritreans who failed asylum due to the threat of imprisonment, torture, and death for returnees, granting most applicants protections under CAT (Convention Against Torture). Additionally, the Eritrean Embassy had refused to issue travel documents to deportees. In September 2017, however, the Department of Homeland Security began detaining Eritreans who were denied asylum with the intention of removal. Deportations stopped soon thereafter when a deportee committed suicide en route.

While withholding of removal allowed Kidane to stay in the US, it provided no path to residency and family reunification and could be revoked at any moment. Kidane expressed feeling stuck in limbo, momentarily safe from removal, but unable to plan a future with his family in the US.

I couldn't process family to come here. If the government does not change for the next ten years, I will be here but can't [bring my family].

I have already applied for paperwork. We are not feeling good here. Separated from family for five years or more. I talk with some people and tell them I'm separated from my family. They cannot believe for years. How can you stay like this? Sometimes talking about this makes me feel angry.

I say to my son "I miss you," and he says "if you miss me, why don't you come?"

My father is now eighty-two, eighty-three years old. He's getting old. I've got one brother in Europe, another in Libya.

If I don't have a problem in our country, why wouldn't I go home? My wife is living with her parents. When in Africa, we couldn't separate our home. She shares with her parents. I can't send her money. I would prefer to be home. It's very difficult. She must [get] out from our country illegally if she wants to come.

After the interview in the café, we invited Kidane to join us on our trip to some Houston museums. Our Uber driver was also an African immigrant. He came from Nigeria. He had recently suffered a bad burn in a cooking accident. He wanted to return to his studies. For now, he was driving a nice car and meeting people from all over the world. It was the kind of life we could imagine for Kidane.

The driver took us to the Rothko Chapel. We didn't know much about the chapel, but we were familiar with Rothko's stark, uber-minimalist paintings so it wasn't a great surprise to enter what looked like a grey concrete bunker with a few black and grey panel paintings.

We sat down on the concrete benches and absorbed the strange sense of tranquility that seems to pervade the building. Despite its urban location and its place in the chaotic modern historical era, it is an oasis of calm, a Central Park of the soul.

We had told Kidane that the museum was one of the most famous artistic installations in the country, one that drew visitors from all over the world. He followed the circular path that people use to view the panel paintings.

"What are people looking at?" said Kidane.

"The paintings . . . they're simple, but . . ."

"They're nothing! The paintings are nothing," Kidane said. "They're looking at nothing."

It was a brutally frank assessment of Rothko's work. But surprisingly hard to rebut.

"In Eritrea, we have beautiful cathedrals, with paintings," said Kidane.

"There's something powerful about the stark . . ."

"It's nothing," said Kidane.

There was nothing foolish about the visitors filing through the Rothko chapel, muttering sophisticated notes of appreciation. This was not a question of the "emperor's new clothes." It was more of a commentary on divergent life experiences.

If modern art is defined by the experience that people bring to the work of art, Kidane brought five years of heartache, anguish, and life-or-death struggle. There was nothing to reflect that odyssey in the serene chapel.

The eclectic collection in the Museum of Fine Arts Houston was more to Kidane's taste. The richest cultural experience of the visit, however, turned out to be in a suburban strip mall. There, we had dinner at Lucy Ethiopian Restaurant and Lounge. Ethiopian owner Suzani Grant extended to us the hospitality that Kidane assured us was typical of his homeland.

"Kidane has shared with us his story of traveling through Africa on the back of a motorbike, and then through the Americas," we said.

"Oh, this is nothing," Ms. Grant said. "These days they go by motorbike, by bus. We walked!"

Ms. Grant, as it turned out, had fled the Ethiopian famine and civil war in the 1980s. She spent some time in Europe before meeting and marrying a United States citizen. Together, they had opened the restaurant where we now sat.

She was living proof that the extraordinary migration journeys taken from the Horn of Africa could have a happy ending, once upon a time.

Everybody Cried

For Jane Mtebe, there was no doubt about what the worst part of her journey was. Her two near-death experiences in the Panamanian jungle? The rough-and-ready field hospital at the edge of the jungle?

> [It] was the handcuffs in America. That's when we really felt bad. [The rest of the] journey was OK, just normal journey, enjoying adventure.
>
> The other moment was horrible handcuffs and chains and everything was even worse than the jungle. It was OK, just a scary route . . . route was really scary.
>
> Then when you get before you get to Tijuana, there's a stony valley there it was so beautiful, though the road was scary . . . the scenery was like really beautiful, nature at its best. I have some video of the rocky mountains.
>
> When we got to Tijuana we went straight to the border to pick a number so we can enter.

"Picking a number" is part of Mexico's response to the pressure from the Trump administration, its version of *flujo controlado*. The Trump administration made this public pressure a piece of diplomatic reality television. In the summer of 2019, as Mr. Trump railed against migrant caravans, he pointed the finger at Mexico, claiming the Obrador administration was not doing enough to stop the caravans. The administration publicly threatened to raise tariffs on Mexican imports. With the US already waging tariff wars with China and the European Union, Mexican President Andrés Manuel López Obrador could not afford to dismiss the threat. The Trump administration was effectively vowing to shut export-oriented Mexico out of its main market, unless it could find some way to disrupt the flow of migrants.

As discussed in the previous chapter, the new measures included the painstaking drip-drip-drip of people through Tapachula. At Mexico's northern border, there was an even more stringent method of controlling the flow. Mexico's INM immigration service, or some representative of INM, would now distribute numbers that allow migrants to claim a place in the line to cross into the US, parceling out permission based on the US quota for daily asylum applications mentioned earlier, known as "metering." CBP defends metering as necessary due to the insufficient resources to process more than a small number of applicants daily. However, the Cato Institute has shown that larger numbers of applications were processed under the Obama administration, concluding that "the purpose of metering is to make immigrants so miserable that they give up and go home."[16]

Metering is outsourced to Mexican officials (who, in turn, often outsource the queue to private actors) through MPP, the Orwellian "Migrant Protections Protocol" better known as "Wait in Mexico." Although migrants from non-Spanish-speaking countries are supposed to be exempt from MPP, border officials have discretion to send any nationality back to Mexico—as Ms. Mtebe experienced.[17] While waiting in Mexico, human rights observers have documented high numbers of kidnapping, rape, torture, assault, and extortion of asylum seekers in the program in clear violation of non-refoulement principles of international law.[18]

Whether part of the MPP program or not, many asylum-seekers were forced to stay in Mexico. The new asylum requirements maintained that any non-Mexican migrant should have applied for asylum elsewhere on their way. Through WhatsApp messages and phone conversations, Mr. Tumwine described his daily existence in Tijuana as a dire one. He lived in what he described as a Haitian camp consisting of tents near the border wall. By some estimates, thousands of Haitians are living in makeshift homes in Tijuana in an area known as Little Haiti or the Ciudad de Dios.[19]

Under the eye of Mexican immigration forces, designated migrants took people's information, checking their passports, and the *tramite* from the INM immigration service. The new arrival is then given a number and must check into the marquee regularly to find out their place in the queue. As soon as Ms. Mtebe arrived, she joined a crowd of migrants in a large marquee. Here they were processed, according to reports, not by the INM, but by other migrants. One explanation for the INM's outsourcing of the work is "plausible deniability" on the question of the Mexican immigration service doing the US dirty work of enforcing the refugee quota.

The use of "lists" placed asylum seekers waiting to request protection in the United States at risk of being identified and located in Mexico and susceptible to extortion by "list" managers. In Piedras Negras, where private individuals have run the list on behalf of the municipality, a previous "list" manager allegedly extracted payments from asylum seekers to join a parallel, expedited "list." In Ciudad Acuña, Grupos Beta allegedly extorts between $500 and $1,300 from migrants to move their names to the top of the list. Meanwhile, a private citizen group controls the list in Piedras Negras, while the official INM runs it in Nuevo Laredo.[20]

One exasperated immigration lawyer, Jodi Goodwin, described the chaos of MPP in the following:

> Then there are all the court documents that have fake addresses where CBP puts in an address to a shelter that no one can get in. They are homeless. But the judges buy those fake addresses and use them to deport people. The "tear sheets" which are supposed to instruct refugees how to appear to court are either not given at all or given with wrong information telling them to appear at the bridge at the same time their hearing is supposed to start, which ensures they will not make it to their hearing on time. Then there are those thrown back without even giving them their court documents. . . . How in the world are refugees supposed to know when and where to go to court when CBP won't even give them the court documents? And of course I cannot fail to mention all the defects in the court charging documents . . . it goes on and on.[21]

While she was waiting in Tijuana, Ms. Mtebe asked Kristina, the American hostel owner she had met in Colombia, to forward on the cash that she had left in her care. Kristina had held the money in trust for Ms. Mtebe so that it could not be stolen from the Cameroonian migrant on the route.

This was the first interaction we had with Ms. Mtebe, facilitating this transfer of money. We used the financial firm that does for the shadow migration business what American Express once did for the conventional travel industry—Western Union. The nearest agent to us was the local supermarket. Some locals call the place, with suburban hauteur, the "Murder Kroger." We joined a line of the unbanked, many of them migrants themselves, between the change machine and the lotto advertisements, waiting to cash checks, pay bills, and send remittances. Slowly, the agent gathered the information necessary to print the voluminous receipt, topped by the all-important "MTN number," which the recipient must provide to pick up the money.

On the other end, Ms. Mtebe was not just unbanked, but entirely undocumented. Few of the migrants on the *camino duro* have identification acceptable to merchants unfamiliar with foreign passports and visas. Often, local people act as intermediaries for the Western Union, providing an ID recognizable to the Mexican WU agent. The sender has no way to verify that the name provided by the recipient is a trusted intermediary rather than a bandit posing as such. It's an honor system comparable to the practice of *hawala*, which is widespread in the labor migration networks of the Global South. In the *hawala* system, people send money to one another using middlemen who don't have any documented link to the transaction.

To us, Ms. Mtebe was blunt in her messages—understandably frazzled. Even then, we had no idea what stress she must have been under. We were somewhat taken aback by her "Where was the receipt?" We messaged her a photograph of the receipt. "No!" We had to send one with more information. Despite Kristina's introduction, we had fears regarding fraud. Could the man whose name we were using be seeking personal information like our WU account number? We messaged Ms. Mtebe a picture revealing slightly more information, including the location of the sending office, which is a critical detail. "No!" She needed our full names.

Ms. Mtebe and her friends, who were a few weeks behind Kidane on the trail, experienced the delays in Tijuana that he had wished to avoid.

> When we came they told us that we'd be there between four to six weeks. [I] left I think on the sixth week.
>
> A lot lot lot [of migrants were waiting]. There was a lot. You went to get numbers. I was like, they showed us the list is long. I knew we'd be there four to six weeks. [On the] fourth week, we knew we should be coming to check our numbers because you may enter at any time after the fourth week.
>
> We were checking every day . . . not like one day kind of thing . . . yeah, it was difficult really frustrating you have to feed yourself. You're scared not to run out of money because nobody will feed you. It's very uncertain.

In Tijuana, Ms. Mtebe reunited with Gloria, the friend who had traveled with her to South America from Ghana. The woman was now heavily pregnant. Ms. Mtebe also received bad news about the belongings she'd left in the care of another Cameroonian man in her friend's group, who Ms. Mtebe had lost in the Darién jungle.

"I met the guy that had my bag," said Ms. Mtebe. A *coyote* had tricked the Cameroonian man into giving him Ms. Mtebe's bag, saying that was her request. "That's when I knew I lost everything passport birth certificate . . . everything lost!"

The San Ysidro pedestrian crossing from Tijuana to the San Diego area is the most heavily trafficked border crossing in the Western hemisphere.

YouTube footage shows a long arcade of stores and street cafes on the Mexican side, funneling the foot traffic into the turnstile gates, in an uncanny echo of a Disneyworld entrance.

On the day that her number came up, Ms. Mtebe was taken by a minivan to the pedestrian ramp in northern Tijuana that leads to the San Ysidro crossing.

> You enter by the gate there. Most of the time everyone stands outside. They call their names, enter by a gate. You give them that paper that they give you at Tapachula.

There was a checkpoint on the Mexican side, where border guards checked Ms. Mtebe's *tramite* against her person to make sure it was her. Initially, the clicking of the turnstile did inspire a joyful anticipation.

> There was a small gate like that drop us there have to walk. We walked at [one] side then a lot of cars at the other side people going in and coming out. They really welcome you . . . "Welcome to the United States of America!"

When Ms. Mtebe met with the representatives from the US CBP on the other side of the pedestrian ramp, she was worried they would not let her pass because she lacked her original documents. But the border officer applied a generous reverse-psychology reading to her case.

> I had to explain to them what happened. They were kind of skeptical. They say lot of people saying all their things are lost. Mine was a bit easier because some people say passport is lost, but they have the original of the birth certificate. My case was different because I didn't have originals for anything . . . it was all was just photocopies. So many people were coming with original . . . he believed me, and said "I'm really sorry that you lost everything."
>
> Someone in front of me told them he'd lost his passport, and they asked him, "How have you lost your passport but you have original [state] ID, but the ID is smaller than the passport?"
>
> I told them I don't even have ID or birth certificate. Everything was gone. [The border guard] told the first guy, "this is somebody that lost something."

Ms. Mtebe was waved on, into the US.

It was October 2018, and, just on the other side of the border from Tijuana, Ms. Mtebe was taken to an "ice box," one of the "cage"-like cells that had stirred such controversy that year. In another deliberate effort to discomfit migrants, Immigration and Customs Enforcement utilize crowded holding cells known as "las hieleras" or "iceboxes." Excessively cold air is blown into the make-shift cells. If you have lived an un-air-conditioned life, the blast of filtered air is one of the first and most visceral culture shocks of arrival in the US. Just going to a bank to cash a traveler's check is unpleasant. In the "iceboxes," the refrigerated air is blown incessantly, a discomfort amplified to a form of torture. Migrants are given a single mylar, or thin foil, sheet to warm themselves.

> So they took us there, and took all information, name, they take fingerprints everything. [I] say rooms [but it's] some cell not a room, supposed to give you mat. And the blanket some kind of funny blanket like that.
>
> It was a really cold cell, with like fifteen of you in one small cell. But it's separated, children have their own. If women they have baby they have their own cell. Teenagers, adolescent have theirs. Then they separated me and other women so they don't just mix.

None of this is an accident. Nowhere was the Trump administration's policy of "deterrence" and "zero tolerance" clearer than in the detention centers along the border. It was in the "ice boxes," as Ms. Mtebe observed, where the controversial practice of "child separation," of deliberately separating young children from their parents, was practiced. This is freezing, malnourishment, and overcrowding by design. Ms. Mtebe said the food was notably worse than that provided in Mexico or Costa Rica, far poorer states than the US, who are dealing with the same people.

For Ms. Mtebe, any idea that the turnstile was the way to the end of her trip was immediately shattered. The detention center was closer to hell, filled with the sounds of anguish from lost souls.

> We were there for five days then we left six days. People were crying it was so bad . . . that place was no good.
>
> There was a Turkish girl . . . she was crying every second. She was not used to [such treatment]. She was crying and crying.

Here, Ms. Mtebe gave her first interview to an "asylum officer" from the US CBP agency. She was awoken at two or three in the morning, to her surprise. This interview seemed to be the first step in a screening process used to separate people with legitimate asylum cases from those who do not qualify. Such screening processes were the pretext under which the US began to use migration detention centers in the late nineteenth century.

> This one is the first interview, not the "credible fear" interview, but any information you give there. . . . If they find something that's not credible fear you're done. They had to ask if you have a sponsor. When you enter they ask for the name of anybody in America that they can call.

Some of Ms. Mtebe's cellmates told her their interviewers used harsh interrogation techniques and intimidation. Their interrogators shone lights in their faces, she was told, "and they'd just be like, 'You're lying!'"

> The guy that interviewed me, Ramsay, he was nice to me . . . he really felt my pain. He was nice.
> My sponsor was called but did not pick up. . . . [they were] probably sleeping. The man interviewed me . . . asked how I traveled. He explained everything to me. He didn't ask me what happened to me in Cameroon. He said very soon I would leave this place. "Just know this is not credible fear; this is a [preliminary interview.] What happened in Cameroon . . . I don't want to ask you that. I'm not the one to take a decision on that."

Ms. Mtebe felt relieved because she had heard of worse treatment, but she was still interrogated much as a suspected criminal in the US would be. When it was time to leave the "ice-box," she was treated like a convict on a chain gang. Jane Mtebe was a nurse with postgraduate qualifications. She fit the profile of the skilled immigrants that even the Trump administration has conceded that the US economy desperately needs. Nobody has ever suggested that Ms. Mtebe had anything to do with crime. And, yet, under the Trump administration's policy, she was shackled like a convicted killer. It was painful enough for Ms. Mtebe to talk about her persecution by the police in her home country. But she cannot talk about her departure from the holding cell in San Diego without tears clogging her throat.

> When [we were] supposed to leave, they took us to the corridor. They handcuffed our legs first, then you have to walk with that handcuff on your legs to house where the bus is standing they tie chain around your waist and handcuff your hands. At that point I cried, it was so horrible. [You felt like a] criminal.
> Everybody cried, even me, I was crying. The [ICE officers] were nice they were

like it's a rule, it's a policy they're supposed to follow, not like they really want to do it, but they've been asked to do it.

Not all of the border patrol were so nice. While Ms. Mtebe was in the "ice box" some of the officers taunted her.

> When I was in the cell, some of the officers were good, some were mean. There was a day some people were complaining the food wasn't enough. So one of the officers said "where you people are coming from, you don't have food or water to drink." The [other guards] shunned the officer. Their boss had to talk to him and they took him out.

Another Cameroonian woman who traveled across the Americas from Brazil with her two young children was helped on the Texas border by contacts of Kristina, the American hostel-owner in Colombia. She was not separated from her children because she arrived in June 2017, before that policy was enforced. Like Ms. Mtebe, however, the Cameroonian mother, who had worked as a translator in Cameroon and Nigeria, was made to feel like a criminal.

> We were struggling to go through this one . . . we went there . . . they refused us. For two days, we went to two different border [crossings.] The third one worked. It went well, because when we entered the officer on duty was like, "Where you people from?"
> We said, "from Cameroon." He said, "Oh, Cameroon, I heard you guys are having some trouble there." So he asked for the paper they give in the Mexico camp. So when he asked for that, we gave him [the papers], they took us in, they took our bags took everything. I had to take off my earrings off and everything. They just took us to a room.
> Yeah, so after taking our pictures, handprints and all that they took us to a room where we met other people . . . it was very confined three days. It was not like, very scary, because [the kids] could talk, play, do their things.
> But they have been through a lot. After three days they released us. Then they took us to a place [where they put] a monitor for GPS on my leg.

The Cameroonian mother would wear the GPS monitor for ten months. "It was so traumatizing," she said.

Ms. Mtebe's bus was essentially a prison bus, with bars separating the detainees from the driver. The detainees remained shackled for the entire journey. During the last decade, and particularly during the Trump administration, migrant-detention protocols have taken on many of the trappings of the prison system. (For example, Israel "Izzy" Torres, a Mexican American who was deported in 2016 after decades living in Texas, said he was placed in a "spit hood," a barbaric restraint, when he was transported to Mexico by ICE.[22]) After four hours, they arrived in the San Luis, Arizona, detention center. Here, Ms. Mtebe was happier. The manacles were removed. The food was decent, and the guards were friendly. She was taken to the health center because of her high blood pressure. She was given special medication. She had tuberculosis testing and was administered vaccines.

Like Kidane, she slept in a large dormitory, sharing with up to forty other women at a time. The guards patrolled outside the dormitory. She stayed in Arizona for seventeen days and was then flown in a military plane to another detention center in Colorado, "again in chains and handcuffs . . . and footcuffs."

In Colorado, Ms. Mtebe said, there were "lots of emergencies." There was a fire alarm on the dormitory that regularly sounded in the middle of the night for drills or otherwise. One of Ms. Mtebe's fellow female prisoners suffered from epilepsy, which was consistently triggered by the alarm drills. The ambulance crew who came to pick up the woman warned the guards that she would have to be moved to avoid further fits. The guards ignored the warnings, and the ambulance crew kept coming.

Ms. Mtebe spent Christmas in detention. She remembers it relatively fondly. It was her first time seeing snow. Local volunteers came to sing Christmas songs and hand out gifts. Still, it was not the same. Usually, she made a trip to see her mum in the French-speaking region of Cameroon.

Ms. Mtebe had her "credible fear" interview on December 28, 2019. Arguing for your own "credible fear"—it's a vicious joke that Alexander Solzhenitsyn would surely appreciate. Can someone who is gripped by terror give a credible account of their terror? Remember what Ms. Mtebe had experienced in seeking a place of refuge—near death in a nightmarish jungle, confinement in a cage with weeping strangers, public manacling and confinement in remote prisons. And now, she had to face interrogation about the traumatic flight from her home and convince an unseen "asylum" officer that she had genuine reasons to be afraid. If Ms. Mtebe did not feel fear, she would not be in her right mind.

On the fourth last day of 2019, Ms. Mtebe and a Spanish-speaking woman were taken to a room where they each spoke with an asylum officer by phone.

The interviewer, when the call was connected, asked me if I was there with any-one. I said, "yeah, I'm here with one Spanish girl who doesn't speak English." The interviewer called security and said I was supposed to be in the room alone. Security was mad like am I reporting her? I said, "no, she just asked . . ."

They interviewed me on the phone . . . the interview was OK. They wanted to ask name of my sponsor. The number I had forgotten. They said no it was OK, they had all the information. [They asked] what happened in Cameroon why did I leave. I had to explain everything that I told you before with her. What happened with police, and stuff like that to her.

Two weeks later, Ms. Mtebe was informed that she had passed the credible-fear test. It was a great relief. The fear that she would not be judged sufficiently afraid was alleviated. She was given a choice of continuing the case out on parole or resolving it more quickly by waiting in confinement. She chose the latter. She appeared before an immigration judge one week after the credible-fear interview for a ruling on her asylum application. The judge read four charges against her, relating to her crossing the US border without a visa. She acknowledged each one. The judge gave her two weeks to fill out a form with all the details of her asylum claim.

Like Kidane, Ms. Mtebe had heard bad things about the court-appointed lawyers, who she feared would "waste my time. That's when I told the judge I'll handle myself whatever happens will happen to me," said Ms. Mtebe.

It was a courageous decision, verging on the rash. To a US citizen who has taken Civics 101, US immigration law seems straightforward. Anyone who has been through the ICE wringer knows otherwise. The endless demands for identification, forms, hearings, and fingerprints often appear to be an exercise in red tape as trip wires for exclusion. Certainly, the bureaucratic demands were weaponized during the Trump years. John Stauffer, the advocate for Eritrean refugees in the US, said he had heard of Eritreans having asylum applications rejected because they left fields on their forms blank, instead of writing N/A or not applicable. With more than half of all asylum applications rejected in the US in the five years up to 2019, according to Syracuse University's TRAC, the odds were stacked against Ms. Mtebe, even with expert legal representation. Speaking for herself, the case would not be delayed so she had to figure out the process quickly.

One Mexican [woman] had a lawyer, and I looked at the way the lawyer organized her documents. I went up to library, and filled my form out. My sister sent me affidavits from Cameroon. [She] also [sent me] some letters telling me that the police are still looking for me. . . . I put everything together took it to the court those [were] the only things I had. I didn't have time to go and sign an affidavit.

Any young lawyer would be intimidated by their first confrontation with a highly experienced US government lawyer. Now imagine that you are representing yourself in an unfamiliar setting, without any legal training and scant familiarity with the American dialect of the English language, which is quite different from the English spoken in West Africa. The slim chance of a favorable ruling is often contingent not on *what* you say, but *how* you say it. As analysis of asylum cases has shown, having one's story be considered truthful requires telling it according to a Western literary standard of veracity.[23] In other words, a "truthful" story must be what an American judge considers a "good" story consisting of details, plausibility, consistency, and a narrative arc. Trying to translate cultural understandings of narrative, not to mention the impact of traumatic experiences, rarely make for neat and well-packaged stories.

It was really scary because the first day, when the judge asked the government lawyer where she wanted me to go to, the government lawyer said she wanted me to go back to Cameroon. The judge said, "OK, I'll look into that." The case was just beginning.

The second time when judge of that court has come back, I gave her my documents what I presented [my case]. She was like, "you did all this without a lawyer?" I said, "yes I did it." . . . She was like, "Wow! I really think you want to go home." I said, "yes, I want to go home but I'm scared."

The government lawyer gave Ms. Mtebe a form to fill out and said the fingerprints should be ready to process in seven weeks. Ms. Mtebe left the courtroom feeling encouraged. It sounded like the judge wanted to approve the application. The fingerprint instructions came back five weeks later from a Nebraska office. But the court date was delayed until March 5.

So when we came first the government lawyer came that's when my heart was beating. The government lawyer came to me and said, "are you the lady that needs English translation?" I said, "no I don't need translation." She said, "very sorry." The way she apologized, [which] made my pressure come down. Just three of us in court with security guard. [The] judge asked what happened in Cameroon, my name, age, educational level, which schools I'd gone to, what did I do in school.

She asked when did your problems start in Cameroon? I explained everything to her. We reached [the subject of] prison, and I explained how the prison cell looked like. I explained everything. When I was done, she had to hand over to the government lawyer.

For Ms. Mtebe, talking about her ordeal is painful. She had pushed through trauma to reach the US, and now she had to relive the trauma over and over again, first for the judge and now for the prosecutor's cross-examination. She answered all the prosecutor's questions about events in Tiko, her hometown. When the prosecutor's questions stopped, the judge said, "'I intend to grant her asylum.'"

The government lawyer wanted to continue with the case, and have Ms. Mtebe read the statements from her forms. "The judge was like, 'Why should I let her? She has been consistent, saying the same thing since the day she entered,'" said Ms. Mtebe.

Next, the lawyer raised an issue with fingerprints. There were mistakes on a couple of Ms. Mtebe's prints. This, in the government lawyer's eyes, would become Ms. Mtebe's problem rather than that of the Federal Bureau of Investigation agents who took the fingerprints. Ms. Mtebe's heart must have skipped a beat while the judge considered this technicality. Had Ms. Mtebe gone to the FBI office willingly and allowed herself to be fingerprinted? That was enough for the judge. If the government wished to appeal her decision, they were welcome to. But Ms. Mtebe was granted asylum. Case closed.

Usually, an asylum applicant was released from detention a day or two after their application was approved by a judge. In this case, however, Ms. Mtebe remained in confinement for days, and then more than a week. She was exasperated.

Even the [ICE] officer there, was like, "what are you still doing here? Because, you're still here but you're supposed to have left." They don't know. There was no case [against me.] They didn't know why they were keeping me there. Two weeks after [the hearing] . . . that's when they told me [that I was] supposed to have left two week ago. There was a mistake, an error.

Ms. Mtebe was in bed 20 in her dormitory. The Center confused her with another Cameroonian woman, who was in bed 18. The second woman was later told that she'd have to wait another two months as the release process was started in error.

Finally, the day arrived. Volunteers from the Denver nonprofit organization Casa de Paz picked up Ms. Mtebe outside the detention center's back door, taking her and about four other released detainees in a minivan. They took her to the shelter in Denver, a suburban house that Coloradan Sarah Jackson purchased and opened up to immigrants, calling it the "house that love built." The organization's web site claims that more than 3,100 migrants from seventy-seven countries have stayed there.

> They [took] me to Casa de Paz house. There I met some other volunteers. [Got] food there on the table, and asked me to eat. showed me a room asked me to sleep, gave me hygienic stuff.
>
> They asked me for the number to call the sponsor so I'd have a means of transport so I can go.
>
> Now they call, and my sponsor says "OK," she'll look for a flight. So they check for flight.

Ms. Mtebe stayed in the shelter for about a week. Casa de Paz paid half the $500 airfare to Reagan Airport in the Washington, DC, area, where her US-based friend and sponsor lived.

> It was so refreshing . . . it was good. [I stayed in] Casa de Paz till next day one of volunteers took me to the airport, and even bought me breakfast there. They took me through. I had a cart because [they gave] me a card [to] bypass security checks.

Ms. Mtebe's relief and gratitude at the welcome she found at Casa de Paz are reminiscent of Kidane's feelings on arriving at Mama Africa's, and of a passage in Charlotte Bronte's *Jane Eyre*: "Somehow, now that I had once crossed the threshold of this house, and once was brought face to face with its owners, I felt no longer outcast, vagrant, and disowned by the wide world."[24] Ms. Mtebe stayed with her friend in Maryland for a week, then moved to Massachusetts, where she found work through a nursing agency. She has worked in a center in Rockland for people with disabilities. "We teach them basic things in life—arts and crafts, music, exercise, sewing."

When she got her work permit in September 2019, she started working full time. When the coronavirus crisis hit, she was on the front lines, caring for the disabled in their homes in Canton, Massachusetts.

"It's not like what I expected but it's manageable," said Ms. Mtebe. "I stay with a friend . . . we have our own apartment that we share. The weather . . . it's cold all the time, not hot like where I come from."

Destination Liminal

By early 2019, Kidane Okubay was fed up with his life in Houston. He could not get regular work without a permit, and he had little hope of winning his appeal. An Eritrean friend told him they knew a smuggler who could help. If Kidane took one more leg on the *camino duro*, his friend told him, he could expect better luck in Canada.

The US was long universally considered the preeminent destination for asylum-seekers. For thousands of refugees, during the Trump administration, the US had become just another way station. One of the most striking images on our travels along the *camino* was the façade of an agency in Tapachula advertising visa sales. These private agencies are common sights along all the chokepoints on the route, from Kathmandu to Quito. The preeminent flag on the facades of these offices has always been the stars and stripes. In Tapachula in 2020, however, the largest flag, painted on the wall, mural-style, as Mexican signage often is, was a red maple leaf between two red stripes.

In mid-March 2019, Kidane traveled by Greyhound bus from Houston to Minneapolis, where he and an Eritrean friend met a smuggler who they paid for passage. Together, they traveled by taxi, north to the US-Canada border. The smuggler showed Kidane and his friend an area of farmland and pointed them forward. By then it was 9 p.m. on March 20. The snow still lay thick on the fields. Kidane had seen snow, but never like this. Not a blade of grass penetrated the winter shroud.

The smuggler had told Kidane the snow would have hardened, making it possible to stay on the surface. But it was still powder. They had to wade through the fields with the snow up to their knees. Using the global-positioning service on their phone as a compass, they walked north, trudging through the snow for more than half an hour. Their teeth were chattering.

When Kidane's GPS showed they had crossed the Canadian border, he dialed 911. The smuggler had told them what would come next. The Canadian police picked them up and took them to the nearest border-patrol station at Emerson, Manitoba. Once they had been processed, the group were transported by the border patrol to the nearest large urban center—Winnipeg. For the first time in his five-year journey, Kidane felt welcome somewhere. After the bullets in South Sudan; the windowless warehouses in Dubai; the treacherous *camino duro* through the Americas; and the gulag system of US immigration, he finally felt safe. He was finally someplace that felt like it could one day be home.

> Here in Canada, they do not have any detention center. I write and send all my case to immigration. Then wait for immigration response. For me they accept me after nine months. Till they give my work permit the Canadian government helped me all the expenses. After two months they gave me my work permit and start my job. I arrived Canada on [March 20] 2019 and started job on [May 27] 2019. So Canadian immigration is better for me when I compare with American immigration.

An Eritrean friend of Kidane's, who was already in Winnipeg, gave him a ski jacket and tips for dealing with the cold. He bought himself some warm clothes and a new pair of shoes.

Kidane soon found a job, at a company on the outskirts of Winnipeg called Duxton Windows & Doors. At the weekends, he works another part-time job. The cold weather doesn't bother him after the warm reception.

We asked him whether it was worth it, the years of wandering, the desperate search for a better life, the near-death experiences, the ignominy of the detention centers.

> Yes [it has] been worth it, because at least I get peace. You know I can go wherever I want inside Canada and the rest of the world. At this time I have Canadian travel document. You know in my country even I can not go in everywhere of my country. I need [a] permit from the government to move from one place to another place of my country. So even it was very hard to cross the many countries finally it becomes good for me . . . I decided to live here in Winnipeg. I

am waiting [for] my family to come here. I have enough income, means to feed me and my family.

But Kidane's journey is not at an end. In February 2022, he received his permanent resident card, after a wait of more than two years. Now he's waiting permission to bring his wife Hiwet and his son Yoel, now six years old, to Canada. While Kidane endured the psychological depredations of bureaucracy, Hiwet and Yoel faced physical threats in Addis Ababa, the capital of Ethiopia. The bloodiest war on the planet in 2022, by some estimates, is not in Ukraine but in Ethiopia, where the national army is brutally crushing resistance from the Tigray People's Liberation Front. As part of its fight against the Tigrayan force, Ethiopia and its allies, the Eritrean national army, have blockaded the region. At one stage, it looked as if Addis Ababa would be on the front lines. There are reports that ethnic Tigray like Kidane's wife and son are facing harassment in the capital, with claims on social media of houses searched at random, bank accounts being frozen, and licenses revoked.

In the Tigray region of Ethiopia, not far from Kidane's parents' house across the border in Bihat, there have been several reports of large-scale atrocities. In the village of Mai Kadra, there were two rounds of massacres in November 2020 that claimed hundreds of lives, Reuters reported. First, bands of armed Tigray youths slaughtered ethnic Amhara neighbors. In reprisal, troops from an Amhara province came to Mai Kadra and rounded up Tigray residents for mass killings. The troops burned many ethnic Tigray residents out of their homes. A European Union envoy to Ethiopia said Prime Minister Abiy Ahmed's had vowed to "wipe out" Tigray people. The blockades by Eritrean and Ethiopian troops cutting off aid to Tigrayans has driven at least 400,000 people to the brink of starvation, according to the UN. In November 2021, UN officials warned of the danger that the conflict could lead to genocide. Among the most abhorrent actions is the practice of Eritrean forces raiding refugee camps on the Ethiopian side of the border, the kind of camp where Kidane once stayed. In a sick inversion of international refugee protocols, the Eritrean troops are reportedly seizing refugees and forcing them to return to the country they fled. If Kidane had not undertaken his journey when he did, he could have been one of those seized.

Kidane's Ulysses-like quest to reunite with his family continues. He is still waiting—waiting for consular officials in Kenya to process a visa for his family, waiting for DNA tests, waiting for fingerprints to be processed, waiting for the flight to take off from Addis Ababa. He is still, in a sense, stuck on the road home.

The Other US Border

Kidane is one of thousands of refugees for whom the US became just another way station in the *camino duro* during the Trump administration. If there were a "border crisis" in the US when the Trump administration came to power, that crisis has not ended, but it has been extended to the River Suchiate on the Guatemalan-Mexico border, and, most recently, to the northern frontier. Much of the social rubric associated with the Rio Grande crossings—from *coyotes* to migrant shelters—have emerged in Manitoba and Quebec.

In Manitoba, where Kidane crossed, migrants have been rescued from waist-deep snow, and braved the torrents of Red River, which runs along the border between Canada and the US states of Minnesota and North Dakota.[1]

Frances Ravensbergen lives in Hemmingford, Quebec, a town about five miles from the US border and upstate New York. It's an area where the hilly maple woods of New York, Vermont, and Quebec converge around Lake Champlain—a body of water with the setting and demeanor of a summer-camp pond and the dimensions of a Great Lake. One of her neighbors, who grew up in the area, claims Canadian police once asked him to lift his bike over the indentation on Roxham Road that marked the border, because they were tired of sensors installed on the road alerting them to his movements.

In the age of "the border crisis," Roxham Road still, technically, runs unbroken between the two nations. But the physical transformation of Roxham Road near Hemmingford in the last decade reflects the psychic transformation of border and immigrant visions in North America. The depression in the road has become a full-scale roadblock, with concrete barricades. The temporary trailer where Canadian border patrol officers would fix a cup of coffee while out on patrol has been transformed into a full-fledged police station.

Roxham Road is defined as an "irregular" border crossing, a place that's not an official port of entry, a place where the border between the US and Canada is essentially fudged. If a migrant took the I-87 highway north from Plattsburgh, New York, instead of the route 22 regional road, they would reach the official port of entry near Roxham Road at LaColle, and face an entirely different set of protocols. Here, they would be handed over to US border patrol at the adjoining Champlain station, under the Safe Third Country Agreement signed in 2004.

"We have heard from our sister organization in Plattsburgh, where once people are handed back to the American side, some people have been put in jail," said Ms. Ravensbergen.

At an informal border crossing, officers are not under the same obligation.

With no permanent border patrol stations on Roxham Road, migrants are treated as if they had arrived on Canadian soil, entering the same process that Kidane did in the snowfields of Manitoba.

A trickle of migrants has squeezed through the loophole in the Safe Third Country Agreement for decades, using irregular crossings at Roxham Road and elsewhere. In recent years, the trickle of "irregular" migrants has become a flood. Canadian authorities started to track the numbers in 2017. In 2017 and 2018, about twenty thousand migrants, nearly half of all those who applied for asylum in Canada during those years, used irregular crossings.[2] Since the surge started in 2016, Roxham Road has become militarized and militant-ized.

Roxham Road has seen anti-immigrant right-wing protests and counter protests from pro-immigrant groups like "Bridges Not Borders," on whose coordinating committee Ms. Ravensbergen sits. The road became "short-hand" for the debate over Canada's refugee policy in recent years.[3]

Ms. Ravensbergen talked to border patrol officers she knew in the community about how they were dealing with the influx.

"They were going to Costco and buying muffins because they felt badly for people taken from Roxham Road brought to the [official] border, and then they had to wait until there was enough to get a bus to Montreal. They were asking friends did they have used baby seats." (Sometimes, the Royal Mounted Canadian police transported the migrants in vehicles that were not equipped with baby seats.)

One sculptor from Hemmingford's long-established artistic community made a metal statue he called "Bridges not Borders." In the wake of right-wing protests, Ms. Ravensbergen and other concerned Hemmingford citizens decided to start an immigrant support group, and it seemed natural to take the sculpture's name. Roxham now had its own station in the underground railroad of humanitarians supporting the migrants.

Like all the people in her organization, Ms. Ravensbergen is a volunteer. Yet, when we called her in July 2020, she took great interest in our questions, and made it clear that she would provide all the help she possibly could. In her passion for assisting the migrants, and the affectionate way she spoke about them, she reminded us of Etelvina Hernández López in Tapachula, and of Kristina in Capurganá.

"We just fell into it," Ms. Ravensbergen said. "There was a meeting in November. We put on a pot of lentil soup, and we were making more and more soup the day of. We thought it'd be ten of us, but twenty or thirty people walked in."

Ms. Ravensbergen and other group members would take turns crossing the border at Roxham Road. They would wait for migrants to arrive in taxis from Plattsburgh, New York. They'd make sure the migrants knew their rights and the major steps in the asylum-seeking process. The Bridges Not Borders volunteers observed the arrests, which—although frightening for many migrants—are the first step in entering the Canadian asylum process.

The vast majority of migrants share Kidane's positive experience, as the Canadian border patrol mostly treat them humanely. Ms. Ravensbergen was struck by the sight of an Afghan man striding across the border using a traditional wooden staff as a walking stick, undeterred by the warnings of the heavily armed Canadian police to stop and present himself for arrest. His daughter ran from the taxi, dragging the family's luggage and calling to the police, "'He doesn't speak English, he doesn't speak English!'" On another occasion, a Haitian teenager fled when the police approached; when the police caught the boy, they pinned him face-first to a car, Ms. Ravensbergen said.

The taxis that bring the migrants to Roxham Road come from the airport or bus station in Plattsburgh, the nearest big town in upstate New York, about twenty-five miles from the border. The shadow travel industry has also grown up around Roxham Road. In Plattsburgh, a town hard hit by base closures and rust-belt recessions, the arrival of refugees created the kind of economic boom-let that we had seen in other way stations along the *camino duro*. Taxis were plastered with advertisements for passage to Roxham Road, in Haitian Creole, French, and African languages.

One taxi driver in Plattsburgh, who didn't wish to be named, said he had transported refugees from all over the world, including Latin America, Asia, and Africa. At the height of the influx, he was taking more than one group a day, and he was one of several drivers who specialized in the migrant trade.

The drivers were conducting business in the gray area between legitimate commerce and migrant exploitation, treading the line between smugglers and migrant service providers, a practice we had seen all over Latin America. It was the same when we tried to negotiate with the taxi drivers in Tulcan, Ecuador, on behalf of a Haitian group. There was the price of a taxi, the price of a taxi for foreigners like ourselves, and then there was the price of the taxi for the Haitian migrants. It's the kind of exploitation that those on the *camino duro* see as inevitable. The migrants we met are resigned to paying inflated rates to black-market service providers, but all carefully tracked the prices on that black market.

In Plattsburgh, taxi drivers were charging families as much as $300 for the short ride from the small city in upstate New York to the road. One driver,

Christopher Crowningshield, was fined $10,000 in a Plattsburgh court for overcharging asylum seekers.

As in Ecuador, those facilitating the travel, the taxi drivers in this case, were often migrants themselves.

When we called her in July 2020 to better understand the experience that migrants like Kidane were having on the Canadian border, Ms. Ravensbergen invited us to visit as soon as the border reopened. We put off our visit for a month, but a year later in summer 2021, the border was still sealed due to pandemic control measures.

The border between the US and Canada reopened for people coming north in July 2021, after fifteen months. It was unclear when the irregular crossing would return to use, Ms. Ravensbergen told us. In May 2021, the Canadian parliament passed a bill that would close the informal-border crossing loophole. But asylum-seekers may still follow in Kidane's footsteps because a Canadian court also invalidated the Safe Third Country agreement with the US, citing the treatment of migrants under the Trump administration.

Migration in the Time of COVID

Many of the migrants who arrived in the US and Canada before COVID found themselves in a liminal existence, with transitory jobs and makeshift housing. During the pandemic era, arrival is an even more tentative experience. Mexican, US, and Canadian governments closed borders and further restricted visas. The economic pain of the pandemic disproportionately affected immigrants, who, unable to find work or receive governmental relief, are often also the target of xenophobic outbursts.[4] One undocumented worker in Denton, Texas, told us that day laboring work had dried up by April 2020, and that his family went hungry that month.

The collective research project (Im)Mobility in the Americas has demonstrated how the public health logic of confinement has produced a dangerous cocktail of violence, infection, and severe resource shortages in many of the borderlands on the *camino duro*—US/Mexico, Mexico/Guatemala, Panama/Colombia, and Colombia/Ecuador.[5] For long stretches of the pandemic, the passenger boats stopped going to Capurganá from Turbo, according to Kristina, the hostel-owner.

The Trump administration wasted no time in using the pandemic to further its anti-asylum agenda. In March 2020, the administration ordered the

CDC to issue Title 42, which granted CBP officers the authority to rapidly expel all migrants, including asylum-seekers, arriving at the Mexico border.

Gabriel Aguilar, the Honduran migrant we met on the zocalo in Tapachula in January 2020, experienced the COVID outbreaks in Mexico alongside many migrants from the Global South. He described a lonely existence, with no casual labor available, and efforts to move north becoming increasingly desperate as the border shut completely.

When they closed ACNUR, a lot of migrants took the other route . . . some of them took the train called *La Bestia*. Others begged for money to buy a ticket to their destination. Today, walking through the streets of Monterrey, I see closed shops and closed parks. People with the mask on their face and at the same time their eyes cast down. I don't even know when they will reopen the institutions that support migrants. Africans, Cubans, Haitians, Hondurans, Salvadorans, Guatemalans, Nicaraguans, etc., etc. I almost don't know where to look—the road north to the US or other parts of Mexico? At the same time, there's no business. There are a lot of restrictions in the bus stations, airports, and the empty roads. This has stopped all movement by Mexicans and migrants. I hear people saying from all over, protesting the situation where it looks like the government does the best thing for the people who live in their beautiful country. It's easy to say "stay at home," if you have the money for food and all you need.

There's usually more work for migrants in the industrial city of Monterrey than in other regions of Mexico. But the bustling, cosmopolitan nature of the city also primed it to be one of the hardest hit areas. Mr. Aguilar's other reason for coming to Monterrey, which is less than 150 miles from McAllen, Texas, was to use it as a springboard to the US. For the next six months, Mr. Aguilar waited for opportunities to make the final leg of his journey. He made it as far as the US border, stowed away on a freight train. US border patrol searched the train and promptly sent Mr. Aguilar back to Mexico. He decided to give up on his journey, to go home to Honduras. A little less than a year since we first met him there, Mr. Aguilar returned to Tapachula. Over WhatsApp, he described to us a city that was even more of a trap than when we'd visited. With the US border sealed, there was no way forward for the migrants who had arrived in Tapachula from all over the world. With Guatemala demanding proof of negative COVID-19 tests, there was almost no way back. Mr. Aguilar and others had to swim the Suchiate River once again, this time going south.

The condition of being frozen in transit was accentuated for migrants on the *camino duro*, who had always been versed in US immigration law. By January 2020, many of the migrants we met, including Mr. Aguilar, were following US party politics.

Some migrants asked us whether a new president would mean a new border regime. One migrant had even asked us for whom we planned to vote. The question came from a Dominican man standing in line at a Mexican refugee agency; in theory, the US election should have had little bearing on his life. But American politics has become global politics. The question brought home to us the fact that the lines of migrants in Tapachula were a direct result of policies created in Washington, DC.

Later in 2020, with word spreading about Joe Biden's lead in the polls, hope was gathering that Mr. Biden would end the zero-tolerance era.

With Mr. Biden's victory all but assured in mid-November, the eye of the needle appeared to widen. The mood was jubilant in the migrant camp in the Mexican border town of Matamoros after Biden's victory, according to a report from the magazine *Texas Monthly*.[6] The camp is one of many that sprang up because of MPP, which forced asylum-seekers who entered at the southern border to return to Mexico to await processing of their cases.

Mr. Tumwine, the Ugandan who we also met in Tapachula, was making similar calculations. He had been in Tijuana since March 2020, waiting for the pandemic to end, waiting for a new president to be elected. During text messaging in December 2020, he admitted that although he did not expect the border to open soon, he was planning to cross ("jump") in the next month. We have not heard from him since, and we can only hope that he is safe and did not endure detention for too long.

For a lucky few, this epic journey does have an end, even a happy one. Ms. Mtebe has continued to work in residential health care in Massachusetts, supporting special needs patients. In late 2020, Ms. Mtebe gave birth to a little girl. In mid-2021, she announced on Facebook that she had married the father of her child.

Virtual Destinations

Social media features in every aspect of contemporary life, but perhaps to an even more striking degree on the *camino duro*. There may not be a phone number on earth that would work on every step along this circuitous route. But as long as you can get to a WiFi connection, you will be able to access your social media accounts with any old burner smart phone. In this way, migrants stay in touch with their homelands by WhatsApp or Facebook Messenger. If they are separated from their group on the road or in the detention center, they rely on the WhatsApp group to reconnect. For North Indian and other more affluent migrants, social media is also critical for maintaining one's public image.

When we initially met Akashbir Singh, the young man who was posing as a tourist with his friends in Quito, he seemed very personable. From the outset, however, he was also very image conscious. He was very excited to see the DSLR camera we had brought (although slightly less excited when he had a good look at it.) He carefully stage-managed the shots we took of him and his friends (and their *coyote*, Mr. Guerrero, who looked strangely out of place, a minder in the midst of a boy band) outside the Indian restaurant in Quito. When we parted, Mr. Singh offered the email attached to his Facebook account, rather than a phone number or physical address, as contact information. It was through Facebook Messenger we stayed in touch with Mr. Singh as he made his way to the US. (Social media, with its in-built capacity for finding people with whom you have crossed paths, has also been a vital part of our reporting process.) Mr. Singh was impatient with us whenever we connected on Facebook Messenger. He did not want to talk about the vicissitudes of the route.

How did you travel onward? We asked him. "By boat," he said. What kind of boat? We asked.

"Small boat."

Where did the boat leave from?

"Capurganá," he said. "Why you ask me blady questions? Send me photo."

The only thing Mr. Singh wanted to talk about were the photographs we had snapped of him. This was initially puzzling. He said he had worked as a photographer in the Punjab. But mostly, it appeared, he worked on his image. In the end, he was bitterly disappointed by their quality, and they never appeared on his widely followed Facebook feed.

Mr. Singh did not post publicly for his more than one thousand Facebook friends during the journey north. Unlike the Nepali group in Tapachula and unlike Kidane, all of whom relished the adventure of the trail, Mr. Singh seemed ashamed of its grit and lack of glamor. When Mr. Singh made it to the US, in the fall of 2016, he announced his arrival with a carefully staged photo. There he was, clean-shaven and spiffed up, outside an expensive-looking suburban house in the Chicago area with some affluent-looking friends or relatives. The photograph had arrival written all over it. It's the kind of photograph that could launch a thousand trips along the *camino duro*. But it was an illusion, a carefully choreographed simulation of arrival.

When we reached out to Mr. Singh, he was cagy about his living situation in Illinois. Finally, he agreed to meet us at a certain restaurant in Chicago. When Nelson arrived, there was no sign of him. We finally tracked him down on Messenger. He had left the Chicago area on short notice, he said. Our last contact with Mr. Singh was a video call to his new residence in New Jersey. It was hard to get a feel for his living situation. He didn't want to talk about the details of his journey, or why he had left Illinois. He was sitting in a restaurant, which was apparently closed, accompanied by an infant who seemed to have been left in his care.

His Facebook feed told a very different story, portraying a young man who had made it in New York. There he was, in a stylish zip-top, walking under the lights in Times Square in July 2018. He popped up again brandishing his muscles in front of the Golden Gate Bridge. Another picture showed him in the kind of lustrous black-tie outfit and new haircut that evoked Oscars red carpets. But what came between those pictures? Was Mr. Singh's life in the US as easy as it looked?

Kidane's Facebook profile, meanwhile, is a picture of Yoel, the son he has never met.

EPILOGUE

Joe Biden's defeat of Donald Trump—possibly the most explicitly anti-immigrant president in US history—was greeted by a sigh of relief in much of the world, and particularly from those whose lives are marked by immigration. Trump flags still flap outside many homes in border states such as Texas and throughout the US, an ominous welcome for migrants. Anti-immigrant sentiment remains strong in North America. Reports of a "border crisis" are growing again. The number of undocumented migrants apprehended at the US border exceeded prepandemic levels in March 2022, with the fastest growth coming among migrants from outside Central America. These are people like Kidane and Ms. Mtebe, people who have trekked the *camino duro*, people from Haiti, India, Venezuela; people from all over the Global South.

Rhetoric about the border wall died down in the 2020 campaign, but nobody in the Republican Party has openly repudiated the Trump administration's policies. Even with the Senate in Democratic hands, the "supermajority" requirements for legislation to overcome filibusters means that few immigration laws are likely to be passed.

Hopes that Biden's election would make the *camino duro* any easier were short lived. The president himself may be more tolerant, but the legal architecture remains that of "zero tolerance." Like a retreating army booby-trapping its fortress, the Trump administration made sure this architecture was treacherous to dismantle. Most efforts to reverse anti-immigrant Trump policies are snared in the courts. It may be encouraging to migrants at the Mexican border that the Biden administration wants to hear their asylum claims, but, as a practical matter, they are still stuck.

Through executive order, President Biden ended MPP on June 1, 2021. However, in August 2021, a federal judge ordered the Biden administration to reinstate the policy. Later, in December, after a second attempt to dismantle MPP failed, the administration expanded the program to include Haitians, as well as any nationality in the Western hemisphere other than Mexican. As of writing, the Supreme Court has heard arguments and is expected to make a decision regarding the administration's requirement to uphold MPP. In another major step, in May 2022, the Biden administration ended expulsions under the Title 42 policy, which had made it almost impossible to seek asylum on the Mexican border. As of writing, however, Republican-led lawsuits have effectively kept the policy in place. Many other policies that clash with the UN Human Rights Convention and refugee protocols still stand. And, as we have outlined, these policies are only components of a vast punitive "zero tolerance" machine. The Biden administration has not done enough dismantling of this machine to change the experience of people such as Ms. Mtebe, Kidane, and the other protagonists of our story. Once set in motion, a gulag-like system of punitive machinery will grind people's lives away under its own steam, as Alexander Solzhenitsyn observed. For example, thousands of people languishing in detention centers throughout the US would not be helped by unwinding the MPP. Even without the cooperation of Guatemala, the immigration-court judges installed and empowered by the Trump administration could keep the eye of the needle all but impassable, unless those courts are reformed.[1]

The liminal life is the sting in the tail of the deterrence policy and *flujo controlado*. By making life in the US untenable for Kidane, or for Mr. Singh, the authorities hope to control the message home.

But, the US immigration industrial complex has miscalculated how deterrence incentivizes a profit-seeking industry to recruit more migrants. It has vastly underestimated the resilience, agency, and resourcefulness of migrants like Kidane, Mr. Singh, and Ms. Mtebe, and their ability to curate their own stories.

Beginning with the arrival of the first native people, US history was formed by a series of great migrations. There's another incredible journey happening, but this time the US is spurning the voyagers. Kidane and thousands like him may well shape a great new chapter in a nation's history, but that nation is more likely to be Canada than the US.

Mr. Biden was part of the Obama administration, which both Mr. Trump and many progressive critics of immigration policy have accused of laying the foundation for the gulag system. Mr. Trump has gleefully pointed out that Obama "built the cages" that Ms. Mtebe saw being filled with children torn from their parents. While the specifics of Mr. Trump's claim can be disputed, the larger point cannot be denied—family separation represented the extension of Obama-era policies and practices of deportation and detention.

The Biden administration has removed some of the human-made hurdles we have described that make migrant journeys so painful, but allowed others to stand. Across South Asia and Africa, climate change is threatening to displace millions. India is the first step in almost every Nepali migrant journey, but pandemic regulations have complicated passage to the larger nation. Near Eritrea, the Tigray conflict has brought hundreds of thousands, if not millions, of people to the brink of a manmade famine. Cameroon remains a treacherous place for the Anglophone community, with allegations of civilians killed during military attacks on rebel camps in summer 2021. The flight from political instability and hunger in Venezuela and Haiti continues.

Multicontinental migrant journeys will continue throughout the Biden era. The only question is whether the journeys' endings will be any happier.

NOTES

INTRODUCTION

1. With the exception of Kidane, who asked us to use his name, we have given pseudonyms to all people presented in the book.
2. Based on data extracted from US Customs and Border Protection's 2019 chart of apprehensions at the southwest border. As this data only accounts for "deportable aliens," the actual proportion might be even higher.
3. "Boletín Mensual de Estadísticas Migratorias," Gobierno de México, accessed January 2, 2021, http://portales.segob.gob.mx/es/PoliticaMigratoria/Boletines_Estadisticos.
4. "Migración Estadísticas," República de Panamá, Accessed January 5, 2021, https://www.migracion.gob.pa/inicio/estadisticas.
5. Victoria Stone-Cadena and Soledad Álvarez Velasco, "Historicizing Mobility: *Coyoterismo* in the Indigenous Ecuadorian Migration Industry," *The Annals of the American Academy of Political and Social Science* 676 (2018).
6. Tatiana Seijas, *Asian Slaves in Colonial Mexico: From Chinos to Indians* (New York: Cambridge University Press, 2014); Herbert S. Klein and Ben Vinson III, *African Slavery in Latin America and the Caribbean* (Oxford: Oxford University Press, 2007).
7. Jonathan Blitzer, "The Cuban Migrant Crisis," *New Yorker*, January 16, 2016, https://www.newyorker.com/news/news-desk/the-cuban-migrant-crisis.
8. Facultad Latinoamericana de Ciencias Sociales (FLACSO Costa Rica), "Diagnóstico sobre la situación actual, tendencias y necesidades de protección y asistencia de las personas migrantes y refugiadas extracontinentales en México y América Central," 2011, https://www.corteidh.or.cr/sitios/observaciones/11/Anexo8.pdf; Organización de los Estados Americanos, *Migración Extracontinental en las Américas: Memoria* (Washington, DC: Organización de los Estados Americanos, 2010), https://www.acnur.org/fileadmin/Documentos/BDL/2011/7402.pdf; Organización Internacional para las Migraciones, "Migrantes

extracontinentales en América del Sur: Estudio de casos," 2013, https://
publications.iom.int/books/cuadernos-migratorios-ndeg5-migrantes-extra-
continentales-en-america-del-sur-estudio-de-casos.

9. Susan Bibler Coutin, "Falling Outside: Excavating the History of Central Amer-
ican Asylum Seekers," *Law and Social Inquiry* 36, no. 3 (2011): 574–81; Stephan
Scheel and Vicki Squire, "Forced Migrants as 'Illegal' Migrants," in *The Oxford
Handbook of Refugee and Forced Migration Studies*, ed. Elena Fiddian-Qasmiyeh,
Gil Loescher, Katy Long, and Nando Sigona (Oxford: Oxford University Press,
2014).

10. Anne Garland Mahler, *From the Tricontinental to the Global South: Race, Radicalism, and Transnational Solidarity* (Durham, NC: Duke University Press, 2018).

11. Susan Parnell and Jennifer Robinson, "(Re)theorizing Cities from the Global
South: Looking beyond Neoliberalism," *Urban Geography* 33, no. 3 (2013).

12. Teresa Caldeira, "Peripheral Urbanization: Autoconstruction, Transversal Logics, and Politics in Cities of the Global South," *Environment and Planning D: Society and Space* 35, no. 1 (2016); Seth Schindler, "Towards a Paradigm of Southern Urbanism," *City* 21, no. 1 (2017); Abdoumaliq Simone, *Improvised Lives:
Rhythms of Endurance in an Urban South* (Cambridge, UK: Polity Press, 2019).

13. Jason De León, *The Land of Open Graves: Living and Dying on the Migrant Trail*
(Berkeley: University of California Press, 2015), 66–72.

14. The term "remote border control" was originally coined by Aristide Zolberg to
describe the emergence of visa requirements and restrictions at the point of
embarkation in the nineteenth and early twentieth centuries. Zolberg, "The
Great Wall against China," in *Migration, Migration History, and History: Old Paradigms and New Perspectives*, ed. Jan Lucassen and Leo Lucassen (New York:
Peter Lang, 1997), 308. Scholars have since used the term to theorize the externalization of border patrols beyond a state's territory. In the post-9/11 era, with
the creation of the Department of Homeland Security in the US, and Frontex
in Europe, externalization includes the virtual walls of data information systems, the training and militarizing of security forces, and creation of detention centers and deportation agreements. Ruben Zaiotti, "Mapping Remote
Control: The Externalization of Migration Management in the Twenty-First
Century," in *Externalizing Migration Management: Europe, North America and
the Spread of 'Remote Control' Practices*, ed. Ruben Zaiotti (Abingdon, Oxfordshire: Routledge, 2016), 4.

15. John Gramlich and Luis Noe-Bustamente, "What's Happening at the US-Mexico
Border in 5 Charts," Pew Research Center, November 1, 2019, https://
www.pewresearch.org/fact-tank/2019/11/01/whats-happening-at-the-u-s-
mexico-border-in-5-charts.

16. Antje Missbach and Melissa Phillips, "Reconceptualizing Transit States in an Era of Outsourcing, Offshoring, and Obfuscation." *Migration and Society: Advances in Research* 3 (2020): 27.

17. Ruben Andersson astutely describes the irony of Europe's massive investment in immigration enforcement: "This industry . . . produces what it is meant to eliminate, curtail, or transform—more migrant illegality. In this loop, more funding is assured in a vicious circle reminiscent of the 'war on terror'; the more specter-like the threat at the border, the higher the potential gains from this phantom menace." Andersson, *Illegality, Inc.: Clandestine Migration and the Business of Bordering Europe* (Berkeley: University of California Press, 2014), 8.

18. Luigi Achilli, "The 'Good' Smuggler: The Ethics and Morals of Human Smuggling among Syrians," *Annals of the American Academy of Political and Social Science* 676, no. 1 (2018); Rubén Hernández León, "Conceptualizing the Migration Industry," in *The Migration Industry and the Commercialization of International Migration*, ed. Thomas Gammeltoft-Hansen and Ninna Nyberg Sørenson (Oxford: Routledge, 2013), 32.

19. Stephen Castles, Hein de Haas, and Mark J. Millar, *The Age of Migration*, 5th ed. (London: Palgrave Macmillan, 2013); David Kyle, *Transnational Peasants: Migrations, Networks, and Ethnicity in Andean Ecuador* (Baltimore, MD: John Hopkins University Press, 2000); John Salt and Jeremy Stein, "Migration as a Business: The Case of Trafficking," *International Migration* 35, no. 4 (1997); Thomas Gammeltoft-Hansen and Ninna Nyberg Sørenson, eds. *The Migration Industry and the Commercialization of International Migration* (London: Routledge, 2013).

20. Stone-Cadena and Álvarez Velasco, "Historicizing Mobility," 195.

21. Sheldon X. Zhang, Gabriella E. Sanchez, and Luigi Achilli, "Crimes of Solidarity in Mobility: Alternative Views on Migrant Smuggling," *Annals of the American Academy of Political and Social Science* 676, no. 1 (2018): 11; Stephanie Maher, "Out of West Africa: Human Smuggling as a Social Enterprise," *Annals of the American Academy of Political and Social Science* 676, no. 1 (2018).

22. Achilli, "The 'Good' Smuggler"; Maher, "Out of West Africa"; Kalid Koser, "Why Take the Risk? Explaining Migrant Smuggling," in *Global Migration, Ethnicity and Britishness*, ed. Tariq Modood and John Salt (London: Palgrave Macmillan, 2011), 76; Sheldon X. Zhang, *Smuggling and Trafficking in Human Beings: All Roads Lead to America* (Westport, CT: Praeger/Greenwood, 2007), 86, 98; Wendy Vogt, *Lives in Transit: Violence and Intimacy on the Migrant Journey* (Berkeley: University of California Press, 2018), 154.

23. Ali Nobil Ahmad, *Masculinity, Sexuality and Illegal Migration: Human Smuggling from Pakistan to Europe* (Burlington, VT: Ashgate Publishing, 2011), 7; Theodore Baird and Ilse Van Liempt, "Scrutinising the Double Disadvantage: Knowledge Production in the Messy Field of Migrant Smuggling," *Journal of Ethnic and Migration Studies* 42, no. 3 (2016): 407–9; Stone-Cadena and Álvarez Velasco, "Historicizing Mobility," 200–202; Zhang, Sanchez, and Achilli, "Crimes of Solidarity in Mobility," 13–14.
24. Achilli, "The 'Good' Smuggler"; Zhang, *Smuggling and Trafficking*, 89; Shahram Khosravi, *"Illegal" Traveller: An Auto-ethnography of Borders* (New York: Palgrave Macmillan, 2010), 105–11.
25. Baird and van Liempt, "Scrutinising the Double Disadvantage," 407.
26. Although translated as "brown" in Spanish, *moreno* signifies Black in much of Latin America.
27. Khosravi, *"Illegal" Traveller*, 27; Wendy Vogt, "Crossing Mexico: Structural Violence and the Commodification of Undocumented Central American Migrants," *American Ethnologist* 40, no. 4 (2013): 764.
28. Maher, "Out of West Africa."
29. Michael Collyer and Hein de Haas, "Developing Dynamic Categorisation of Transit Migration," *Population, Space and Place* 18 (2012); Franck Düvell, "Transit Migration: A Blurred and Politicised Concept," *Population, Space and Place* 18 (2012); Sabine Hess, "De-naturalising Transit Migration: Theory and Methods of an Ethnographic Regime Analysis," *Population, Space and Place* 18 (2012); Melissa Phillips and Antje Missbach, "Introduction," *International Journal of Migration and Border Studies* 3, nos. 2–3 (2017).
30. Michael Collyer, "In-between Places: Trans-Saharan Transit Migrants in Morocco and the Fragmented Journey to Europe," *Antipode* 394 (2007): 668–70; Phillips and Missbach, "Introduction," 114.
31. For transit literature focused on movements from Africa or Asia toward Europe, see Andersson (2014); Collyer (2007); Düvell, Molodikova, and Collyer (2014); Mainwaring and Brigden (2016); Papadopoulou (2004); Schapendonk (2017); for texts on Central America toward the US, see Coutin (2005) and Vogt (2018); for Southeast Asia toward Australia, see Missbach (2015).
32. Jonathan Echeverri Zuluaga, "Errance and Elsewheres among Africans Waiting to Restart Their Journeys in Dakar, Senegal," *Cultural Anthropology* 30, no. 4 (2015).
33. Dimitris Papadopoulos and Vassilis S. Tsianos, "After Citizenship: Autonomy of Migration, Organisational Ontology and Mobile Commons," *Citizenship Studies* 17, no. 2 (2013): 190.

34. Tekalign Ayalew Mengiste further defines migrant protection from below as the "diverse and dynamic strategies collectively devised and mobilized by migrants, their cotravelers, families and friends settled en route and in the diaspora, and friendly strangers and diverse facilitators to reduce risks in clandestine journeys and who allow for successful transits, while not discounting the violence and suffering encountered by migrants and refugees on their paths. The accumulated body of information pertaining to and allowing for past, ongoing, and future experiences of migration to be transmitted constitutes a collective system of knowledge, in which communities are vital in guiding migrants in the negotiation and performance required at various stages of the migration process." Mengiste, "Refugee Protections from Below: Smuggling in the Eritrea-Ethiopia Context," *Annals of the American Academy of Political and Social Science* 676, no. 1 (2018): 63–64.

CHAPTER 1

1. "World Report 2014: Eritrea," Human Rights Watch, accessed March 5, 2020, https://www.hrw.org/world-report/2014/country-chapters/eritrea#.
2. Abraham T. Zere, "Democracy According to Eritrea's Afwerki, Then and Now," *Al Jazeera*, May 24, 2018, https://www.aljazeera.com/opinions/2018/5/24/democracy-according-to-eritreas-afwerki-then-and-now.
3. Fatma Naib, "Slavery in Libya: Life inside a Container," *Al Jazeera*, January 26, 2018, https://www.aljazeera.com/news/2018/01/26/slavery-in-libya-life-inside-a-container; Laurie Lijnders and Sara Robinson, "From the Horn of Africa to the Middle East: Human Trafficking of Eritrean Asylum Seekers across Borders," *Anti-Trafficking Review* 2 (2013): 137–40.
4. The US justifies its support for BIR, in spite of its record of human rights abuses and war crimes in the Anglophone regions, as part of the war on terror against Boko Haram. Joe Penney, "Cameroonian Asylum-Seekers at the Border Are Fleeing a US-Backed Military Force," *The Intercept*, December 1, 2019, https://theintercept.com/2019/12/01/us-asylum-seekers-cameroon. While the US did suspend much of its military aid to Cameroon in 2019, asylum success rates for Cameroonians in US courts decreased from 81 percent in 2018 to 62 percent in 2019. Human Rights Watch, "US: Protect Cameroonians from Deportation," December 18, 2020, https://www.hrw.org/news/2020/12/18/us-protect-cameroonians-deportation.
5. Sanjay Sharma, Shibani Pandey, Dinesh Pathak and Bimbika Sijapati-Basnet, "State of Migration in Nepal," Kathmandu: Centre for the Study of Labour and Mobility, Research Paper VI, 2014, 32.

6. Tristan Bruslé, "Choosing a Destination and Work: Migration Strategies of Nepalese Workers in Uttarakhand, Northern India," *Mountain Research Development* 28 no. 3/4 (2008): 242; Jeevan Raj Sharma, *Crossing the Border to India: Youth, Migration and Masculinities in Nepal* (Philadelphia, PA: Temple University Press, 2018), 12.

7. The phrase "middle space of migration" comes from Johan Lindquist, Biao Xiang, and Brenda S. A. Yeoh, "Opening the Black Box of Migration: Brokers, the Organization of Transnational Mobility and the Changing Political Economy in Asia," *Pacific Affairs* 85, no. 1 (2012): 11.

8. Bandita Sijapati and Amrita Limbu, *Governing Labour Migration in Nepal: An Analysis of Existing Policies and Institutional Mechanisms*, 2nd ed. (Kathmandu: Himal Books, 2017), 120.

9. Alice Kern and Ulrike Müller-Böker, "The Middle Space of Migration: A Case Study of Brokerage and Recruitment Agencies in Nepal," *Geoforum* 65 (2015).

10. Tristan Bruslé, "The Nepali-Qatari Migrant World," *Himal South Asian*, May 1, 2008, https://www.himalmag.com/the-nepali-qatari-migrant-world.

11. Sarah Paoletti, Eleanor Taylor-Nicholson, Bandita Sijapati, and Bassina Farbenblum, *Migrant Workers' Access to Justice at Home: Nepal* (New York: Open Society Foundations, 2014).

12. Thanks to the anthropologist Heather Hindman for pointing out to Nelson how state-regulated migration patterns, such as between South Korea and Nepal, are often less trusted than the more informal arrangements of Gulf labor migration.

13. Asia Foundation, *Labour Migration Trends and Patterns: Bangladesh, India, and Nepal 2013* (Kathmandu: The Asia Foundation, 2013), 13.

14. Bandita Sijapati, Ashim Bhattarai, and Dinesh Pathak, *Analysis of Labour Market and Migration Trends in Nepal*, (Kathmandu: Deutsche Gesellschaft für Internationale Zusammenarbeit and International Labour Organization, 2015), 54.

15. Asia Foundation, *Labour Migration Trends*, 9.

16. Janakraj Sapkota, "Amerika jaana khojda bandhak," *Kantipur*, November 13, 2019.

17. Echeverri Zuluaga, "Errance and Elsewheres," 590.

18. Anju Mary Paul, "Stepwise International Migration: A Multistage Migration Pattern for the Aspiring Migrant," *American Journal of Sociology* 116, no. 6 (2011): 1843.

19. Echeverri Zuluaga, "Errance and Elsewheres."

20. Nanneke Winters and Franziska Reiffen, "Haciendo-lugar vía huellas y apegos: Las personas migrantes africanas y sus experiencias de movilidad, inmovilidad

e inserción local en América Latina." *REMHU: Revista Interdiciplinar da Mobilidade Humana* 27, no. 56 (May–August 2019), https://doi.org/10.1590/1980-85852503880005602.

21. In the short story "Paper and Being," Sienna Craig tells a fictional account of a Nepali immigrant (with Tibetan/Mustangi heritage) in New York obtaining a Tibetan green book, or *deb jangu*, to improve his chances of obtaining residency in the US. Issued by the Tibetan government in exile, the green book is used to prove one's Tibetan identity outside of the People's Republic of China. Craig writes, "he needed to be Tibetan in order to become American." Craig, *The Ends of Kinship: Connecting Himalayan Lives between Nepal and New York* (Seattle: University of Washington Press, 2020), 99.

CHAPTER 2

1. Mario Vargas Llosa, *The Dream of the Celt*, trans. Edith Grossman (New York: Farrar, Straus and Giroux, 2012).
2. The anthropologist Shahram Khosravi compares the cross-cultural dehumanization of smuggled migrants, *pollo* in Spanish, *renshe* (human snakes) in Chinese, and *gosfand* (sheep) in Farsi (also sheep, or *bheda*, in Nepali) to point out the sacrificial and ritual aspect of border crossing. *"Illegal" Traveler*, 27.
3. Soledad Álvarez Velasco, interpersonal communication.

CHAPTER 3

1. Brad Jokisch and David Kyle, "Ecuadorian International Migration," in *The Ecuador Reader*, ed. Carlos de la Torre and Steve Striffler (Durham, NC: Duke University Press, 2008); Kyle, *Transnational Peasants*.
2. By the 1990s, there were so many Ecuadorians in New York (specifically Queens), that it was jokingly called the "third biggest Ecuadorian city" behind Quito and Guayaquil.
3. Stone-Cadena and Álvarez Velasco, "Historicizing Mobility."
4. Álvarez Velasco demonstrates that Ecuador's recent transformation into a transit country is rooted in a legacy dating back to the 1970s. Soledad Álvarez Velasco, "From Ecuador to Elsewhere: The (Re)Configuration of a Transit Country," *Migration and Society: Advances in Research* 3 (2020): 39.
5. Diego Acosta Arcarazo and Luisa Feline Freier, "Turning the Immigration Policy Paradox Upside Down? Populist Liberalism and Discursive Gaps in South America," *International Migration Review* 49, no. 3 (2015); Luisa Feline Freier, "Open Doors (for Almost All): Visa Policies and Ethnic Selectivity in Ecuador," Working Paper 188, UC San Diego: Center for Comparative Immigration Studies, 2017, https://escholarship.org/uc/item/4m18b9tc; Ana Margheritis, "'Todos

somos migrantes' (We Are All Migrants): The Paradoxes of Innovative State-Led Transnationalism in Ecuador," *International Political Sociology* 5, no. 2 (2018); Paul Mena, "Ecuador: Crece Flujo de Inmigrantes Surasiáticos," *BBC News*, August 31, 2010, http://www.bbc.co.uk/mundo/america_latina/2010/08/100825_ecuador_inmigrantes_asia_pea.shtml; Jeffrey Pugh, "Universal Citizenship through the Discourse and Policy of Rafael Correa," *Latin American Politics and Society* 59, no. 2 (2017).

6. Manuel Góngora-Mera, Gioconda Herrera, and Conrad Müller, "The Frontiers of Universal Citizenship: Transnational Social Spaces and the Legal Status of Migrants in Ecuador," Working Paper No. 71, Berlin: desiguALdades.net, International Research Network on Interdependent Inequalities in Latin America, 2014, 22. However, these fears were clearly exaggerated. Freier shows that the total number of Asian and African, excluding Chinese, entries was 2,609 between 2008 and 2010, far lower than the 45,934 Colombians and 33,851 Peruvians who entered during the same period. Freier, "Open Doors," 8.

7. Freier, "Open Doors," 10.

8. Freier, "Open Doors," 13.

9. Soledad Álvarez Velasco, "From Ecuador to Elsewhere," 37.

10. Acosta Arcarazo and Freier, "Turning the Immigration."

11. Bernarda Zubrzycki, "Recent African Migration to South America: The Case of Senegalese in Argentina," *International Journal of Humanities and Social Sciences* 2, no. 22 (2012); Rosana Baeninger, Natália Belmonte Demétrio, and Jóice Domeniconi, "Espaços das migrações transnacionais: Perfil sociodemográfico de imigrantes da África para o Brasil no século XXI," *REMHU: Revista Interdisciplinar da Mobilidade Humana* 27, no. 56 (2019), http://dx.doi.org/10.1590/1980-85852503880005603.

12. While immigration to Chile gradually increased throughout the 2000s, from about 40,000 to 80,000 admissions per year, it greatly accelerated in the 2010s, growing from 81,578 in 2011 to a peak of 438,222 in 2018. Gobierno de Chile, "Estadísticas Migratorias," accessed March 20, 2020, https://serviciomigraciones.cl/estadisticasmigratorias. But, in spite of Bachelet's attempts to legislate immigration reforms, the Pinochet-era immigration law has remained and xenophobic public sentiment has become entrenched. Christian Doña Reveco, "Amid Record Numbers of Arrivals, Chile Turns Rightward on Immigration," January 17, 2018, https://www.migrationpolicy.org/article/amid-record-numbers-arrivals-chile-turns-rightward-immigration.

13. Herédia Merlotti, Vania Beatriz, Santos Gonçalves, and Maria do Carmo, "Deslocamentos populacionais no sul do Brasil: O caso dos senegaleses," in *Imigração*

senegalesa no Brasil e na Argentina: Multiplos olhares, ed. João Carlos and Gisele Kleidermacher (Porto Alegre: Est Edições, 2017); Winters and Reiffen, "Haciendo-lugar vía huellas y apegos."

14. Álvarez Velasco, "From Ecuador to Elsewhere," 43.
15. Álvarez Velasco, "From Ecuador to Elsewhere," 43.
16. "Pakistani Citizen Sentenced to 50 Months in Prison for Conspiracy to Provide Material Support to the Pakistani Taliban," US Department of Justice, last modified January 5, 2012, https://www.justice.gov/opa/pr/pakistani-citizen-sentenced-50-months-prison-conspiracy-provide-material-support-pakistani.
17. Ecuador added Senegal and Cuba to the list in 2015 and North Korea in 2017.
18. Freier, "Open Doors," 13–18.
19. Pugh, "Universal Citizenship," 117.
20. Álvarez Velasco, "From Ecuador to Elsewhere," 44.
21. Jonathan Echeverri Zuluaga and Liza Acevedo Saenz, "Pensando a travesías y esperas de viajeros africanos en Quito y Dakar," *Antípoda: Revista de Antropología ye Arqueología* 32 (2018).

CHAPTER 4

1. Motlagh, in his feature expose of the Darién for *Outside* magazine, found the "tourist charade" to be used even deep into the jungle. Jason Motlagh, "A Terrifying Journey through the World's Most Dangerous Jungle," *Outside Online*, July 19, 2016, https://www.outsideonline.com/outdoor-adventure/exploration-survival/skull-stake-darien-gap.
2. Khosravi, in his retelling of his own migration from Iran to Sweden, narrates a similar "performance" of disguising himself as a tourist. To learn his European part while waiting in India, he closely observed the tourists in Delhi's Connaught Place and studied Hollywood movies. *"Illegal" Traveler*, 63.
3. Emily Gogolak, "Haitian Migrants Turn toward Brazil," *New Yorker*, August 20, 2014, https://www.newyorker.com/news/news-desk/haitian-migrants-turn-toward-brazil.
4. Heloisa Harumi Miura, "The Haitian Migration Flow to Brazil: Aftermath of the 2010 Earthquake," in *The State of Environmental Migration 2014,* ed. François Gemenne, Pauline Brücker, and Dina Ionesco (Liége, Belgium: Presses Universitaires de Liége, 2014), http://labos.ulg.ac.be/hugo/wp-content/uploads/sites/38/2017/11/The-State-of-Environmental-Migration-2014-149-165.pdf.
5. "Migrants, Authorities Clash on Peru-Brazil Border," *La Prensa Latina*, February 16, 2021, https://www.laprensalatina.com/migrants-authorities-clash-on-peru-brazil-border.

CHAPTER 5

1. César Chaparro, "Víctimas de tráfico de migrantes cuentan el horror en manos del Clan del Golfo," *Noticias Caracol*, February 28, 2018, https://noticias. caracoltv.com/colombia/victimas-de-trafico-de-migrantes-cuentan-el-horror-en-manos-del-clan-del-golfo; Nelson Matta and Julio Herrera, "Clan del Golfo tapona a migrantes en el Darién," *El Colombiano*, February 19, 2019, https:// www.elcolombiano.com/colombia/clan-del-golfo-tapona-a-migrantes-en-el-darien-la10238641. According to Telesur, The Clan reportedly became the largest paramilitary force in Colombia by filling the void created by the demobilization of the paramilitary force, United Self-Defenses Forces, in 2005. Telesur, "A Look into 'Clan del Golfo,' Colombia's Largest Paramilitary Group," April 2, 2018, https://www.telesurenglish.net/news/Exclusive-Gulf-Clan-Colombias-Biggest-Paramilitary-Group-20180402-0026.html.
2. Matta and Herrera, "Clan del Golfo."
3. Vogt, *Lives in Transit*, 85.
4. Julián Amorocho and Esteban Vanegas, "Una estampida humana cruza por Capurganá," *El Colombiano*, March 2, 2018, https://www.elcolombiano.com/colombia/el-refugio-de-los-migrantes-ilegales-en-capurgana-choco-HK8286900.
5. Sijapati et al., *Analysis of Labour Market and Migration Trends in Nepal*, 54.
6. Thomas Faist, "Brokerage in Cross-Border Mobility: Social Mechanisms and the (Re)Production of Social Inequalities," *Social Inclusion* 2, no. 4 (2014): 39.
7. The fluctuations in policy and enforcement often produce alterations in the journey's route. At the time of writing, it appears that the pre-Darién stopover has shifted, again, from Capurganá to Acandí, approximately sixteen kilometers to the south.

CHAPTER 6

1. Juan Arturo Gómez Tobón, "Más de una decena de Cubanos mueren ahogados por la crecida de un río en el Darién," Diario de Cuba, June 7, 2019, https:// diariodecuba.com/cuba/1559868692_46826.html.
2. Laureen Fagan, "For African Migrants, Will Panama Become the New Libya?" *Africa Times*, August 30, 2019, https://africatimes.com/2019/08/30/for-african-migrants-will-panama-become-the-new-libya.
3. Peter Herlihy, "Opening Panama's Darién Gap," *Journal of Cultural Geography* 9, no. 2 (1989): 42.
4. Stephanie C. Kane, *The Phantom Gringo Boat: Shamanic Discourse and Development in Panama* (Washington, DC: Smithsonian Institution Press, 1994), 30.
5. Kane, *The Phantom Gringo Boat*, 96.

6. Herlihy, "Opening Panama's Darién Gap," 48.
7. Herlihy, "Opening Panama's Darién Gap," 48.
8. Peter Herlihy, "Chocó Indian Relocation in Darién," *Cultural Survival Quarterly* (1985), https://www.culturalsurvival.org/publications/cultural-survival-quarterly/choco-indian-relocation-darien-panama.
9. Sara Trab Nielsen, "The Spillover Effect of the Colombian Conflict Ecological Damage in the Darién Gap," Mandala Project, 2006, http://mandalaprojects.com/ice/ice-cases/darien.htm.
10. Ashoka Mukpo, "Harrowing Video Shows Indigenous Colombians Fleeing Gunfire," *Mongabay*, May 28, 2020, https://news.mongabay.com/2020/05/harrowing-video-shows-indigenous-colombians-fleeing-gunfire.
11. Motlagh, "A Terrifying Journey."
12. "Migración Estadísticas," República de Panamá.
13. "Panama: Locking in Success," World Bank, 2015, https://documents1.worldbank.org/curated/en/180611468100727814/pdf/947060SCD0P1510ICodisclosedo3030150.pdf.
14. Vogt, *Lives in Transit*, 208.
15. De León, *The Land of Open Graves*, 66–68.
16. De León, *The Land of Open Graves*, 3–4.
17. De León, *The Land of Open Graves*, 68–72.
18. Papadopoulos and Tsianos, "After Citizenship," 190.
19. Jean-Philippe Chippaux, "Incidence and Mortality Due to Snakebite in the Americas," *Neglected Tropical Diseases* 11, no. 6 (2017), https://journals.plos.org/plosntds/article?id=10.1371/journal.pntd.0005662.

CHAPTER 7

1. Nanneke Winters, "Haciendo-lugar en tránsito: Reflexión sobre la migración africana y trabaja de campo en Darién, Panama," *REMHU: Revista Interdisciplinar da Mobilidade Humana* 27, no. 56 (2019), https://doi.org/10.1590/1980-85852503880005613.
2. Abraham Teran, "Panama Isolates Migrants in Remote Jungle Coronavirus Unit," *Reuters*, June 9 2020, https://www.reuters.com/article/us-health-coronavirus-panama/panama-isolates-migrants-in-remote-jungle-coronavirus-unit-idUSKBN23G1HC.
3. Winters, "Haciendo-lugar en tránsito."
4. Caitlyn Yates, "A Case Study in the Outsourcing of US Border Control," *Lawfare Blog*, April 11, 2019, https://www.lawfareblog.com/case-study-outsourcing-us-border-control.

5. Nanneke Winters and Cynthia Mora Izaguirre, "Es cosa suya: Entanglements of Border Externalization and African Transit Migration in Northern Costa Rica," *Comparative Migration Studies* 7, no. 27 (2019), https://doi.org/10.1186/s40878-019-0131-9.

6. Caitlin Fouratt, "'Those who come to do harm': The Framings of Immigration Problems in Costa Rican Immigration Law," *International Migration Review* 48, no. 1 (2014): 161.

7. Shiri Noy and Koen Voorend, "Social Rights and Migrant Realities: Migration Policy Reform and Migrants' Access to Health Care in Costa Rica, Argentina, and Chile," *Journal of International Migration and Integration* 17, no. 2 (2016): 609.

8. Winters and Mora Izaguirre, "Es cosa suya."

9. Noelia Esquivel Solano, "Mama Africa: The Woman Investigated of Crossing African Migrants from Guanacaste to Nicaragua," *Voice of Guanacaste*, May 28, 2020, https://vozdeguanacaste.com/en/mama-africa-the-woman-investigated-of-crossing-african-migrants-from-guanacaste-to-nicaragua.

10. Dianne Solis and Julieta Chiquillo, "Sister Norma, the Border Battle's Fiercest Fighter, Is 'Astute as a Serpent and Gentle as a Dove,'" *Dallas Morning News*, June 21, 2018, https://www.dallasnews.com/news/immigration/2018/06/21/sister-norma-the-border-battle-s-fiercest-fighter-is-astute-as-a-serpent-and-gentle-as-a-dove.

11. Dánae Vílchez, "Antimotines reprimen a comunidad por auxiliar a migrantes," *Confidencial*, October 16, 2016, https://confidencial.com.ni/antimotines-reprimen-comunidad-auxiliar-migrantes.

12. Vílchez, "Antimotines reprimen."

13. José Adán Silva, "Migrantes atrapados en muro de contención de Nicaragua," *Inter Press Service, Agencia de Noticias*, February 12, 2018, http://www.ipsnoticias.net/2018/02/migrantes-atrapados-muro-contencion-nicaragua.

14. UNHCR has stipulated that a "safe third country" entails the "ability to provide access to full and fair procedure for determining a claim to asylum or equivalent temporary protection." Such third country agreements should not take place if there exists a risk of refoulement (persecution in the third country), indirect or chain refoulement (removal from third country to country of origin), or lack of access to fair hearing, health, education, basic services, and protection in the third country.

15. Yael Schacher, Rachel Schmidtke, and Ariana Sawyer, "Deportation with a Layover: Failure of Protection under the US-Guatemala Asylum

Cooperative Agreements," Human Rights Watch. May 19, 2020, https://www.hrw.org/report/2020/05/19/deportation-layover/failure-protection-under-us-guatemala-asylum-cooperative.

CHAPTER 8

1. Maureen Meyer and Adam Isacson, "The 'Wall' before the Wall: Mexico's Crackdown on Migration at its Southern Border," Washington, DC: Washington Office on Latin America, December 17, 2019, 38–39. https://www.wola.org/analysis/mexico-southern-border-report.

2. It should be noted that a main part of Obrador's crackdown on immigration at the southern border was sending nearly 12,000 members of the newly created National Guard, consisting mostly of active soldiers and military police, to southern border enforcement. Meyer and Isacson "The 'Wall' before the Wall," 8.

3. Mexico more than doubled its humanitarian visas (TVRH) from 2018 (17,722) to 2019 (40,966). Importantly, nearly half of the 2019 visas were issued in January (11,833) and February (7,216). Similarly, deportations and returns significantly dropped in Obrador's first three months in office, from an average of 11,000 per month in 2018 to 6,207 in December 2018, 6,144 in January 2019, 8,228 in February 2018, and 9,629 in March. Gobierno de México, "Boletín Mensual."

4. After a short decline at the start of 2019, the number of deportations and returns quickly grew in response to the threats of the Trump administration: April (17,144), May (17,644), June (24,125), and July (17,130). Gobierno de México, "Boletín Mensual." In Chiapas (the state in which Tapachula is located) alone, 66 percent more migrants were detained through September 2019 than for the same period in 2018. Priya S. Morley, *A Journey of Hope: Haitian Women's Migration to Tapachula, Mexico* (San Francisco: University of California, Hastings College of Law, Center for Gender and Refugee Studies, 2021), 11, https://imumi.org/attachments/2020/A-Journey-of-Hope-Haitian-Womens-Migration-to%20-Tapachula.pdf.

5. Maria Verza, "Overcrowding, Abuse Seen at Mexico Migrant Detention Center," *AP News*, June 17, 2019, https://apnews.com/article/immigration-caribbean-ap-top-news-international-news-cuba-cae4919e5d5d4d6eb280785618dfa865.

6. A research report by the Black Alliance for Just Immigration confirms the discriminatory treatment against Black immigrants in Siglo XXI. They are consistently given less food and medical care. Priya S. Morley, *"There Is a Target on Us": The Impact of Anti-Black Racism on African Migrants at Mexico's Southern Border* (Brooklyn, NY: Black Alliance for Just Immigration, 2020), 40, https://imumi.org/attachments/2020/The-Impact-of-Anti-Black-Racism-on-African-Migrants-at-Mexico.pdf.

7. Morley, *"There Is a Target on Us,"* 40.

8. Michael Agier, *Managing the Undesirables: Refugee Camps and Humanitarian Government*, trans. David Fernbach (Cambridge: Polity Press, 2011).

9. However, the asylum success rate is drastically lower for Haitians (13 percent). Morley, *A Journey of Hope*, 12.

10. *Reuters*, "Mexico Flies 300 Indian Migrants to New Delhi in 'Unprecedented' Mass Deportation," October 17, 2019, https://www.reuters.com/article/us-usa-immigration-mexico-india/mexico-flies-300-indian-migrants-to-new-delhi-in-unprecedented-mass-deportation-idUSKBN1WW2KV.

11. De Genova refers to border scenes as "spectacles" that frame illegality as a self-evident category. This spectacle renders the migrant body hyper-visible while obscuring the political history of immigration laws, policy, and recruitment of migrant laborers. The threat of detainment and deportation thus serves not to seal the border, but to place migrant workers in a permanent and exploitable state of "subordinate inclusion." Nicholas De Genova, "Border, Scene and Obscene," in *A Companion to Border Studies*, eds. Thomas Wilson and Hastings Donnan (Chichester, UK: Blackwell Publishing, 2012).

12. Robert J. Kaiser, "Performativity and the Eventfulness of Bordering Practices" in *A Companion to Border Studies*, eds. Thomas Wilson and Hastings Donnan (Chichester, UK: Blackwell Publishing, 2012), 523.

13. The externalization of border control often entails an asymmetrical relationship in which dominant states outsource enforcement to or impose extra-territorial controls on subordinate states, who, in turn, internalize the former's agenda through detection, detention and deportation practices. Cecilia Menjívar, "Immigration Law beyond Borders: Externalizing and Internalizing Border Controls in an Era of Securitization," *Annual Review of Law and Social Science* 10 (2014). Although dating back to early twentieth-century visa requirements, in the post-9/11 emergence of the Department of Homeland Security in the US, and Frontex in Europe, externalization now includes the virtual walls of data information systems, the training and militarizing of security forces, and creation of detention centers and deportation agreements. Zaiotti, "Mapping Remote Control," 4.

14. The exception was Nicaraguan migrants fleeing the violence between the leftist Sandinista state and the US-supported Contras. While asylum-denied Guatemalans and Salvadorans were likely to be deported, Nicaraguans were much more likely to be allowed to remain. Coutin, "Falling Outside," 572.

15. Vogt, *Lives in Transit*.

16. Rebecca Galemba, *Contraband Corridor: Making a Living at the Mexico-Guatemala Border* (Palo Alto, CA: Stanford University Press, 2018).

17. The simultaneous easing of transborder movement for goods while placing increasing control over the movement of people speaks to the larger contradictions of the post-Cold War neoliberal era in which exploitable labor is countered by security concerns of migration. Menjívar, "Immigration Beyond Borders," 354.

18. Carmen Boullosa and Mike Wallace, *A Narco History* (New York: OR Books, 2015).

19. Lynn Stephen, "Gendered Transborder Violence in the Expanded United States-Mexico Borderlands," *Human Organization* 75, no. 2 (2016); Vogt, *Lives in Transit*, 155–80.

20. Varela Huerta credits Central American migrants for coining the term "vertical border" to describe the "policies put in place to prevent Central American migrants and asylum-seekers from reaching their intended destination and ostensibly to deter future undocumented immigration from the region." Amarela Varela Huerta, "Migrants Trapped in the Mexican Vertical Border," University of Oxford, Faculty of Law, Border Criminologies Blog, June 21, 2018, https://www.law.ox.ac.uk/research-subject-groups/centre-criminology/centre-border-criminologies/blog/2018/06/migrants-trapped. Vogt prefers the term "arterial border" to conceptualize the non-linear "layers of enforcement that permeate highways, roads, and railways, spreading like arteries throughout Mexico's interior." Vogt, *Lives in Transit Violence*, 54.

21. Translated from "La frontera de Guatemala con México, que para los centroamericanos es el inicio del infierno, para los africanos es el último tramo de su odisea" in Carlos Dada, "El último viaje del señor Ngu," *El Faro/El País*, December 7, 2019, https://especiales.elfaro.net/es/frontera_sur/el_ultimo_viaje_del_senor_ngu.

22. According to the Department of Homeland Security's website (2019), an SIA is defined as "a non-US person who, based on an analysis of travel patterns, potentially poses a national security risk to the United States or its interests. Often such individuals or groups are employing travel patterns known or evaluated to possibly have a nexus to terrorism. DHS analysis includes an examination of travel patterns, points of origin, and/or travel segments that are tied to current assessments of national and international threat environments. This does not mean that all SIAs are 'terrorists,' but rather that the travel and behavior of such individuals indicates a possible nexus to nefarious activity (including terrorism) and, at a minimum, provides indicators that necessitate heightened screening and further investigation. The term SIA does not indicate any specific derogatory information about the individual—and DHS has never indicated that the SIA designation means more than that." In practicality though, SIAs

are almost always designated due to countries of origin that are, or have been, on the ever-fluctuating list of twenty-one to sixty-three "countries of interest" with suspected terrorist activity. David J. Bier, and Alex Nowrasteh, "45,000 'Special Interest Aliens' Caught since 2007, but No US Terrorist Attacks from Illegal Border Crossers," CATO Institute, December 17, 2018, https://www.cato.org/blog/45000-special-interest-aliens-caught-2007-no-us-terrorist-attacks-illegal-border-crossers.

23. Bier and Nowrasteh, "45,000 'Special Interest Aliens.'"

24. Morley, *"There Is a Target on Us,"* 38.

25. Two judges decided that the lack of diplomatic representation of most African countries in Mexico rendered the migrants effectively "stateless," and thus, in need of protection in and the right to travel through Mexico. Dada, "El último viaje del señor Ngu." It remains unclear, however, how many migrants beyond the 350 plaintiffs in the case have received the exit permits allowing them to transit out of Chiapas.

26. Morley *"There Is a Target on Us,"* 41–44.

27. Andersson, *Illegality, Inc.*, 229.

28. For more on anti-black racism in Tapachula, see the excellent report by Morley, *"There Is a Target on Us."*

29. *En el Camino* (November 4, 2019), a pamphlet published by migrant rights organization Sin Fronteras.

30. Didier Fassin, "Noli Me Tangere: The Moral Untouchability of Humanitarianism," in *Forces of Compassion: Humanitarianism between Ethics and Politics*, ed. Erica Bornstein and Peter Redfield (Santa Fe, NM: School of Advanced Research, 2011).

31. Andersson, *Illegality, Inc.*, 183.

32. Zhang, *Smuggling and Trafficking*, 86.

33. Elizabeth Nimmons, "Forming Spontaneous Ties in Dangerous Terrain: African Refugee Migration through Latin America," MA Thesis, University of Texas at Austin, 2019, 30.

34. Amy Bracken, "Mexico's 'Mama Africa' welcomes migrants on a long journey," *Public Radio International*, April 19, 2017, https://www.pri.org/stories/2017-04-19/mexico-s-mama-africa-welcomes-migrants-long-journey; Patrick McDonnell, "Traversing the Rio Suchiate," *Los Angeles Times*, December 23, 2016, https://www.latimes.com/projects/la-fg-immigration-trek-america-mexico.

35. Patricia de Santana Pinho, *Mama Africa: Reinventing Blackness in Bahia* (Durham, NC: Duke University Press, 2010).

36. Isaias Alvarado, "Los codiciados migrantes que pagan $50,000 para llegar a EEUU: Así operan los 'coyotes' los guían," *Univision*, September 1, 2019, https://www.univision.com/noticias/inmigracion/los-codiciados-migrantes-que-pagan-50-000-para-llegar-a-eeuu-asi-operan-los-coyotes-que-los-guian.

CHAPTER 10

1. Neena Satija, "Port Isabel Detention Center, Where Immigrants Will Be Sent before Reuniting with Children, Has Long History of Problems," *Texas Tribune*, June 27, 2018, https://www.texastribune.org/2018/06/27/port-isabel-detention-center-long-history-problems-immigrants-reunific.
2. Robert S. Kahn, *Other People's Blood: US Immigration Prisons in the Reagan Decade* (Boulder, CO: Westview Press, 1996).
3. "Immigration Detention in the United States by Agency," American Immigration Council, Washington, DC, last modified January 2, 2020, https://www.americanimmigrationcouncil.org/research/immigration-detention-united-states-agency.
4. Stephen Legomsky, "Learning to Live with Unequal Justice: Asylum and the Limits of Consistency," *Stanford Law Review* 60, no. 2 (2007).
5. US Government Accountability Office. "Significant Variation Existed in Asylum Outcomes across Immigration Courts and Judges," GAO-08–940. Washington, DC: GAO, 2008.
6. Jaya Ramji-Nogales, Andrew I. Schoenholtz, and Philip G. Schrag, "Refugee Roulette: Disparities in Asylum Adjudication," *Stanford Law Review* 60, no. 2 (2007).
7. Linda Camp Keith, Jennifer S. Holmes, and Banks P. Miller, "Explaining the Divergence in Asylum Grant Rates among Immigration Judges: An Attitudinal and Cognitive Approach," *Law and Policy* 35, no. 4 (October 2013), 263; Marc R. Rosenblum and Idean Salehyan, "Norms and Interests in US Asylum Enforcement," *Journal of Peace Research* 41 (2004), 683.
8. Coutin, "Falling Outside," 572.
9. Tal Kopan, "Outgoing SF Immigration Judge Blasts Courts as 'Soul-Crushing,' Too Close to ICE," *San Francisco Chronicle*, May 18, 2021, https://www.sfchronicle.com/politics/article/Exclusive-Outgoing-SF-immigration-judge-blasts-16183235.php.
10. Timothy J. Dunn, *The Militarization of the US-Mexico Border, 1978–1992: Low-Intensity Conflict Doctrine Comes Home* (Austin: University of Texas Press, 1996).
11. De León, *The Land of Open Graves*, 31.

12. Reece Jones, *Violent Borders: Refugees and the Right to Move* (New York: Verso Books, 2016), 35.

13. Josiah M. Heyman, "Constructing a Virtual Wall: Race and Citizenship in US-Mexico Border Policing," *Journal of the Southwest* 50, no. 3 (2008).

14. Border scholar Josiah M. Heyman makes a compelling argument for understanding securitization beyond deterrence, as a strategy of centralizing state power in service of certain elite interests. Particularly in the post-9/11 era, the state has militarized the border to create what he calls the homeland security-industrial complex. This complex benefits three groups. One, it justifies the ballooning of defense, intelligence, and surveillance budgets. Two, ratcheting up anti-migrant border rhetoric creates a "convenient distraction" for right-wing ideologues, who, in 2005 needed to redirect public attention away from the failing Iraq War. Finally, corporate elites benefit from how migrant criminalization produces vulnerable and disciplined workers. Josiah M. Heyman, "Constructing a Virtual Wall," 319–20.

15. Jezmin Fuentes, Henry L'Esperance, Raul Perez, and Caitlin White, "Impacts of US Immigration Policies on Migration Behavior," in *Impacts of Border Enforcement on Mexican Migration: The View from Sending Communities*, ed. Wayne A. Cornelius and Jessa M. Lewis (La Jolla, CA: Center for Comparative Immigration Studies, 2007).

16. David J. Bier, "Despite More Staff, CBP Says 'No Resources' to Process Asylum Applicants at Ports," Cato Institute, December 5, 2019, https://www.cato.org/blog/despite-more-staff-cbp-says-no-resources-process-asylum-applicants-ports.

17. Of the nationalities covered in this book, only Cuba records a blip on the MPP program, accounting for 28.9 percent of cases. Syracuse University's Transactional Records Access Clearinghouse, "MPP Transfers into United States Slow and Nationality Inequities Emerge," June 17, 2021, https://trac.syr.edu/immigration/reports/650.

18. "Q&A: Trump Administration's 'Stay in Mexico Program,'" Human Rights Watch, last modified January 29, 2020, https://www.hrw.org/news/2020/01/29/qa-trump-administrations-remain-mexico-program#.

19. Jasmine Aguilera, "Caught between US Policies and Instability at Home, Haitian Migrants in Tijuana Are in a State of Limbo," *Time*, July 22, 2021, https://time.com/6080579/haitian-migrants-tijuana-us-policy; Nancy Moya, "Haitianos rechazados por EEUU se establecen en Tijuana," *Associated Press*, June 11, 2018, https://apnews.com/article/f25135c24cf5479187c76f823a68c79f.

20. "Barred at the Border." Human Rights First, last modified April 2019, https://www.humanrightsfirst.org/sites/default/files/BARRED_AT_THE_BORDER.pdf.

21. "Jodi Goodwin Exposes Realities of Remain in Mexico," *ImmigrationProf Blog*, September 19, 2019. https://lawprofessors.typepad.com/immigration/2019/09/jodi-goodwin-exposes-realities-of-remain-in-mexico-part-1.html.

22. Rob Curran, "The Brutal Deportation of Mexican Immigrants Is a Crime against Humanity," *Dallas Morning News*, May 17, 2016, https://www.dallasnews.com/opinion/commentary/2016/05/17/rob-curran-the-brutal-deportation-of-mexican-immigrants-is-a-crime-against-humanity.

23. Madeline Holland, "Stories for Asylum: Narrative and Credibility in the United States' Political Asylum Application," *Refuge: Canada's Journal on Refugees* 34, no. 2 (2018).

24. Charlotte Brontë, *Jane Eyre* (Dover Thrift Editions, 1857 [2002]), 315.

CONCLUSION

1. Mila Koumpilova, "Minnesota Becomes a Gateway to Canada for Rejected African Migrants," *Minneapolis Star Tribune*, February 4, 2017, https://www.startribune.com/minnesota-becomes-a-gateway-to-canada-for-rejected-african-migrants/412771883.

2. Stephanie Levitz, "More than 16,000 People Nabbed by RCMP between Border Crossings in 2019," *Canadian Press*, January 16, 2020, https://www.ctvnews.ca/canada/more-than-16-000-people-nabbed-by-rcmp-between-border-crossings-in-2019-1.4770504; Mireille Paquet, and Robert Schertzer, *Irregular Border Crossings and Asylum Seekers in Canada: A Complex Intergovernmental Problem*, IRPP Study 80 (Montreal: Institute for Research on Public Policy, 2020).

3. David Sommerstein, "'Refugee Taxis' from Plattsburgh to Canada Subject of New Doc." *North Country Public Radio*, June 22, 2020, https://www.northcountrypublicradio.org/news/story/41725/20200622/refugee-taxis-from-plattsburgh-to-canada-subject-of-new-doc.

4. Soledad Álvarez Velasco and Lucia Pérez Martínez, "Pandemic and (Im)Mobility in the Americas," *Antipode Online*, August 11, 2020, https://antipodeonline.org/2020/08/11/pandemic-and-immobility-in-the-americas.

5. See the Immobility in the Americas website, https://en.inmovilidadamericas.org.

6. Cat Cardenas, "Asylum Seekers in Matamoros Celebrated Joe Biden's Victory. But the Final Weeks of the Trump Administration Are Bringing Fresh Anxiety," *Texas Monthly*, December 14, 2020, https://www.texasmonthly.com/news/matamoros-asylum-seekers-biden-victory.

EPILOGUE

1. The Trump administration filled two-thirds of the 520 lifetime judge positions in immigration courts. Judges appointed by Trump ordered deportations in 69 percent of cases as opposed to the 58 percent average of judges previously appointed. Reade Levinson, Kristina Cooke, and Mica Rosenberg, "How Trump Administration Left Indelible Mark on US Immigration Courts," *Reuters*, March 8, 2021, https://www.reuters.com/article/us-usa-immigration-trump-court-special-r/special-report-how-trump-administration-left-indelible-mark-on-u-s-immigration-courts-idUSKBN2B0179.

REFERENCES

Achilli, Luigi. "The 'Good' Smuggler: The Ethics and Morals of Human Smuggling among Syrians." *Annals of the American Academy of Political and Social Science* 676, no. 1 (2018): 77–96.

Acosta Arcarazo, Diego, and Luisa Feline Freier. "Turning the Immigration Policy Paradox Upside Down?: Populist Liberalism and Discursive Gaps in South America." *International Migration Review* 49, no. 3 (2015): 659–96.

Agier, Michael. *Managing the Undesirables: Refugee Camps and Humanitarian Government.* Translated by David Fernbach. Cambridge, UK: Polity Press, 2011.

Aguilera, Jasmine. "Caught between US Policies and Instability at Home, Haitian Migrants in Tijuana Are in a State of Limbo." *Time*, July 22, 2021. https://time.com/6080579/haitian-migrants-tijuana-us-policy.

Ahmad, Ali Nobil. *Masculinity, Sexuality and Illegal Migration: Human Smuggling from Pakistan to Europe.* Burlington, VT: Ashgate Publishing, 2011.

Alvarado, Isaias. "Los codiciados migrantes que pagan $50,000 para llegar a EEUU: Así operan los 'coyotes' los guían." *Univision*, September 1, 2019. https://www.univision.com/noticias/inmigracion/los-codiciados-migrantes-que-pagan-50-000-para-llegar-a-eeuu-asi-operan-los-coyotes-que-los-guian.

Álvarez Velasco, Soledad. "From Ecuador to Elsewhere: The (Re)Configuration of a Transit Country." *Migration and Society: Advances in Research* 3 (2020): 34–49.

Álvarez Velasco, Soledad, and Lucia Pérez Martínez. "Pandemic and (Im) Mobility in the Americas." *Antipode Online*, August 11, 2020. https://antipodeonline.org/2020/08/11/pandemic-and-immobility-in-the-americas.

American Immigration Council. "Immigration Detention in the United States by Agency." Washington, DC. Last modified January 2, 2020. https://www.americanimmigrationcouncil.org/research/immigration-detention-united-states-agency.

Amorocho, Julián, and Esteban Vanegas. "Una estampida humana cruza por Capurganá." *El Colombiano*, March 2, 2018. https://www.elcolombiano.com/colombia/el-refugio-de-los-migrantes-ilegales-en-capurgana-choco-HK8286900.

Andersson, Ruben. *Illegality, Inc.: Clandestine Migration and the Business of Bordering Europe*. Berkeley: University of California Press, 2014.

Asia Foundation. *Labour Migration Trends and Patterns: Bangladesh, India, and Nepal 2013*. Kathmandu: The Asia Foundation, 2013.

Baeninger, Rosana, Natália Belmonte Demétrio, and Jóice Domeniconi. "Espaços das Migrações Transnacionais: Perfil sociodemográfico de imigrantes da África para o Brasil no século XXI." *REMHU: Revista Interdiciplinar da Mobilidade Humana* 27, no. 56 (2019). http://dx.doi.org/10.1590/1980-85852503880005603.

Baird, Theodore, and Ilse Van Liempt. "Scrutinising the Double Disadvantage: Knowledge Production in the Messy Field of Migrant Smuggling." *Journal of Ethnic and Migration Studies* 42, no. 3 (2016): 400–417.

Bier, David J. "Despite More Staff, CBP Says 'No Resources' to Process Asylum Applicants at Ports." Cato Institute. December 5, 2019. https://www.cato.org/blog/despite-more-staff-cbp-says-no-resources-process-asylum-applicants-ports.

Bier, David J., and Alex Nowrasteh. "45,000 'Special Interest Aliens' Caught since 2007, but No US Terrorist Attacks from Illegal Border Crossers." CATO Institute, December 17, 2018. https://www.cato.org/blog/45000-special-interest-aliens-caught-2007-no-us-terrorist-attacks-illegal-border-crossers.

Blitzer, Jonathan. "The Cuban Migrant Crisis." *New Yorker*, January 16, 2016. https://www.newyorker.com/news/news-desk/the-cuban-migrant-crisis.

Boullosa, Carmen, and Mike Wallace. *A Narco History*. New York/London: OR Books, 2015.

Bracken, Amy. "Mexico's 'Mama Africa' Welcomes Migrants on a Long Journey." Public Radio International, April 19, 2017. https://www.pri.org/stories/2017-04-19/mexico-s-mama-africa-welcomes-migrants-long-journey.

Brontë, Charlotte. *Jane Eyre*. 1857. New York: Dover Thrift Editions, 2002.

Bruslé, Tristan. "Choosing a Destination and Work: Migration Strategies of Nepalese workers in Uttarakhand, Northern India." *Mountain Research Development* 28 no. 3/4 (2008): 240–47.

———. "The Nepali-Qatari Migrant World." *Himal South Asian*, May 1, 2008. https://www.himalmag.com/the-nepali-qatari-migrant-world.

Caldeira, Teresa. "Peripheral Urbanization: Autoconstruction, Transversal Logics, and Politics in Cities of the Global South." *Environment and Planning D: Society and Space* 35, no. 1 (2016): 3–20.

Cardenas, Cat. "Asylum Seekers in Matamoros Celebrated Joe Biden's Victory. But the Final Weeks of the Trump Administration Are Bringing Fresh Anxiety." *Texas Monthly*, December 14, 2020. https://www.texasmonthly.com/news/matamoros-asylum-seekers-biden-victory.

Castles, Stephen, Hein de Haas, and Mark J. Millar. *The Age of Migration*, 5th ed. London: Palgrave Macmillan, 2013.

Chaparro, César. "Víctimas de tráfico de migrantes cuentan el horror en manos del Clan del Golfo." *Noticias Caracol*, February 28, 2018. https://noticias.caracoltv.com/colombia/victimas-de-trafico-de-migrantes-cuentan-el-horror-en-manos-del-clan-del-golfo.

Chippaux, Jean-Philippe. "Incidence and Mortality Due to Snakebite in the Americas." *Neglected Tropical Diseases* 11, no. 6 (2017): https://journals.plos.org/plosntds/article?id=10.1371/journal.pntd.0005662.

Collyer, Michael. "In-between Places: Trans-Saharan Transit Migrants in Morocco and the Fragmented Journey to Europe." *Antipode* 394 (2007): 668–90.

Collyer, Michael, and Hein de Haas. "Developing Dynamic Categorisation of Transit Migration." *Population, Space and Place* 18 (2012): 468–81.

Coutin, Susan B. "Being En Route." *American Anthropologist* 107, no. 2 (2005): 195–206.

———. "Falling Outside: Excavating the History of Central American Asylum Seekers." *Law and Social Inquiry* 36, no. 3 (2011): 569–96.

Craig, Sienna. *The Ends of Kinship: Connecting Himalayan Lives between Nepal and New York*. Seattle: University of Washington Press, 2020.

Curran, Rob. "The Brutal Deportation of Mexican Immigrants Is a Crime against Humanity." *Dallas Morning News*, May 17, 2016. https://www.dallasnews.com/opinion/commentary/2016/05/17/rob-curran-the-brutal-deportation-of-mexican-immigrants-is-a-crime-against-humanity.

Dada, Carlos. "El último viaje del señor Ngu." *El Faro/El Pais*, December 7, 2019. https://especiales.elfaro.net/es/frontera_sur/el_ultimo_viaje_del_senor_ngu.

De Genova, Nicholas. "Border, Scene and Obscene." In *A Companion to Border Studies*, edited by Thomas Wilson and Hastings Donnan, 492–504. Chichester, UK: Blackwell Publishing, 2012.

De León, Jason. *The Land of Open Graves: Living and Dying on the Migrant Trail.* Berkeley: University of California Press, 2015.

Doña Reveco, Christián. "Amid Record Numbers of Arrivals, Chile Turns Rightward on Immigration." January 17, 2018. https://www.migrationpolicy.org/article/amid-record-numbers-arrivals-chile-turns-rightward-immigration.

Dunn, Timothy J. *The Militarization of the US-Mexico Border, 1978–1992: Low-Intensity Conflict Doctrine Comes Home.* Austin: University of Texas Press, 1996.

Düvell, Franck. "Transit Migration: A Blurred and Politicised Concept." *Population, Space and Place* 18 (2012): 415–27.

Düvell, Franck, Irina Molodikova, and Michael Collyer. *Transit Migration in Europe.* Amsterdam: Amsterdam University Press, 2014.

Echeverri Zuluaga, Jonathan. "Errance and Elsewheres among Africans Waiting to Restart Their Journeys in Dakar, Senegal." *Cultural Anthropology* 30, no. 4 (2015): 589–610.

Echeverri Zuluaga, Jonathan, and Liza Acevedo Saenz. "Pensando a travesías y esperas de viajeros africanos en Quito y Dakar." *Antípoda: Revista de Antropología ye Arqueología* 32 (2018): 105–23.

Esquivel Solano, Noelia. "Mama Africa: The Woman Investigated of Crossing African Migrants from Guanacaste to Nicaragua." *Voice of Guanacaste*, May 28, 2020. https://vozdeguanacaste.com/en/mama-africa-the-woman-investigated-of-crossing-african-migrants-from-guanacaste-to-nicaragua.

Facultad Latinoamericana de Ciencias Sociales (FLACSO Costa Rica). *Diagnóstico sobre la situación actual, tendencias y necesidades de protección y asistencia de las personas migratnes y refugiadas extracontinentales en México y América Central.* Mexico City: Regional Office for Central America and Mexico of the International Organization for Migration (IOM) and United Nations High Commissioner for Refugees (UNHCR), 2011. https://www.corteidh.or.cr/sitios/observaciones/11/Anexo8.pdf.

Fagan, Laureen. "For African Migrants, Will Panama Become the New Libya?" *Africa Times*, August 30, 2019. https://africatimes.com/2019/08/30/for-african-migrants-will-panama-become-the-new-libya.

Fassin, Didier. "Noli Me Tangere: The Moral Untouchability of Humanitarianism" In *Forces of Compassion: Humanitarianism between Ethics and Politics*, edited by Erica Bornstein and Peter Redfield, 35–52. Santa Fe, NM: School of Advanced Research, 2011.

Faist, Thomas. "Brokerage in Cross-Border Mobility: Social Mechanisms and the (Re)Production of Social Inequalities." *Social Inclusion* 2, no. 4 (2014): 38–52.

Fouratt, Caitlin. "'Those who come to do harm': The Framings of Immigration Problems in Costa Rican Immigration Law." *International Migration Review* 48, no. 1 (2014): 144–80.

Freier, Luisa Feline. "Open Doors (For Almost All): Visa Policies and Ethnic Selectivity in Ecuador." Working Paper 188. UC San Diego: Center for Comparative Immigration Studies, 2017. https://escholarship.org/uc/item/4m18b9tc.

Fuentes, Jezmin, Henry L'Esperance, Raul Perez, and Caitlin White. "Impacts of US Immigration Policies on Migration Behavior." In *Impacts of Border Enforcement on Mexican Migration: The View from Sending Communities*, edited by Wayne A. Cornelius and Jessa M. Lewis, 53–73. La Jolla, CA: Center for Comparative Immigration Studies, 2007.

Galemba, Rebecca. *Contraband Corridor: Making a Living at the Mexico-Guatemala Border*. Palo Alto, CA: Stanford University Press, 2018.

Gammeltoft-Hansen, Thomas, and Ninna Nyberg Sørenson, eds. *The Migration Industry and the Commercialization of International Migration*. London: Routledge, 2013.

Gobierno de Chile. "Estadísticas Migratorias." 2020. Accessed March 20, 2021. https://serviciomigraciones.cl/estadisticasmigratorias.

Gobierno de México. "Boletín Mensual de Estadísticas Migratorias." Accessed January 2, 2021. http://portales.segob.gob.mx/es/PoliticaMigratoria/Boletines_Estadisticos.

Gogolak, Emily. "Haitian Migrants Turn toward Brazil." *New Yorker*, August 20, 2014. https://www.newyorker.com/news/news-desk/haitian-migrants-turn-toward-brazil.

Gómez Tobón, Juan Arturo. "Más de una decena de Cubanos mueren ahogados por la crecida de un río en el Darién." Diario de Cuba, June 7, 2019. https://diariodecuba.com/cuba/1559868692_46826.html.

Góngora-Mera, Manuel, Gioconda Herrera, and Conrad Müller. "The Frontiers of Universal Citizenship: Transnational Social Spaces and the Legal Status of Migrants in Ecuador." Working Paper No. 71, Berlin: desiguALdades.net, International Research Network on Interdependent Inequalities in Latin America, 2014. https://www.desigualdades.net/Resources/Working_Paper/71-WP-Gongora-Mera-Herrera-Mueller-Online.pdf.

Goodwin, Jodi. "Jodi Goodwin Exposes Realities of Remain in Mexico." *ImmigrationProf Blog*. September 19, 2019. https://lawprofessors.typepad.

com/immigration/2019/09/jodi-goodwin-exposes-realities-of-remain-in-mexico-part-1.html.

Gramlich, John, and Luis Noe-Bustamente. "What's Happening at the US-Mexico Border in 5 Charts." Pew Research Center, November 1, 2019. https://www.pewresearch.org/fact-tank/2019/11/01/whats-happening-at-the-u-s-mexico-border-in-5-charts.

Herlihy, Peter. "Chocó Indian Relocation in Darién." *Cultural Survival Quarterly* (1985) https://www.culturalsurvival.org/publications/cultural-survival-quarterly/choco-indian-relocation-darien-panama.

———. "Opening Panama's Darién Gap." *Journal of Cultural Geography* 9, no. 2 (1989): 42–59.

Hernández León, Ruben. "Conceptualizing the Migration Industry." In *The Migration Industry and the Commercialization of International Migration*, edited by Thomas Gammeltoft-Hansen and Nina Nyberg Sørenson, 24–44. Oxford: Routledge, 2013.

Hess, Sabine. "De-naturalising Transit Migration: Theory and Methods of an Ethnographic Regime Analysis." *Population, Space and Place* 18 (2012): 428–40.

Heyman, Josiah M. "Constructing a Virtual Wall: Race and Citizenship in US-Mexico Border Policing." *Journal of the Southwest* 50, no. 3 (2008): 305–33.

Holland, Madeline. "Stories for Asylum: Narrative and Credibility in the United States' Political Asylum Application." *Refuge: Canada's Journal on Refugees* 34, no. 2 (2018): 85–93.

Human Rights First. "Barred at the Border." April 2019. https://www.humanrightsfirst.org/sites/default/files/BARRED_AT_THE_BORDER.pdf.

———. "World Report 2014: Eritrea." Accessed March 5, 2020. https://www.hrw.org/world-report/2014/country-chapters/eritrea#.

———. "Q&A: Trump Administration's "Stay in Mexico Program." January 29, 2020. https://www.hrw.org/news/2020/01/29/qa-trump-administrations-remain-mexico-program#.

———. "US: Protect Cameroonians from Deportation." December 18, 2020. https://www.hrw.org/news/2020/12/18/us-protect-cameroonians-deportation.

Jokisch, Brad and David Kyle. "Ecuadorian International Migration." In *The Ecuador Reader*, edited by Carlos de la Torre and Steve Striffler, 350–58. Durham, NC: Duke University Press, 2008.

Jones, Reece. *Violent Borders: Refugees and the Right to Move*. New York: Verso Books, 2016.

Kahn, Robert S. *Other People's Blood: US Immigration Prisons in the Reagan Decade*. Boulder, CO: Westview Press, 1996.

Kaiser, Robert J. "Performativity and the Eventfulness of Bordering Practices." In *A Companion to Border Studies*, edited by Thomas Wilson and Hastings Donnan, 522–37. Chichester, UK: Blackwell Publishing, 2012.

Kane, Stephanie C. *The Phantom Gringo Boat: Shamanic Discourse and Development in Panama*. Washington, DC: Smithsonian Institution Press, 1994.

Keith, Linda Camp, Jennifer S. Holmes, and Banks P. Miller. "Explaining the Divergence in Asylum Grant Rates among Immigration Judges: An Attitudinal and Cognitive Approach." *Law and Policy* 35, no. 4 (October 2013): 261–89.

Kern, Alice, and Ulrike Müller-Böker. "The Middle Space of Migration: A Case Study of Brokerage and Recruitment Agencies in Nepal." *Geoforum* 65 (2015): 158–69.

Khosravi, Shahram. *"Illegal" Traveller: An Auto-ethnography of Borders*. New York: Palgrave Macmillan, 2010.

Klein, Herbert S., and Ben Vinson III. *African Slavery in Latin America and the Caribbean*. Oxford: Oxford University Press, 2007.

Kopan, Tal. "Outgoing SF Immigration Judge Blasts Courts as 'Soul-Crushing,' Too Close to ICE." *San Francisco Chronicle*, May 18, 2021. https://www.sfchronicle.com/politics/article/Exclusive-Outgoing-SF-immigration-judge-blasts-16183235.php.

Koser, Khalid. "Why Take the Risk?: Explaining Migrant Smuggling." In *Global Migration, Ethnicity and Britishness*, edited by Tariq Modood and John Salt, 65–83. London: Palgrave Macmillan, 2011.

Koumpilova, Mila. "Minnesota Becomes a Gateway to Canada for Rejected African Migrants." *Minneapolis Star Tribune*, February 4, 2017. https://www.startribune.com/minnesota-becomes-a-gateway-to-canada-for-rejected-african-migrants/412771883.

Kyle, David. *Transnational Peasants: Migrations, Networks, and Ethnicity in Andean Ecuador*. Baltimore, MD: John Hopkins University Press, 2000.

La Prensa Latina. "Migrants, Authorities Clash on Peru-Brazil Border." *La Prensa Latina*, February 16, 2021. https://www.laprensalatina.com/migrants-authorities-clash-on-peru-brazil-border.

Legomsky, Stephen H. "Learning to Live with Unequal Justice: Asylum and the Limits of Consistency," *Stanford Law Review* 60, no. 2 (2007): 413–75.

Levinson, Reade, Kristina Cooke and Mica Rosenberg. "How Trump Administration Left Indelible Mark on US Immigration Courts." *Reuters*, March 8, 2021. https://www.reuters.com/article/us-usa-immigration-trump-court-special-r/special-report-how-trump-administration-left-indelible-mark-on-u-s-immigration-courts-idUSKBN2B0179.

Levitz, Stephanie. "More than 16,000 People Nabbed by RCMP between Border Crossings in 2019." *Canadian Press*, January 16, 2020. https://www.ctvnews.ca/canada/more-than-16-000-people-nabbed-by-rcmp-between-border-crossings-in-2019-1.4770504.

Lijnders, Laurie, and Sara Robinson. "From the Horn of Africa to the Middle East: Human Trafficking of Eritrean Asylum Seekers across Borders." *Anti-Trafficking Review* 2 (2013): 137–54.

Lindquist, Johan, Biao Xiang, Brenda S.A. Yeoh. "Opening the Black Box of Migration: Brokers, the Organization of Transnational Mobility and the Changing Political Economy in Asia." *Pacific Affairs* 85, no. 1 (2012): 7–19.

Maher, Stephanie. "Out of West Africa: Human Smuggling as a Social Enterprise." *Annals of the American Academy of Political and Social Science* 676, no. 1 (2018): 35–56.

Mahler, Anne Garland. *From the Tricontinental to the Global South: Race, Radicalism, and Transnational Solidarity*. Durham, NC: Duke University Press, 2018.

Mainwaring, Cetta, and Noelle Brigden. "Beyond the Border: Clandestine Migration Journeys." *Geopolitics* 21, no. 2 (2016): 243–62.

Margheritis, Ana. "'Todos somos migrantes' (We Are All Migrants): The Paradoxes of Innovative State-Led Transnationalism in Ecuador." *International Political Sociology* 5, no. 2 (2018): 198–217.

Matta, Nelson, and Julio Herrera. "Clan del Golfo tapona a migrantes en el Darién." *El Colombiano*, February 19, 2019. https://www.elcolombiano.com/colombia/clan-del-golfo-tapona-a-migrantes-en-el-darien-la10238641.

McDonnell, Patrick. "Traversing the Rio Suchiate." *Los Angeles Times*, December 23, 2016. https://www.latimes.com/projects/la-fg-immigration-trek-america-mexico.

Mena, Paul. "Ecuador: Crece Flujo de Inmigrantes Surasiáticos." *BBC News*, August 31, 2010. http://www.bbc.co.uk/mundo/america_latina/2010/08/100825_ecuador_inmigrantes_asia_pea.shtml.

Mengiste, Tekalign Ayalew. "Refugee Protections from Below: Smuggling in the Eritrea-Ethiopia Context." *Annals of the American Academy of Political and Social Science* 676, no. 1 (2018): 57–76.

Menjívar, Cecilia. "Immigration Law beyond Borders: Externalizing and Internalizing Border Controls in an Era of Securitization." *Annual Review of Law and Social Science* 10 (2014): 353–69.

Merlotti Herédia, Vania Beatriz, Santos Gonçalves, and Maria do Carmo. "Deslocamentos populacionais no sul do Brasil: O caso dos senegaleses." In *Imigração senegalesa no Brasil e na Argentina: Multiplos olhares*, edited by João Carlos and Gisele Kleidermacher, 209–28. Porto Alegre: Est Edições, 2017.

Meyer, Maureen and Adam Isacson. "The 'Wall' before the Wall: Mexico's Crackdown on Migration at Its Southern Border." Washington, DC: Washington Office on Latin America, December 17, 2019. https://www.wola.org/analysis/mexico-southern-border-report.

Missbach, Antje. *Troubled Transit: Asylum Seekers Stuck in Indonesia*. Singapore: ISEAS, 2015.

Missbach, Antje, and Melissa Phillips. "Reconceptualizing Transit States in an Era of Outsourcing, Offshoring, and Obfuscation." *Migration and Society: Advances in Research* 3 (2020): 19–33.

Miura, Heloisa Harumi. "The Haitian Migration Flow to Brazil: Aftermath of the 2010 Earthquake." In *The State of Environmental Migration 2014*, edited by François Gemenne, Pauline Brücker, and Dina Ionesco, 149-165. Liége, Belgium: Presses Universitaires de Liége, 2014. http://labos.ulg.ac.be/hugo/wp-content/uploads/sites/38/2017/11/The-State-of-Environmental-Migration-2014-149-165.pdf.

Morley, S. Priya. *"There Is a Target on Us": The Impact of Anti-Black Racism on African Migrants at Mexico's Southern Border*. Brooklyn, NY: Black Alliance for Just Immigration, 2020. https://imumi.org/attachments/2020/The-Impact-of-Anti-Black-Racism-on-African-Migrants-at-Mexico.pdf.

———. *A Journey of Hope: Haitian Women's Migration to Tapachula, Mexico*. San Francisco: University of California, Hastings College of Law, Center for Gender and Refugee Studies, 2021. https://imumi.org/attachments/2020/A-Journey-of-Hope-Haitian-Womens-Migration-to%20-Tapachula.pdf.

Motlagh, Jason. "A Terrifying Journey through the World's Most Dangerous Jungle." *Outside Online*, July 19, 2016. https://www.outsideonline.com/outdoor-adventure/exploration-survival/skull-stake-darien-gap.

Moya, Nancy. "Haitianos rechazados por EEUU se establecen en Tijuana." *Associated Press*, June 11, 2018. https://apnews.com/article/f25135c24cf5479187c76f823a68c79f.

Mukpo, Ashoka. "Harrowing Video Shows Indigenous Colombians Fleeing Gunfire." *Mongabay*, May 28, 2020. https://news.mongabay.com/2020/05/harrowing-video-shows-indigenous-colombians-fleeing-gunfire.

Naib, Fatma. "Slavery in Libya: Life inside a Container." *Al Jazeera*, January 26, 2018, https://www.aljazeera.com/news/2018/01/26/slavery-in-libya-life-inside-a-container.

Nielsen, Sara Trab. "The Spillover Effect of the Colombian Conflict Ecological Damage in the Darién Gap." Mandala Project, December 2006. http://mandalaprojects.com/ice/ice-cases/darien.htm.

Nimmons, Elizabeth. "Forming Spontaneous Ties in Dangerous Terrain: African Refugee Migration through Latin America." MA Thesis, University of Texas at Austin, 2019.

Noy, Shiri, and Koen Voorend. "Social Rights and Migrant Realities: Migration Policy Reform and Migrants' Access to Health Care in Costa Rica, Argentina, and Chile." *Journal of International Migration and Integration* 17, no. 2 (2016): 605–29.

Organización de los Estados Americanos. *Migración Extracontinental en las Américas: Memoria*. Washington, DC: Organización de los Estados Americanos, 2010. https://www.acnur.org/fileadmin/Documentos/BDL/2011/7402.pdf.

Organización Internacional para las Migraciones. "Migrantes extracontinentales en América del Sur: Estudio de casos." 2013. https://publications.iom.int/books/cuadernos-migratorios-ndeg5-migrantes-extracontinentales-en-america-del-sur-estudio-de-casos.

Paoletti, Sarah, Eleanor Taylor-Nicholson, Bandita Sijapati, and Bassina Farbenblum. *Migrant Workers' Access to Justice at Home: Nepal*. New York: Open Society Foundations, 2014.

Papadopoulos, Dimitris, and Vassilis S. Tsianos. "After Citizenship: Autonomy of Migration, Organisational Ontology and Mobilie Commons." *Citizenship Studies* 17, no. 2 (2013): 178–96.

Papadopoulou, Aspasia. "Smuggling into Europe: Transit Migrants in Greece." *Journal of Refugee Studies* 17, no. 2 (2004): 167–84.

Paquet, Mireille, and Robert Schertzer. *Irregular Border Crossings and Asylum Seekers in Canada: A Complex Intergovernmental Problem*. IRPP Study 80. Montreal: Institute for Research on Public Policy, 2020.

Parnell, Susan, and Jennifer Robinson. "(Re)theorizing Cities from the Global South: Looking beyond Neoliberalism." *Urban Geography* 33, no. 3 (2013): 593–617.

Paul, Anju Mary. "Stepwise International Migration: A Multistage Migration Pattern for the Aspiring Migrant." *American Journal of Sociology* 116, no. 6 (2011): 1842–86.

Penney, Joe. "Cameroonian Asylum-Seekers at the Border Are Fleeing a US-Backed Military Force." *The Intercept*, December 1, 2019. https://theintercept.com/2019/12/01/us-asylum-seekers-cameroon.

Phillips, Melissa, and Antje Missbach. "Economies of Transit: Exploiting Migrants and Refugees in Indonesia and Libya." *International Journal of Migration and Border Studies* 3, nos. 2–3 (2017): 139–57.

———. "Introduction." *International Journal of Migration and Border Studies* 3, nos. 2–3 (2017): 113–20.

Pugh, Jeffrey. "Universal Citizenship through the Discourse and Policy of Rafael Correa," *Latin American Politics and Society* 59, no. 2 (2017): 98–121.

Ramji-Nogales, Jaya, Andrew I. Schoenholtz, and Philip G. Schrag. "Refugee Roulette: Disparities in Asylum Adjudication." *Stanford Law Review* 60, no. 2 (2007): 295–411.

República de Panamá. "Migración Estadísticas." Accessed January 5, 2021. https://www.migracion.gob.pa/inicio/estadisticas.

Reuters. "Mexico Flies 300 Indian Migrants to New Delhi in 'Unprecedented' Mass Deportation." October 17, 2019. https://www.reuters.com/article/us-usa-immigration-mexico-india/mexico-flies-300-indian-migrants-to-new-delhi-in-unprecedented-mass-deportation-idUSKBN1WW2KV.

Rosenblum, Marc R., and Idean Salehyan. "Norms and Interests in US Asylum Enforcement." *Journal of Peace Research* 41 (2004): 677–97.

Salt, John and Jeremy Stein. "Migration as a Business: The Case of Trafficking." *International Migration* 35, no. 4 (1997): 467–94.

Santana Pinho, Patricia de. *Mama Africa: Reinventing Blackness in Bahia.* Durham, NC: Duke University Press, 2010.

Sapkota, Janakraj. "Amerika jaana khojda bandhak." *Kantipur*, November 13, 2019.

Satija, Neena. "Port Isabel Detention Center, Where Immigrants Will Be Sent before Reuniting with Children, Has Long History of Problems." *Texas Tribune*, June 27, 2018. https://www.texastribune.org/2018/06/27/port-isabel-detention-center-long-history-problems-immigrants-reunific.

Schacher, Yael, Rachel Schmidtke, and Ariana Sawyer. "Deportation with a Layover: Failure of Protection under the US-Guatemala Asylum Cooperative Agreements." Human Rights Watch, May 19, 2020. https://www.hrw.org/report/2020/05/19/deportation-layover/failure-protection-under-us-guatemala-asylum-cooperative.

Schapendonk, Joris. "The Multiplicity of Transit: The Waiting and Onward Mobility of African Migrants in the European Union." *International Journal of Migration and Border Studies* 3, nos. 2–3 (2017): 208–27.

Scheel, Stephan, and Vicki Squire. "Forced Migrants as 'Illegal' Migrants." In *The Oxford Handbook of Refugee and Forced Migration Studies*, edited by Elena

Fiddian-Qasmiyeh, Gil Loescher, Katy Long, and Nando Sigona, 188–99. Oxford: Oxford University Press, 2014.

Schindler, Seth. "Towards a Paradigm of Southern Urbanism." *City* 21, no. 1 (2017): 47–64.

Seijas, Tatiana. *Asian Slaves in Colonial Mexico: From Chinos to Indians.* New York: Cambridge University Press, 2014.

Sharma, Jeevan Raj. *Crossing the Border to India: Youth, Migration and Masculinities in Nepal.* Philadelphia, PA: Temple University Press, 2018.

Sharma, Sanjay, Shibani Pandey, Dinesh Pathak and Bimbika Sijapati-Basnet. "State of Migration in Nepal." Kathmandu: Centre for the Study of Labour and Mobility, Research Paper VI, 2014. https://www.ceslam.org/uploads/backup/STATE%20OF%20MIGRATION%20IN%20NEPAL1404964819.pdf.

Sijapati, Bandita, and Amrita Limbu. *Governing Labour Migration in Nepal: An Analysis of Existing Policies and Institutional Mechanisms*, 2nd edition. Kathmandu: Himal Books, 2017.

Sijapati, Bandita, Ashim Bhattarai, and Dinesh Pathak. *Analysis of Labour Market and Migration Trends in Nepal.* Kathmandu, Nepal: Deutsche Gesellschaft für Internationale Zusammenarbeit and International Labour Organization, 2015.

Silva, José Adán. "Migrantes atrapados en muro de contención de Nicaragua." *Inter Press Service, Agencia de Noticias*, February 12, 2018. http://www.ipsnoticias.net/2018/02/migrantes-atrapados-muro-contencion-nicaragua.

Simone, Abdoumaliq. *Improvised Lives: Rhythms of Endurance in an Urban South.* Cambridge, UK: Polity Press, 2019.

Solis, Dianne and Julieta Chiquillo. "Sister Norma, the Border Battle's Fiercest Fighter, Is as Astute as a Serpent and Gentle as a Dove." *Dallas Morning News*, June 21, 2018. https://www.dallasnews.com/news/immigration/2018/06/21/sister-norma-the-border-battle-s-fiercest-fighter-is-astute-as-a-serpent-and-gentle-as-a-dove.

Sommerstein, David. "'Refugee Taxis' from Plattsburgh to Canada Subject of New Doc." *North Country Public Radio*, June 22, 2020. https://www.northcountrypublicradio.org/news/story/41725/20200622/refugee-taxis-from-plattsburgh-to-canada-subject-of-new-doc.

Stephen, Lynn. "Gendered Transborder Violence in the Expanded United States-Mexico Borderlands." *Human Organization* 75, no. 2 (2016): 159–67.

Stone-Cadena, Victoria, and Soledad Álvarez Velasco. "Historicizing Mobility: *Coyoterismo* in the Indigenous Ecuadorian Migration Industry." *Annals of the American Academy of Political and Social Science* 676 (2018): 194–211.

Syracuse University's Transactional Records Access Clearinghouse. "MPP
    Transfers into United States Slow and Nationality Inequities Emerge." June
    17, 2021. https://trac.syr.edu/immigration/reports/650.

Telesur. "A Look into 'Clan del Golfo,' Colombia's Largest Paramilitary Group."
    April 2, 2018. https://www.telesurenglish.net/news/Exclusive-Gulf-Clan-
    Colombias-Biggest-Paramilitary-Group-20180402-0026.html.

Teran, Abraham. "Panama Isolates Migrants in Remote Jungle Coronavirus
    Unit." *Reuters*, June 9 2020. https://www.reuters.com/article/us-health-
    coronavirus-panama/panama-isolates-migrants-in-remote-jungle-
    coronavirus-unit-idUSKBN23G1HC.

US Border and Customs Protection. "US Border Patrol Nationwide
    Apprehensions by Citizenship and Sector." 2019. https://www.cbp.gov/sites/
    default/files/assets/documents/2020-Jan/U.S.%20Border%20Patrol%20
    Nationwide%20Apprehensions%20by%20Citizenship%20and%20
    Sector%20%28FY2007%20-%20FY%202019%29_1.pdf.

US Government Accountability Office. "Significant Variation Existed in
    Asylum Outcomes across Immigration Courts and Judges," GAO-08–940.
    Washington, DC: GAO, 2008.

US Department of Homeland Security. "MYTH/FACT: Known and
    Suspected Terrorists/Special Interest Aliens." Department of Homeland
    Security, January 7, 2019. https://www.dhs.gov/news/2019/01/07/
    mythfact-known-and-suspected-terroristsspecial-interest-aliens.

US Department of Justice. "Pakistani Citizen Sentenced to 50 Months in Prison
    for Conspiracy to Provide Material Support to the Pakistani Taliban."
    Department of Justice, January 5, 2012. https://www.justice.gov/opa/pr/
    pakistani-citizen-sentenced-50-months-prison-conspiracy-provide-material-
    support-pakistani.

Varela Huerta, Amarela. "Migrants Trapped in the Mexican Vertical
    Border." University of Oxford, Faculty of Law, Border Criminologies
    Blog. Last modified 2018. https://www.law.ox.ac.uk/research-subject-
    groups/centre-criminology/centreborder-criminologies/blog/2018/06/
    migrants-trapped

Vargas Llosa, Mario. *The Dream of the Celt.* Translated by Edith Grossman. New
    York: Farrar, Straus and Giroux, 2012.

Verza, Maria. "Overcrowding, Abuse Seen at Mexico Migrant Detention Center."
    AP News, June 17, 2019. https://apnews.com/article/immigration-caribbean-
    ap-top-news-international-news-cuba-cae4919e5d5d4d6eb280785618
    dfa865.

Vílchez, Dánae. "Antimotines reprimen a comunidad por auxiliar a migrantes." *Confidencial*, October 16, 2016. https://confidencial.com.ni/antimotines-reprimen-comunidad-auxiliar-migrantes.

Vogt, Wendy. "Crossing Mexico: Structural Violence and the Commodification of Undocumented Central American Migrants." *American Ethnologist* 40, no. 4 (2013): 764–80.

———. *Lives in Transit: Violence and Intimacy on the Migrant Journey*. Berkeley: University of California Press, 2018.

Winters, Nanneke. "Haciendo-lugar en tránsito: Reflexión sobre la migración africana y trabaja de campo en Darién, Panama." *REMHU: Revista interdisciplinar da mobilidade humana* 27, no. 56 (2019). https://doi.org/10.1590/1980-85852503880005613.

Winters, Nanneke, and Cynthia Mora Izaguirre. "Es cosa suya: Entanglements of Border Externalization and African Transit Migration in Northern Costa Rica." *Comparative Migration Studies* 7, no. 27 (2019). https://doi.org/10.1186/s40878-019-0131-9.

Winters, Nanneke, and Franziska Reiffen. "Haciendo-lugar vía huellas y apegos: Las personas migrantes africanas y sus experiencias de movilidad, inmovilidad e inserción local en América Latina." *REMHU: Revista Interdiciplinar da Mobilidade Humana* 27, no. 56 (May-August 2019). https://doi.org/10.1590/1980-85852503880005602.

World Bank. "Panama: Locking in Success. A Systematic Country Diagnostic." Washington, DC: World Bank and International Finance Corporation, January 16, 2015. https://documents1.worldbank.org/curated/en/180611468100727814/pdf/947060SCD0P1510ICodisclosed03030150.pdf.

Yates, Caitlyn. "A Case Study in the Outsourcing of US Border Control." *Lawfare Blog*, April 11, 2019. https://www.lawfareblog.com/case-study-outsourcing-us-border-control.

Zaiotti, Ruben. "Mapping Remote Control: The Externalization of Migration Management in the Twenty-First Century." In *Externalizing Migration Management: Europe, North America and the Spread of 'Remote Control' Practices*, edited by Ruben Zaiotti, 3–31. Abingdon, Oxfordshire: Routledge, 2016.

Zere, Abraham T. "Democracy According to Eritrea's Afwerki, Then and Now." *Al Jazeera*, May 24, 2018. https://www.aljazeera.com/opinions/2018/5/24/democracy-according-to-eritreas-afwerki-then-and-now.

Zhang, Sheldon X. *Smuggling and Trafficking in Human Beings: All Roads Lead to America*. Westport, CT: Praeger/Greenwood, 2007.

Zhang, Sheldon X., Gabriella E. Sanchez, and Luigi Achilli. "Crimes of Solidarity in Mobility: Alternative Views on Migrant Smuggling." *Annals of the American Academy of Political and Social Science* 676, no. 1 (2018): 6–15.

Zolberg, Aristide R. "The Great Wall against China." In *Migration, Migration History, and History: Old Paradigms and New Perspectives*, edited by Jan Lucassen and Leo Lucassen, 291–316. New York: Peter Lang, 1997.

Zubrzycki, Bernarda. "Recent African Migration to South America: The Case of Senegalese in Argentina." International Journal of Humanities and Social Sciences 2, no. 22 (2012): 86–94.

INDEX

Printed in the USA
CPSIA information can be obtained
at www.ICGtesting.com
CBHW031417070324
5069CB00004B/470